Mary Norwak was born in London and now lives in Norfolk. She has been a journalist for over twenty years, contributing regularly to the food columns in the national press and to other magazines. She is at present cookery editor of *Farmers Weekly* and is the editor of *Freezer World*.

English Puddings
Sweet and Savoury

MARY NORWAK

'No mean woman can cook well. It calls for a
generous spirit, a light hand and a large heart'
Eden Phillpotts.

SPHERE BOOKS LIMITED
London and Sydney

First published in Great Britain by
B. T. Batsford Ltd, London 1981
Copyright © 1981 by Mary Norwak
Published by Sphere Books Ltd 1984
30–32 Gray's Inn Road, London WC1X 8JL

Cookery Advisor: Jane Grigson

Illustrations by Juliet Stanwell Smith

Set in Zapf

**Printed and bound in Great Britain by
Cox & Wyman Ltd, Reading**

Contents

Preface

Domestic food is wholesome, though 'tis homely,
And foreign dainties poisonous, though tasteful.
Sir Walter Scott

When the subject of this book was suggested to me, I felt that the term 'English' might be restrictive. How could there be enough to fill a book on one type of dish from just one small country? Little did I guess that I would embark on research that could fill many books and would prove to be a kind of culinary detective story.

English cooking has never been carefully structured like that of France, where dishes are carefully recorded and each permissible variation noted. There simply seems to be no 'right' way to cook in England, and any suggestion of the one-and-only recipe for a favourite or regional dish will always be countered by dozens of equally correct versions. The English have always been sturdy individualists with a loathing for rigid rules, and their cooks have never worried about adding a bit of this and that to any recipe. In both printed and handwritten recipe books there has been a long tradition of footnotes indicating that the reader may do as she pleases when judging texture or colour, or adding flavouring or garnishing. The important thing in the English kitchen has been to make the best of whatever is available, and adaptation has been the secret of survival. When new ingredients were imported, they were simply added to favourite old dishes; when times were hard, substitutions were made for expensive ingredients, so that bread replaced cake, or milk replaced cream, and new dishes evolved.

English recipes have therefore never been static, but have changed subtly in the past eight hundred years, popular dishes often merging together or being influenced by foreign fashions introduced by continental cooks employed in great houses, or by the mixture of French, Portuguese, Spanish, Dutch and German kings and queens who ruled the land. Dishes have also moved up and down the social scale, with medieval court favourites being adapted to everyday use, rustic country dishes being improved for the gentry, and grand recipes imitated by the aspiring lower classes. Further richness has been added by the regional variations, which originally depended on local agriculture, but were often shared with neighbouring counties or given to relatives on marriage, and then became adapted to new local conditions.

All these threads have woven together into a fascinating story, for almost every dish has a small part in English history. For those who wonder why anyone has bothered to tell the story of puddings, I can do no better than quote Thackeray: 'All people who have natural, healthy appetites, love sweets; all children, all women, all Eastern people, whose tastes are not corrupted by gluttony and strong drink.'

My particular thanks are due to Jane Grigson for suggesting the original idea, and to Paula Shea for being an enthusiastic editor. Carolyn Newman has been a tolerant and efficient typist, and kept control of my ever-growing collection of cookery books and bulging files. In preparing this manuscript I have consulted such authorities as Hannah Glasse, Eliza Acton and numerous other cookery writers of bygone years for guidelines on the dating and development of recipes, and, of course, the magnificent work of C. Anne Wilson *Food and Drink in Britain* (1973). In particular, I must record my most grateful thanks to those ordinary housewives who carefully wrote down their favourite family recipes over the centuries in the many beautiful books that I am now happy to own, and which have given me the key to what the English people really enjoyed eating.

1 The Story of Puddings

Let us seriously reflect of what a pudding is composed. It is composed of flour that once waved in the golden grain, and drank the dews of the morning; of milk pressed from the swelling udder by the gentle hand of the beauteous milkmaid, whose beauty and innocence might have recommended a worse draught; who, while she stroked the udder, indulged no ambitious thoughts of wandering in palaces, formed no plans for the destruction of her fellow-creatures: milk, which is drawn from the cow, that useful animal, that eats the grass from the field, and supplies us with that which made the greatest part of the food of mankind in the age which the poets have agreed to call golden. It is made with an egg, that miracle of nature, which the theoretical Burnet has compared to creation. An egg contains water within the beautiful smooth surface; and an unformed mass, by the incubation of the parent, becomes a regular animal, furnished with bones and sinews and covered with feathers. Let us consider; can there be more wanting, more may be found. It contains salt, which keeps the sea from putrefaction: salt, which is made the image of intellectual excellence, contributes to the formation of a pudding.

Dr Johnson's rhapsody on puddings reminds one of the restaurant menus that extol the virtues of dew-fresh morning-gathered mushrooms, but this great man was expressing a proper pride in that unique institution — the pudding. It is now difficult to describe what we mean by a pudding, for today's language is sloppy and inexact. 'Dessert' is an inept refinement, for the word applies only to fresh fruit, nuts and sweetmeats offered to end a grand dinner. 'Sweet' is a niminy-piminy shortening of the sweet course that now ends a meal, but does not apply to the whole magnificent range of puddings, and seems to indicate something rather small and nasty that forms the anticlimax of a meal. The workmanlike schoolboy slang of 'afters' or 'seconds' more nearly describes the dish we have in mind, but gives no hint of its glory. Let us then take the word of M. Misson, a French visitor of 1690:

The pudding is a dish very difficult to be described because of the several sorts there are of it; flour, milk, eggs, butter, sugar, suet, marrow, raisins, etc. etc. are the most common ingredients of a pudding. They bake them in an oven, they boil them with meat, they make them fifty several ways: BLESSED BE HE THAT INVENTED PUDDING, for it is a manna that hits the palates of all sorts of people; a manna better than that of the wilderness, because the people are never weary of it. Ah, what an excellent thing is an English pudding! To come in pudding-time, is as much as to say, to come in the most lucky moment in the world. Give an English man a pudding, and he shall think it a noble treat in any part of the world.

Exactly. Trust a food-loving Frenchman to produce the perfect description of the pudding, analysed in all its diversity of ingredients and methods, its classlessness and timelessness. In this book, therefore, I will retain the good English name of 'pudding' to cover that unique confection that is scarcely known in other countries. The Scandinavians have their sweet porridges and pancakes, the Germans and Austrians their dumplings, the Italians their fruit and ices, and the French have their tarts and the creamy confections of the great chefs. All these individual specialities have been introduced to British shores in the past two thousand years and have been absorbed and improved to form a unique contribution to the culinary history of the world. The English are seldom complimented for their savoury dishes, with the possible exception of roasts, but nobody can fault a true English pudding.

Part of the reason for this passion for puddings has been climatic. The British were always able to grow a wide variety of cereals, to herd milk animals such as sheep, goats and cows, to husband pigs and egg-laying fowls, and to cultivate stone fruit and soft fruit. In addition, as a seafaring nation, England built up a thriving trade with Eastern countries, which sent dried fruit, spices and citrus fruit, and later built up Western trade with the cultivation of sugar cane and the popular importation of rum. Because of this, English cooks were able to diversify the old medieval pottages and custards that were common to many countries, and experiments with flavourings and cooking methods encouraged their creative activity in this particular branch of cookery.

The roots of the English pudding tradition lie in the period after the Norman Conquest, when the traditional peasant cereal dishes began to be refined by the cooks from northern France, who often reintroduced ideas that had originally come from the Romans a thousand years before, but had died out in Britain in the Dark Ages. The original pottages eaten by rich and poor alike were made from cereal softened in water, into which milk and sweetening could be stirred, or which might be enlivened by pieces of meat, spices and dried fruit. The pottage could easily be cooked over an open fire, and gave rise to the cereal-thickened milk puddings that are still eaten today.

The word pudding was originally applied to mixtures of spiced meat, sometimes mixed with cereal, which were stuffed into skins made from animal intestines, like the sausages beloved of the Romans. The original meaning is still retained in Black Puddings, but the word gradually came to mean any kind of stuffing. By the fourteenth century more refined mixtures of suet, cream, breadcrumbs and spices were being put into the skins, and soon this gave way to richer mixtures like thick pottages sweetened with dried fruits, which became the ancestors of our rich plum puddings, Christmas pudding and even fruit mincemeat.

Elizabethan cooks began to experiment with methods of preparing these puddings other than using the inconvenient animal gut. The pudding cloth came into use at the very beginning of the seventeenth century, enclosing the fruit, cereal and fat mixtures, or lighter batter puddings of eggs, milk and thickening cereal. By the end of the century paste made from flour and fat in the form of suet was being wrapped around fruit and meat and could be boiled in the cooking pot along with broth.

All cooking had to be done over an open fire, except in great houses and some farms where bread ovens were available, and this restricted the development of the pudding for the poorer classes, who continued to depend on the liquid cereal dishes, or the firmer bag puddings wrapped in cloths. In richer households cooks experimented with milk puddings and thicker pottages baked in ovens, and also used this method for cooking batters, which had developed from a favourite old Roman dish. In cottages the thick iron plate known as a griddle was a development of the earlier bakestone, and became the implement for cooking pastry-enclosed fruit and batters. Fried pancakes or crisp batters basted with fat from a spit-roasted joint had been medieval favourites, but needed skilful cooking and good fat, which was denied to the peasants with their smoky, uncontrollable fires and lumps of suet. Likewise the subtle egg-thickened custards and creams were not available to those who were unable to afford the chafing dish of coals, a useful small-scale cooker for the elegant cook.

It is important to stress the role of the yeoman in the later development of good English food. Elegant and subtle, but rich, dishes had been the prerogative of the highest social classes, while the poor agricultural or town workers had to manage on the most basic food that would give some degree of instant nourishment, warmth and energy for heavy manual work. The yeomen farmers, however, were privileged men, freed from the slavery of the manor, able to keep horses and honoured to provide fighting men for their superiors. The yeomen provided the nucleus of county regiments and the cavalry, and always maintained a sturdy independence. They provided a valuable link between the rulers and the ruled, and their way of life was much envied. The men and their wives lived comfortably in decent farmhouses, cultivating their land and herding their animals, and they were famous for their good but simple hospitality. Their children were sent to the new grammar schools and even to boarding schools, and the women were skilled housekeepers. They were not too proud to work alongside their maids, and often took on the role of mother to poorer girls. These housewives had their own good produce and were able to be lavish in their cooking. In their little stillrooms near the big kitchens they concocted their own medicines and beauty preparations, and cooked the more delicate dishes. They had access to flowers, soft fruit, cream and eggs, herbs and spices, and the delicate flower-scented waters and essences, and accordingly were able to give subtlety to hearty country dishes.

Their influence is strong from the sixteenth century onwards, when dishes began to develop in the way they are known today. Early cookery books had been written for court circles, but now they were being written for the housewife cooks, for few of their employees were literate. At the same time, these women were able to write down their own favourite recipes and began the pleasant habit of swopping them with friends or other members of the family.

Stimulated by competition, inspired by the elaborate dishes of famous chefs in great houses, and helped by the invention of machines and the importation of new ingredients, cookery

4

became the proud art of the housewife, often with dire results. The simpler dishes, such as milk puddings and boiled bag-puddings, still remained in favour, but a taste for the curious and complicated dish began to develop. Guests at a medieval banquet had enjoyed the cunning subtleties built by pastry-cooks from marzipan and jellies, and now these were imitated in baroque confections set in moulds with decorated towers and gaudy trimmings. Even the traditional boiled pudding had taken to elaborately castellated moulds.

The traditional pudding, however, was safe in the hands of some descendants of the yeoman class. Following the Industrial Revolution in the eighteenth century, there was a drift to the towns not only by manual workers, but also by many families who had made money in farming or rural trade. By the middle of the nineteenth century this new middle class had settled in town houses and, from the evidence of both handwritten and printed books, was experimenting with elegant French dishes. However, these families took with them country girls to staff nurseries and kitchens, and while Cook might go along with the new-fangled dishes for upstairs use, she was still preparing her favourite and easy milk puddings, batters and boiled puddings for the nursery and below-stairs staff. The tradition of wholesome nursery food continued well into the twentieth century, so that men retained their early memories of these comforting dishes, which remain the backbone of catering in London clubs, university colleges and such institutions as the House of Lords.

In country areas and poorer households meals were simple affairs. When the entire meal was cooked in one pot, it might start with broth and plain pudding to assuage appetites, followed by boiled meat and vegetables, and then more pudding with sweetening or perhaps fruit cooked in the same cauldron.

More sophisticated dinners retained the medieval habit of serving large mixed courses until the middle of the nineteenth century. Each course included a number of dishes – there might be meat, fish, game and poultry on the table at the same time, surrounded by side dishes of vegetables, sweet tarts, jellies and other delicacies. Two or three courses would be served, and each might contain this mixture of savoury and sweet dishes. Men eating on their own, however, tended to eat much simpler meals, such as the 'ordinary' in taverns, which consisted of a plain roast and a pudding or tart. The same type of meal was favoured by people living on their own and by writers and artists dining in clubs.

Even where the formal course system was followed, there had been a place for sweetmeats, sometimes known as *quelquechoses* or 'kickshaws', at the end of a meal. The English loved sweet dishes (and are still renowned as a nation for their sweet tooth) and considered this additional sweet course the best part of the meal. The name of banquet was originally applied only to this type of dessert, consisting of tarts, fruit and sweets, and special rooms were reserved to which the guests moved for this treat.

The pudding course as it is known today evolved in the middle of the nineteenth century when smart hostesses began to serve '*Diner à la Russe*', a simplified course system in which one dish followed another, and the structure of soup, fish, meat and sweet course came into being. Grand meals might still be huge if poultry, game and vegetable dishes were included. A sorbet (water ice) might be served between courses to clear the palate, and the meal was completed with a relic of the medieval dessert of fruit, nuts and sweetmeats. In simple households the two- or three-course meal continued as it had done for generations.

Puddings became less fashionable after the First World War. Fewer domestic staff were available, and many housewives had to learn to cook and to simplify the preparation and serving of meals. Many felt, along with Lady Jekyll, that 'jazzing jellies and castellated cakes show misdirection of energy,' and others were concerned with keeping slim figures. A time of mean cooking was beginning, and Sir Harold Nicolson lamented the fact:

One of the to me more distressing manifestations of the changing world in which I live, is that the fashion for pudding has almost wholly faded. As a child, when staying at Clandboys or Shanganagh, there were always two different puddings at every meal. We were offered College Pudding, Bachelor's Pudding, Hasty Pudding, Tipsy Pudding, Treacle Pudding, Lemon Sponge, Pancakes, Junket, Coconut Custard, Marmalade Pie, Roly Poly, Suet Pudding, Toffee Pudding, Almond Sponge, Cherry Whirl, Coffee Honeycomb, Apple Charlotte, Macaroon Hasties, Meringues, Marshmallows, Smyrna Mould and all manner of tarts and creams. Moreover, before the first war, a 'luncheon cake' was always handed round with the cheese. V. [his wife, Vita Sackville-West] does not herself care for sweet dishes and prefers those sour concoctions which are called 'savouries' although they so seldom are. In fact I feel that she regards my passion for puddings as effeminate or perhaps Scottish, or perhaps middle class ... I must therefore resign myself in future to the fact that the puddings of my childhood have, even as four-wheelers, passed from circulation.

Thankfully, the pendulum is swinging again, and that roll-call of puddings is a clarion call for today's good cooks. There is some reaction against the minginess and dullness of packaged foods, girls are taking a pride in learning to cook again, and there is a fascination with the dishes of times gone by. In the following chapters I have given greater details about the historical development of each type of pudding along with recipes, which sometimes have had to be slightly adapted to suit today's methods and ingredients. In order to get the most delicious results, please take time to read the following notes on raw materials.

Ingredients

Bread was a popular ingredient in old-fashioned puddings, but today's factory-baked variety gives poor results, as it tends to become slimy when damp. For white slices or crumbs, use a good home-baked loaf or one from an individual baker. For brown crumbs, use a granary or wholemeal loaf to give the correct texture.

Butter is now mainly sold salted. Before the Second World War, the unsalted variety was more popular, but butter had to be more heavily salted for wartime transport and storage. It can be very salty indeed, particularly if stored in the refrigerator or freezer. For pudding recipes, try to use unsalted butter, as it gives a much better flavour to sweet dishes.

Suet was carefully skinned and chopped by hand or minced by our ancestors. Today's shredded suet gives good results and is much easier to use, but if you have a supply of suet from the purchase of carcass meat for the freezer it may be used. Be sure to chop it very finely to avoid those little jelly-like lumps that used to upset the sensitive eater.

Spongecakes were widely used, but were made in the kitchen rather than brought in packets. Sponge fingers used to be light and sugary confections and there is no exact equivalent available commercially. Homemade Victoria sponge may be used where indicated, but otherwise 'trifle-sponges' may be used – sponge finger biscuits, sometimes known as boudoir biscuits, are too hard and sweet to be useful.

Macaroons are available from some bakers, but be sure to check whether they are made with almonds. A cheaper type is made with coconut and is very unattractive in trifles. Ratafia biscuits, which are like tiny macaroons, are available in packets from good grocers.

Sugar is not quite as used by our forebears, who had to break up huge sugar loaves. Caster sugar has the best texture for pudding-making; light or dark soft brown sugar gives a deliciously rich flavour where specified. Demerara sugar has a somewhat gritty texture and should only be used where indicated.

Milk comes in many varieties. In recipes where creamy milk is specified, use Gold Top or Channel Islands milk, or add some single cream to the ordinary variety. Cream is available fresh, ultra-heat-treated, or frozen, which are all suitable for use in recipes. Clotted cream in bottles has a slightly cooked flavour, but the frozen variety is identical with the fresh.

Flavourings should be as pure as possible. Use a vanilla pod instead of essence, and fresh lemon or orange rind and juice instead of commercially prepared substitutes, for instance. Use cocoa where specified and not sweetened drinking chocolate powder; and always use plain chocolate, not the milk variety. When brandy is specified, an inexpensive one will do; sherry should be medium unless a sweet type is specified; medium cider is also best; white wine should be light and slightly sweet (most German wines are ideal).

Rosewater and orange-flower water were used a great deal to give a delicate flavouring to sweet dishes. They are obtainable in grocers and chemists, and may sometimes be found in beauty departments of stores.

2 Jellies, Blancmanges and Flummeries

At such times as the merchants do make their ordinary or voluntary feasts, it is a world to see what great provision is made of all manner of delicate meats, from every quarter of the country. In such cases also gellies of all colours, mixed with a variety in the representation of sundry flowers, herbs, trees, forms of beasts, fish, fowls and fruits, and thereunto marchpane wrought with no small curiosity, tarts of divers hues, and sundry denominations, conserves of old fruits, foreign and home-bred, suckets, marmalades, marchpanes, sugar-bread, gingerbread, florentines, wild-fowl, venison of all sorts, and sundry outlandish confections, altogether seasoned with sugar.

William Harrison, rector of a north Essex village, *Description of England* (1587).

These overwrought dishes were direct descendants of the 'subtleties' of the late Middle Ages, confected from almond paste, sugar paste and jelly for the delight of guests at the end of each course of a medieval feast. There were allegorical figures with written mottoes and gilded birds alongside spiced fruit pastes and other sweetmeats. Although the elaborate marzipan confections began to die out because they needed skilled preparation and were beyond the scope of family cooks, there was a long-abiding passion for elaborate representational dishes on special occasions. Tudor and Stuart cooks began to develop the art of thickening liquids so that they could be set firmly. By the eighteenth century elaborate china and metal moulds were being manufactured, and the thickened liquids could be set in a diversity of shapes that echoed the medieval representations.

Writing in *Wine and Food* (No. 25), John Diemuke described the sort of dish that the sophisticated hostess offered in the eighteenth and early nineteenth centuries:

There was a 'Solomon's Temple' in flummery, a magnificent architectural monument in brightly coloured stiff jellies. Or such a fancy dish as one young bride wrote in her cook book of 1801– 'A Hen's Nest'. To make this, first a blancmange was prepared laboriously, with isinglass to congeal it; then several dozen eggs were blown and filled with it. A nest was made by partly filling a bowl with jelly, on the top of which a straw made of shredded orange and lemon peel was placed – then the eggs were laid in the straw and jelly was poured over it to hold them in place. The realistic sculpture in jelly was then turned out in a china dish and garnished with green sweetmeats.

The three basic ingredients of these dishes were jelly, blancmange and flummery, each with an honourable history from medieval times, but now totally debased by modern versions offered in packets. Perhaps the decline began with their use in these elaborate representational dishes, for the ingenious Victorians developed a number of thickening ingredients that gave rise to culinary shortcuts. These produced dishes that set firmly, were clear and brightly coloured, and highly suitable for the sweet cold dishes that still graced dinner parties and ball suppers. The flavours became highly artificial, the decorative moulds became unfashionable in the bustling twentieth century, and we were left with bowls of tasteless rubbery milk or water dreaded by school-children and sensitive adults.

The art of thickening began to develop in medieval times with savoury jellies, made by extracting the setting agent from fish or meat bones. Fish jelly was a favourite feast dish, made by boiling a mixture of fish in wine or wine and vinegar. The fish pieces were put into dishes, the liquid coloured and strained, and poured over the fish to set; the result must have been not unlike the Cockney jellied eels. By the sixteenth century the savoury jelly had become sweetened, with a basis of calves' feet liquor mixed with wine and sugar. The jelly was cleared with egg whites, in the same way that good cooks still clear aspic jelly, and could be coloured and spiced to taste. In the same period isinglass (made from sturgeon's sounds) was brought to England from Russia by Dutch traders, and remained in use as a setting agent until the twentieth century. In the seventeenth century jelly was also sometimes set with hartshorn (the shavings of deers' antlers) and fruit juice flavourings were introduced. Colour was more important than flavour in the making of jellies, however, and the inclusion of fruit juices did not become popular until the middle of the eighteenth century.

Blancmange and flummery developed along parallel lines until they merged imperceptibly into a moulded dish of milk or cream. The original blancmange (roughly meaning 'white food') was a thick pottage introduced from Norman France that was distinguished from other similar pottages by its lack of strong spices. The ingredients were chicken flesh, picked into small pieces with a pin, mixed with whole boiled rice, almond milk and sugar. The almond milk was made by soaking ground almonds in water. The surface of the original blancmange was scattered with little aniseed sweets or blanched almonds. Sometimes at feasts the blancmange was divided into two parts, one remaining white and the other being coloured red or yellow as a contrast. A blancmange of fish was eaten on fast days.

The blancmange survived to Elizabethan times as chicken meat, but sometimes the almonds were omitted, or were supplemented by rosewater. Slices were served with a sprinkling of sugar. An alternative version developed without meat, made with cream, sugar and rosewater thickened with egg yolks or beaten egg whites. Late in the seventeenth century a new French version of the dish arrived which was based on a chicken boiled with calves' feet, the resulting jelly being thickened with ground almonds and flavoured with rosewater and allowed to set. Another version omitted the chicken and was thickened with hartshorn, like jelly and flummery. By the eighteenth century the blancmange was a kind of jelly made with hartshorn or isinglass and included milk, cream, or beaten egg whites, still flavoured with almonds. In the 1820s arrowroot arrived in Britain from the West Indies, and sweetened milk flavoured with cinnamon and lemon peel and thickened with arrowroot became known as American blancmange. The final debasement came with the sale of flavoured cornflour later in the nineteenth century.

Flummery was a similar dish, derived from a medieval confection called *leach*, which was made with almond milk and calves' feet liquor and set, then cut in slices and served with wine sauce. This dish could be pale cream, or coloured red, and was soon made with cow's milk. It became a favourite Tudor dish and continued to be eaten until the eighteenth century. Later it became a cream thickened with calves' feet liquor, isinglass or hartshorn. Sometimes the cream was replaced by ground almonds, making it closer to the original dish, as well as to another dish that had been a staple food in country areas. This was the Welsh *llymru* (from which the name flummery derives). It was a kind of oatmeal porridge that became popular in the northern counties, and was sometimes known as 'wash brew'.

The oatmeal was soaked in water for 24 hours, then simmered until thick, and sweetened to taste. It was considered very wholesome and a quantity was often made, as it would keep if boiled daily. It began to be improved with the addition of orange-flower water, and was eaten with honey, wine, beer, milk or fruit and cream. A more ambitious version of the dish was made in Scotland about 1700, with wine, cream and orange-flower water thickened by a jelly made from hartshorn (occasionally pieces of ivory or ivory dust were boiled in water to serve the same purpose). Sometimes eggs were added, which gave it a golden colour. This rich Scottish dish is similar to a dish known as Dutch Flummery or *Jaune-Manger*, a version of blancmange. It may have derived its name from the Dutch traders who introduced isinglass to Britain. The word flummery came to mean a dish thickened with cereal, so that later variations of the traditional porridge-type dish were made with pearl barley, semolina, sago, flour or cornflour. Fruit was often incorporated to produce a result rather like a thin fruit fool.

Summer Flummery

½ pint (300 ml) water
5 tablespoons white wine or cider
3 oz (75 g) fine semolina
2 oz (50 g) caster sugar
2 egg whites

Sauce
8 oz (225 g) raspberries or strawberries
2 teaspoons lemon juice
2 oz (50 g) caster sugar

Heat the water and wine together until just under boiling point. Sprinkle on the semolina, bring to the boil and then lower the heat. Stir over low heat for 3 minutes. Add sugar and continue heating and stirring for 5 minutes. Remove from heat and leave until cool. Whisk the egg whites to stiff peaks and fold into the mixture. Pour into a mould rinsed in cold water and leave until cold and set. Turn out on a serving dish and garnish with a few of the berries. Sieve the remaining fruit and stir in the lemon juice and sugar until dissolved. Chill and serve separately.

Gooseberry Flummery

1 lb (450 g) gooseberries
¼ pint (150 ml) water
6 oz (150 g) sugar

1 teaspoon lemon juice
½ pint (300 ml) milk
2 oz (50 g) fine semolina

As this pudding looks very pale, some people like to add a little green vegetable colouring. I prefer to leave the colour alone, but to sprinkle the surface with crumbled macaroons or digestive biscuits, which give a good contrast of colour and texture.

Top and tail the berries. Put into a pan with water and stir in the sugar. Simmer gently until the skins burst and the fruit is soft. Take off the heat and stir in the lemon juice. Heat the milk to lukewarm and sprinkle the semolina on it. Bring just to the boil and then simmer for 3 minutes, stirring well. Remove from the heat and stir in the gooseberries. Mix well and pour into a bowl. Chill and serve with cream.

Lemon Flummery

Serves 4

½ pint (300 ml) water
Grated rind and juice of 1
    lemon
1 oz (25 g) unsalted butter

1 oz (25 g) plain flour
4 oz (100 g) caster sugar
1 egg

This is a very light flummery which includes whisked egg white and is thickened with flour. It is inexpensive to make, and may be made suitable for a party by sprinkling the top with crushed macaroons and serving with single cream.

Put the water into a pan and add the grated rind of the lemon, and the butter. Bring to the boil. Meanwhile, stir the flour and sugar together in a bowl and make a well in the centre. Pour in the boiling liquid, whisking well to break up any lumps. Separate the egg. Return the liquid to the saucepan and stir over low heat for 3 minutes. Pour a little of the liquid onto the egg yolk and mix well, then stir into the saucepan again. Simmer gently for 10 minutes. Remove from the heat and add the strained juice of the lemon. Cool to lukewarm. Whisk the egg white to stiff peaks and fold into the lemon mixture. Pour into a serving dish and chill before serving.

Blancmange

Serves 6

Grated rind of 1 lemon
1 pint (600 ml) milk
2 oz (50 g) sugar
2 oz (50 g) ground almonds

1½ oz (40 g) gelatine
2 tablespoons water
¾ pint (450 ml) double cream
3 fl oz (75 ml) brandy

The slow decline of this dish can be traced in the thoughts of three of England's most delightful writers. Chaucer in The Canterbury Tales *described the Cook's disability:*

But great harm was it, as it seemed to me,
That on his shin a sore wound had he;
For blankemange he made with the beste

and the loss to the Pilgrims was obviously a sad one. By the nineteenth century Richard Surtees, a keen observer of fashionable customs through his character Mr Jorrocks, noted the innocent hostess who 'never listened for the answer for the blancmange having landed with the loss only of a corner tower, for it was in the castellated style of confectionery, she was now all anxiety to see what sort of a savoury omelette her drunkard job-cook would furnish.'

The even keener observers George and Weedon Grossmith probably expressed everybody's feelings on the last gasp of a debased sweetmeat in The Diary of a Nobody:

In spite of my instructions, that blancmange was brought up again for supper. To make matters worse, there had been an attempt to disguise it, by placing it in a glass dish with jam around it. Carrie asked Lupin if he would have some, and he replied 'No second-hand goods for me, thank you'. I told Carrie, when we were alone, that if the blancmange were placed on the table again I should walk out of the house.

Put the grated lemon rind and milk into a pan and leave to stand for 1 hour so that the flavour of lemon infuses the milk. Add the sugar and ground almonds and bring to the boil. Simmer and stir for 10 minutes, then cool to lukewarm. Meanwhile, stir the gelatine into the water in a cup. Stand the cup in a pan of hot water and stir while heating gently until the gelatine is syrupy. Remove from the heat, cool and stir into the milk. Keep stirring until the mixture is almost cold, and then stir in the cream. Stir in the brandy and pour into a mould. When cold, turn out and decorate with flowers, either fresh or crystallised.

Milk Jelly   *Serves 4*

1 pint (600 ml) creamy milk   ³⁄₄ oz (20 g) gelatine
2 oz (50 g) caster sugar   2 tablespoons water
Grated rind of 1 lemon

This pudding is very delicately flavoured and makes an excellent accompaniment to soft fruit and cream.

Put the milk, sugar and lemon rind into a pan and heat gently for 10 minutes. Stir the gelatine into the water in a cup, and stand the cup in a small pan of hot water. Heat gently, stirring until the gelatine is syrupy. Strain the milk and cool to lukewarm. Stir in the gelatine and pour into a mould rinsed in cold water. Leave until cold and set before turning out.

Lemon Jelly

1 pint (600 ml) water
4 oz (100 g) sugar
2 cloves

3 tablespoons lemon juice
Thinly peeled rind of 1 lemon
½ oz (15 g) gelatine

The original sweet jellies were made with calves' feet liquor flavoured with the juice of lemons or Seville oranges. Today we are able to make them more easily with gelatine. Sometimes a 'jelly sponge' was made by whisking the nearly-set jelly on its own or with egg whites. This sort of dish was described by a late Victorian writer as 'particularly fairylike and dainty'.

Reserve 3 tablespoons water and put the rest into a pan with the sugar, cloves, lemon juice and rind. Bring slowly to boiling point, stirring to dissolve the sugar. Dissolve the gelatine in the remaining water in a cup. Stand the cup in a pan of hot water, and stir while heating gently until the gelatine is syrupy. Remove the lemon liquid from the heat and stir in the gelatine. Stir well and strain into a mould rinsed in cold water. Leave until cold and set before turning out.

Port Wine Jelly

1 pint (600 ml) port
4 oz (100 g) caster sugar
1 oz (25 g) gelatine
¼ pint (150 ml) water

1 teaspoon lemon juice
Pinch of ground nutmeg
Pinch of ground cinnamon

Jelly made with port or claret was supposed to be strengthening for invalids, but obviously it was so delicious that the rest of the family were happy with it too.

Put half the port into a pan with the caster sugar and heat gently until the sugar has dissolved. Put the gelatine into a cup with the water and put the cup into a pan of hot water. Stir gently while heating until the gelatine is very syrupy. Stir into the hot port with the lemon juice and spices. Strain into a bowl. Stir in the remaining port. Leave in the bowl or pour into glasses and leave until cold and set. Serve with whipped cream and small sweet biscuits.

Victorian Apple Jelly

2 lb (900 g) cooking apples
Sugar

Water
Grated rind of 1 lemon

This Victorian jelly comes halfway between a preserve and a pudding. For centuries it was common practice to cook high-pectin fruit to make a stiff jelly that could be reduced to a thick paste, which was then cut into attractive shapes to serve as sweetmeats for medieval banquets. This practice remained popular until the eighteenth century, when housewives discovered that the fruit need not be reduced to a stiff paste. They evolved a kind of fruit jelly or 'cheese', which made a valuable emergency pudding, as it could be stored for months or even years. In some stillrooms it was customary to turn these 'cheeses' out of their moulds, which would be needed for other purposes in the days before mass-produced jars, and stack the stiff fruit preserves on shelves. This apple jelly was usually turned out and stuck with blanched almonds before being surrounded by custard. Similar dishes were sometimes known as Apple Hedgehog because of their shape and decoration (see Chapter 8).

Peel and core the apples and slice them into a pan. Add just enough water to cover them. Simmer until the apples have broken up completely, and beat them with a wooden spoon to a smooth pulp. Weigh the apple pulp and allow 12 oz (350 g) sugar for each 1 lb (450 g) fruit. Put the sugar into a pan and add ¼ pint (150 ml) water for each 12 oz (350 g) sugar. Heat gently, stirring until the sugar dissolves, and then simmer for 10 minutes. Stir this syrup into the apples with the lemon rind and stir over medium heat for 25 minutes until the apples do not stick to the bottom of the pan. For immediate use, pour into a mould rinsed in cold water. Leave until set and turn out onto a serving dish. Serve with cream or custard. For storage, pour into sterilized jars without 'shoulders' and cover as for jam. Turn out when needed and serve as above; the jelly will stiffen during storage.

Little Orange Jellies

Makes 12 pieces

4 Oranges
Grated rind and juice of
   1 lemon
2 tablespoons medium sherry

4 oz (100 g) caster sugar
¾ oz (20 g) gelatine
4 tablespoons water

Charles II was supposed to have been fond of jelly served in this way, but the fashion for jellies set in fruit skins continued for centuries. Eliza Acton (1855) described the making of fruit jellies set in alternate stripes in orange skins. These were cut in quarters and arranged on a stand decorated with 'a few light branches of myrtle'. She also gave detailed instructions for making orange baskets, complete with handles, which were filled with jellies or ratafia biscuits – I can remember jelly-filled orange baskets being the highlight of children's parties of my youth. The jelly for the following little confections is richly-flavoured and firm.

Cut the oranges in neat halves. Scoop out all the flesh and wash the orange skins. Squeeze all the juice from the orange flesh into a pan. Add the grated lemon rind and juice. Add the sherry and sugar. Heat gently and stir until the sugar has dissolved. Dissolve the gelatine in the water in a cup. Put the cup into a pan of water and stir gently while heating until the gelatine is syrupy. Stir into the hot juice. Strain and pour into the orange skins. This quantity will fill about 6 of them, and you must be sure that the skins are completely filled. Leave until completely cold and set. Dip a very sharp knife into hot water and cut each orange skin in half to produce large jelly segments.

Cider Jelly

Serves 4

1 pint (600 ml) dry still cider
½ oz (15 g) gelatine

4 oz (100 g) sugar

Jelly made with cider has a beautiful golden colour and a delicious flavour. If you like to put fruit into jellies, try this one with peeled and stoned white grapes stirred in just before setting.

Mix the gelatine with 3 tablespoons cold cider in a cup. Put the cup into a small pan of hot water and heat gently, stirring until the gelatine is syrupy. Heat the remaining cider and sugar together, stirring until the sugar has dissolved. Bring to the boil and remove from the heat. Stir in the gelatine and pour into a mould rinsed in cold water. Leave until cold and set before turning out.

Stone Cream
Serves 4–6

4 oz (100 g) apricot, plum or
    strawberry jam
1 pint (600 ml) double cream

1 oz (25 g) caster sugar
$^3/_4$ oz (20 g) gelatine

This recipe was written down by Mrs Garden of Redisham, Suffolk, in her personal recipe book in 1847. A similar recipe is included in Mary Byron's Pudding Book *(1923), but using preserved apricots or cherries instead of jam at the bottom of the dish. The fruit was sprinkled with lemon juice and grated peel. Cassell's* Dictionary of Cookery *(late nineteenth century) uses jam in the recipe, sprinkled with lemon rind and juice, and topped with 'liquid blancmange ornamented with pink sugar, knobs of redcurrant jelly, or strips of preserved fruit, or blanched almonds', and it was suggested the blancmange might be thickened with isinglass, gelatine or fine arrowroot – a sad debasement of the earlier dish.*

Cover the bottom of a glass dish with a thick layer of jam. Put the cream and sugar into a thick-bottomed pan and heat very gently until the sugar has dissolved and the cream is lukewarm. Meanwhile, put the gelatine in a cup with 2 tablespoons water and stand the cup in a pan of hot water. Heat, stirring gently, until the gelatine is like thick syrup. Stir into the cream and pour over the jam. Leave until cold. The original recipe says 'you can put any ornaments you please on the top'.

Audrey Slaughter's Honeycomb Mould   *Serves 4–6*

3 large eggs
3 oz (75 g) sugar
½ oz (15 g) gelatine
2 lemons

1 pint (600 ml) less 4 tablespoons
  creamy milk
6 tablespoons single cream

This delectable dish, sometimes known as Honeycomb Cream, seems to have slipped from favour in recent years, but it was a great favourite between the wars. It was oddly difficult to track down a recipe for it from friends or printed sources, until Audrey Slaughter, describing her family alternative to Christmas Pudding, published this version in the Sunday Times. *Certainly the dish reminds me of happy childhood days, but I have often wondered if the original was the result of a happy mistake, like the original Bakewell Pudding (see Chapter 13). Who first discovered that the simple-sounding mixture of eggs, sugar, gelatine, lemons and creamy milk would divide itself into the enchanting layers of bubbly base, creamy middle and lemon jelly top? Michael Smith, that fine writer on English cookery, likes to serve this pudding with a sauce of rich egg custard folded into whipped cream, but I prefer the unadorned nursery version. Michael also makes the important point that the pudding is best chilled in a cool place rather than the refrigerator to prevent the rubberiness of some gelatine dishes, and he recommends that the dish should be served on the day on which it is made, with which I heartily agree.*

Separate the eggs. Put the yolks into a basin, and add the sugar and gelatine. Peel the rind thinly from the lemons, using a sharp knife or potato peeler so that no white pith is included. Add to the egg yolk mixture. Put the milk into a pan and heat almost to boiling point. Add to the egg mixture with the cream and whisk well. Put the basin over a saucepan of simmering water and heat until the mixture is like thick cream. Remove the lemon peel and leave until lukewarm. Whisk the egg whites to stiff peaks. Squeeze out the lemon juice and stir into the creamy mixture. Strain into the egg whites and fold in with a metal spoon. Rinse a decorative 1½ pint (900 ml) mould with cold water. Put in the mixture and chill. Turn out carefully just before serving.

Brown Bread Cream

¾ pint (450 ml) milk
3 egg yolks
1 oz (25 g) caster sugar
½ oz (15 g) gelatine
3 tablespoons water

3 rounded tablespoons fresh
   brown breadcrumbs
2 fl oz (50 ml) double cream
Grated rind of ½ lemon

Another Victorian favourite, this recipe makes use of breadcrumbs and the old principle of thickening milk with cereal. It has a nice 'nutty' flavour, which goes very well with a lightly sweetened purée of summer fruit and whipped cream

Put the milk into a pan and bring just to boiling point. Whisk the egg yolks and caster sugar in a bowl. Pour on the hot milk, whisking well, and put the bowl over a pan of hot water. Heat gently, stirring well until the mixture will coat the back of a spoon. Mix the gelatine and water in a cup and stand in a small pan of hot water. Heat gently and stir until the gelatine is syrupy. Stir the gelatine into the warm milk mixture until well blended. Strain into a bowl and leave to cool. Spread the crumbs on a baking sheet and bake at 325°F/170°C/Gas Mark 3 for 5 minutes until the crumbs are crisp and lightly coloured. Leave until cold. Whip the cream to soft peaks. When the milk mixture is cold but not set, stir in the breadcrumbs and lemon rind and fold in the cream. Put into a serving bowl and chill before serving.

Queen Mab's Pudding

Serves 6

1 pint (600 ml) creamy milk
Grated rind of 1 lemon
8 blanched almonds
4 oz (100 g) caster sugar
6 egg yolks
½ pint (300 ml) single cream

¾ oz (20 g) gelatine
3 tablespoons water
2 oz (50 g) glacé cherries
1 oz (25 g) pistachio nuts
2 oz (50 g) chopped candied
   lemon peel

This creamy set custard is named after the Queen of the Fairies, and is a Victorian version of the earlier decorative flummeries.

Put the milk, lemon rind, almonds and sugar into a pan and bring just to boiling point. Take off the heat and leave to stand for 15 minutes. Whisk the egg yolks in a bowl and strain in the milk. Stir in the cream and put the bowl over a pan of hot water. Stir over gentle heat until the mixture is thick enough to coat the back of a spoon. Dissolve the gelatine in the water in a cup. Put the cup into a pan of hot water, and stir gently while heating until the gelatine is syrupy. Stir into the lukewarm custard. Chop the cherries and all the nuts. Stir the cherries, peel and nuts into the cream just before setting, and pour into a mould. The pudding was often served with the well-sweetened juice of apricots, strawberries or raspberries. Sometimes chopped preserved ginger was used in place of the cherries, and ginger syrup poured round the pudding.

3 Custards, Creams and Fools

The Greeks are credited with the invention of the custard, a simple mixture of milk thickened with eggs, which was either cooked gently in a earthenware pot, or fried in oil. The Romans later borrowed this idea since they kept domestic fowl, and eggs were more plentiful than in earlier times, when wild birds' eggs were eaten. When the Romans left Britain, such culinary refinements died out, although vestiges of their dishes remained in France. The strong Norman influence on English medieval kitchens re-introduced these egg and milk dishes, and 'custards' were baked in pastry cases. It is said that the name derives from the *croustade*, or pastry container. The Elizabethans loved such confections and used eggs and thick cream for their tarts, but in the seventeenth century, the pastry began to be discarded in favour of deep dishes or little custard cups.

These custards were flavoured with spices and delicate scents, such as ambergris and musk, and were cooked gently in a dish over a chafing-dish of coals, for they could not stand the intense heat of an open fire. The Tudors sometimes discarded the eggs, and simply heated thick cream with sweetening, spices and rosewater, and this was known as a 'trifle' (see Chapter 5). Another favourite was the 'fool', or fresh or boiled cream mixed with fruit pulp, sweetened and sometimes spiced. The name is supposed to be derived from the French *fouler*, to mash, and in the early dishes the fruit was only broken up and not sieved. An in-between dish was the fruit custard, which seems always to have been made from gooseberries, and consisted of mashed fruit cooked in a rich creamy custard not unlike the tansy (see Chapter 10). These delicate custards and creams became great favourites in the seventeenth and eighteenth centuries, when cream and eggs were plentiful and the newly-prosperous farmers and gentry could discard the heavier puddings of their poorer forebears. The housewife could show her skill in the stillroom, confecting delicate morsels in silver dishes over a chafing dish of coals, flavouring the creams with fragrant rosewater, orange-flower water, almonds, pistachio nuts, musk and ambergris.

Two other medieval egg-thickened dishes were also popular until the nineteenth century. The caudle was hot ale, sweetened with honey or sugar and thickened with eggs, and was considered to be soothing and nourishing, and particularly good for those with weak digestions. The posset was a similar drink made with milk curdled with an acid liquid such as beer, wine or fruit juice. The milk was just warmed but not boiled (which would have made the curd hard) and then sweetened with honey or sugar. An 'eating posset' was an ale or beer posset thickened with bread. These two nourishing drinks could be served in the morning or evening, but developed in slightly different ways. The caudle became the hot ale nightcap, mulled (gently warmed) in front of the fire with spices, and particularly favoured by university colleges, and now commemorated in festive drinks such as Lambswool and Wassail. The posset became grander as the gentry began to add cream and sack or brandy, along with eggs, almonds and spongecake crumbs. The Sack Posset was a particular favourite and soon ceased to be a comforting bedtime or invalid drink, and turned into an elegant cream dish similar to syllabub (see Chapter 4).

Gooseberry Custard

Serves 4–6

1 lb (450 g) gooseberries
2 tablespoons water
3 eggs

1 teaspoon rosewater
3 oz (75 g) caster sugar

The original recipe comes from an eighteenth century East Anglian manuscript, and indicates that the custard is to be made in a chafing dish over coals, a sure sign that this was a special dish to be prepared by the lady of the house in her stillroom, not left to the cook and her roaring open fire.

Top and tail the gooseberries. Wash the fruit and put into a saucepan with the water. Simmer until the berries are soft and then put the fruit and juice through a sieve. Break the eggs into a basin and beat them until the yolks and whites are well mixed. Stir in the fruit purée, rosewater and sugar. Put the basin over a pan of boiling water and stir over heat until the mixture is thick and creamy. Remove from the heat and pour into a serving dish. Chill before serving.

Gooseberry Custard Cream

Serves 6

2 lb (900 g) gooseberries
½ pint (300 ml) water
1 oz (25 g) butter
1 tablespoon rosewater

8 oz (225 g) sugar
½ pint (300 ml) double cream
4 eggs

This recipe has been handed down in a Suffolk family for over 300 years, and is an early version of today's Gooseberry Fool (see below). The fruit in early fools was mashed and included in the custard cream, instead of being sieved, as is more common today.

Wash the gooseberries and top and tail them. Put into a pan with the water and simmer until soft and broken. Stir in the butter, rosewater and sugar and heat gently until the sugar has dissolved. Beat the cream and eggs together in a bowl until well mixed. Stir the egg mixture into the gooseberries over low heat and cook gently until just thickened. Pour into a serving bowl and chill. Serve with small, sweet biscuits.

Baked Custard

1 pint (600 ml) single cream
1 vanilla pod
3 eggs

2 oz (50 g) sugar
Pinch of ground nutmeg

This baked custard is best made with single cream, but for economy it may be made with creamy milk. It is very good served with fresh raspberries or strawberries and cream. Instead of sugar and nutmeg, a flavouring of 2 tablespoons of honey may be used.

Heat the cream with the vanilla pod until it just comes to boiling point. Beat the eggs lightly with the sugar in a bowl. Remove the vanilla pod and pour the cream onto the eggs, whisking thoroughly. Strain into a lightly buttered pie dish or straight-sided soufflé dish. Put this dish into a roasting tin of hot water. If liked, sprinkle with a pinch of ground nutmeg. Bake at 325°F/170°C/Gas Mark 3 for 1 hour. Serve hot or cold.

Baked Coffee Custard
Omit vanilla pod and nutmeg, and flavour with 2 tablespoons coffee essence.

Baked Chocolate Custard
Add 2 oz (50 g) plain chocolate to cream and vanilla pod before heating. Omit nutmeg.

Caramel Pudding

Caramel
3 oz (75 g) cube sugar
4 tablespoons water

Custard
4 eggs
1½ oz (40 g) caster sugar
¾ pint (450 ml) creamy milk
1 vanilla pod

When made with cream, this is the French crème caramel, but the simpler version appears in many Victorian handwritten books as Caramel Pudding or Caramel Custard. The proportion of eggs is higher than in a baked custard so that the pudding will unmould without breaking.

Use a metal mould to make this dish. If a charlotte mould is not available, use a 6 in (15 cm) round cake tin. Warm the mould in boiling water and dry well. Wrap the mould with a thick cloth or band of newspaper so that it can be held firmly in one hand. Make the caramel by putting the sugar and water into a small pan and heating together. Stir until the mixture boils, and then do not stir again while the sugar boils until it is golden brown. Pour into the mould, twisting the mould quickly with the other hand so that the base and sides are well coated.

To make the custard, whisk the eggs and sugar together until they are just mixed. Heat the milk and vanilla pod just to boiling point and pour onto the eggs. Strain this mixture into the caramel-lined mould. Cover with greased greaseproof paper and steam for 45 minutes. Turn out and serve with cream.

Seville Orange Creams
Serves 4–6

1 Seville orange
1 tablespoon brandy
4 egg yolks

4 oz (100 g) caster sugar
1 pint (600 ml) single cream
1 oz (25 g) flaked almonds

Seville (bitter marmalade oranges) were a favourite fruit for eighteenth and nineteenth century dishes. They are only available for a week or two in January, but freeze well and it is worth keeping a few to use during the year for their distinctive flavour in sweet and savoury dishes.

Peel the rind from the orange very thinly with a vegetable peeler or sharp knife so that no white pith is left on the rind. Cut into very thin matchstick lengths and soak in the brandy overnight. Squeeze out the orange juice and mix with the brandy. Strain into a basin and whisk well with the egg yolks and sugar. Bring the cream to just under boiling point and pour gradually onto the egg yolk mixture, whisking well. Continue whisking until the mixture is lukewarm. Pour into 4–6 individual ovenware dishes and stand them in a pan containing 1 in (2.5 cm) hot water. Bake at 250°F/130°C/Gas Mark ½ for 45 minutes. Cool and sprinkle with flaked almonds.

Burnt Cream

Serves 4–6

½ pint (300 ml) double cream   4 egg yolks
½ pint (300 ml) single cream   Caster sugar

This rich custard with the toffee-like sugar topping is often called Trinity Pudding or Trinity Cream after a Cambridge college. There is a story that the recipe came from an Aberdeenshire country house and was offered to the college kitchens in 1860 by an undergraduate. It was refused without trial, but happily the undergraduate became a fellow, the recipe was accepted, and the pudding became a great favourite. However, the recipe was certainly given in Elizabeth Raffald's The Experienced English Housekeeper *in 1769, and it appears in many handwritten books that predate the Trinity College story. Mary Kettilby in her* Collection of Receipts *(1719) gave a recipe for a rich baked egg-thickened cream flavoured with orange-flower water, and another one for a boiled egg-cream flavoured with sack and made in a bowl over hot water. It seems but a short step for an enterprising cook to sprinkle these rather pale creams with sugar and to glaze them to give a more appetizing appearance. Whatever the origins of the dish, it is delicious, particularly when served with fresh raspberries or strawberries and thick cream.*

I sometimes wonder if this dish was the result of yet another happy kitchen mistake, like the original Bakewell Pudding (see Chapter 13). Did some cook forget to sweeten her cream-custard, hastily sprinkle sugar on top and quickly brown it with a salamander to disguise her mistake?

Put the creams into a pan and bring just to the boil. Whisk the egg yolks in a bowl and whisk in the cream. Put bowl over a pan of hot water and stir over gentle heat until the mixture coats the back of a spoon. Pour into a shallow heat-proof dish and leave until completely cool, then chill.

Sprinkle with a thin, even layer of caster sugar. Put under a very hot grill until the sugar caramelizes into a thin sheet of toffee.

Brandy Orange Cream

4 eggs
1 oz (25 g) caster sugar
6 tablespoons brandy
1 pint (600 ml) creamy milk

1 oz (25 g) candied orange peel
3 tablespoons dark chunky
orange marmalade
½ pint (300 ml) double cream

This custard is richly flavoured with brandy and oranges, which provide a contrast to the cream on top.

Whisk the eggs with the sugar and the brandy. Heat the milk to just under boiling point and stir into the egg mixture. Strain into a greased straight-sided ovenware dish. Slice the peel very thinly and stir into the milk. Put the ovenware dish into a roasting tin containing 1 in (2.5 cm) water. Cover with foil and bake at 325°F/170°C/Gas Mark 3 for 1 hour. Remove from the pan and leave to stand until cold. Gently spread the marmalade on top. Whip the cream to soft peaks and spoon all over the marmalade.

Bath Orange Creams

Serves 4–6

1 pint (600 ml) water
8 oz (225 g) caster sugar
2 oranges

2 lemons
4 eggs

This recipe from a late eighteenth-century East Anglian manuscript is headed 'To make Orange Creams – Bath' and was perhaps a souvenir of a trip to that fashionable spa.

Put the water and sugar into a pan. Grate the rind from the oranges and one of the lemons, and add to the pan. Stir over low heat until the sugar has dissolved and then bring to the boil. Reduce the heat and simmer for 5 minutes. Squeeze the juice from the oranges and lemons. Remove the syrup from the heat and add the fruit juice. Leave to stand until lukewarm. Beat the eggs and add to the fruit mixture. Strain into a basin and put over a pan of boiling water. Heat and stir until the mixture is like thick cream. Cool and put into serving glasses. Serve chilled.

Suck Cream

1 pint (600 ml) single cream   Grated rind of ½ lemon
1½ oz (40 g) caster sugar   3 tablespoons dry white wine
2 egg yolks

This creamy custard used to be eaten with pieces of dry toast, which were dipped into it and sucked – hence the name, although in some recipe books it is called Sack Cream after the alcohol originally used. Serve it today with shortbread, sponge fingers or ginger biscuits.

Put the cream into a pan with the sugar and bring gently to simmering point, but do not let the cream boil. Put the egg yolks into a basin and whisk with a balloon whisk. Pour on the hot cream, whisking all the time. Whisk in the lemon rind and wine. Put over a pan of hot water, or transfer to the top of a double saucepan, and heat gently, stirring until the mixture is thick enough to coat the back of a spoon. Cool slightly and pour into glasses. Cool and then chill in the refrigerator before serving.

Sack Posset

This must have been an incredibly popular dish. One seventeenth-century handwritten book from Suffolk contains no less than 12 recipes, of which this is one.

Take 2 quarts of Cream and a quarter of a pount of Almons. Stamp them in the Cream and boyl amber and musk therein, then take a pint of sack put it into a bason and set it over a chaffin dish of coles. Let it stand till it be blod warm then take the yelks of 12 eggs with 4 whits. Beat them well together and put them into your sack and make it hot and when your Cream is almost cold put it to your sack and keep it with stirring over coles till it be as thick as you would have it. If you take some amber and musk and grate on it with some sugar it will give it a very good tast.

The dish continued into the nineteenth century, but lost many of its nourishing eggs, and became a wine-flavoured custard rather like a cooked syllabub, and was renamed Sack Cream or Suck Cream.

Ginger Cream

½ pint (300 ml) milk
3 egg yolks
2 oz (50 g) caster sugar
1 oz (25 g) gelatine
4 tablespoons water

4 tablespoons syrup from
    preserved ginger
½ pint (300 ml) double cream
3 oz (75 g) preserved ginger
    chopped very finely

Put the milk into a saucepan and heat just to boiling point. Whisk
the egg yolks and sugar together and pour on the milk, whisking
well. Return to the pan and stir gently over low heat until the
custard is creamy. Leave until lukewarm, stirring occasionally. Put
the gelatine into a cup with the water and stand it in a pan of hot
water. Heat gently, stirring until the gelatine is syrupy. Remove
from the heat and stir in the ginger syrup. Leave until lukewarm.
Whip the cream to soft peaks. Stir the gelatine into the custard, and
then pour the custard slowly into the cream, whisking all the time.
When the mixture is thick and cool, add the finely chopped ginger.
Stir to prevent the ginger from sinking and pour into a glass dish.
Stir again and leave until firm and chilled.

Snow Cheese

1 pint (600 ml) double cream
3 oz (75 g) caster sugar
Juice of 1½ lemons

1 oz (25 g) ground almonds
1 tablespoon rosewater
2 teaspoons brandy

*This recipe produces a light, soft cream cheese, which is delicious
with sugar and cream, or with fruit. It was very popular in the
eighteenth and early nineteenth centuries.*

Put the cream into a bowl with sugar, and stir to dissolve the sugar.
Add the juice from the lemons to the cream with the almonds,
rosewater and brandy. Whisk to soft peaks. Line a 6 in (15 cm) hair
or fine nylon sieve with a piece of muslin and put in the cream.
Leave in a cool place (not the refrigerator) for 12 hours. Turn out on
a serving place and serve with sugar and cream.

Geranium Cream

½ pint (300 ml) double cream
3 oz (75 g) caster sugar

2 rose-geranium leaves
6 oz (150 g) cream cheese

This rich cream which is like a sweetened cream cheese, is scented with leaves from cottage geraniums. These pot plants have pretty indented leaves that are slightly furry to the touch and very strongly scented, although the flowers are insignificant. There are lemon-, peppermint-, orange-, ginger-, and rose-scented varieties, the last providing the best flavour for cooking. They are often used in the country to flavour spongecakes and crabapple jelly.

Put the cream into a bowl with the sugar and geranium leaves. Put the bowl over a pan of hot water, and heat gently until the cream is hot but not boiling. Remove from the heat and leave until just cold. Gradually add the cream to the cheese, mixing together until smooth and creamy. Put into a bowl, cover and leave in a cool place (not the refrigerator) for 12 hours. Take out the leaves and put the mixture into a serving bowl. Serve with sugar and cream. This is delicious with fresh raspberries or blackberries.

Almond Cream

4 egg yolks
3 oz (75 g) caster sugar
4 oz (100 g) ground almonds

1 pint (600 ml) single cream
2 teaspoons orange-flower
water

Put the egg yolks and sugar into a basin and whisk until thick and creamy. Stir in the almonds. Heat the cream to just under boiling point. Stir in the orange-flower water and pour gradually onto the eggs, beating well. Put the basin over a pan of hot water and stir over gentle heat until the mixture is like whipped cream. Cool slightly and put into glasses. Chill for 1 hour before serving.

Wine Cream

3 eggs
2 oz (50 g) caster sugar
1 tablespoon redcurrant jelly

6 tablespoons red wine
¼ pint (150 ml) double cream

Separate the eggs. Put the egg yolks, sugar, jelly and wine into a basin over a pan of hot water. Stir over gentle heat until the mixture is thick and creamy. Remove from the heat. Whip the cream to soft peaks. Whisk the egg whites to stiff peaks. Fold the cream into the wine mixture. Fold in the egg whites. Spoon into glasses and chill before serving with small sweet biscuits.

Orange Mousse   Serves 4

4 oranges or lemons   4 eggs
2 oz (50 g) caster sugar

The earliest mousses were not gelatine-set mixtures, but simple cooked mixtures of fruit juice and egg yolks, lightened with egg whites. This eighteenth-century mousse is light and creamy, and seems to be a development of the earlier recipe for Bath Orange Creams.

Grate the rinds from half the fruit and mix with the sugar. Add the juice from the fruit and heat gently until the sugar has dissolved. Leave until cool. Separate the eggs and put the yolks into a basin. Pour over a pan of hot water, and stir over gentle heat until the mixture thickens and will coat the back of a spoon. Remove from the heat and cool to lukewarm. Whisk the egg whites to soft peaks and fold into the fruit mixture. Pour into a serving dish and chill, stirring once or twice during the first hour's cooking.

Strawberry Fool   Serves 4–6

1 lb (450 g) strawberries   1 tablespoon clear honey
½ pint (300 ml) double cream   1 oz (25 g) flaked almonds

The strawberries should be very ripe, but not squashy for the dish. Reserve a dozen of the best berries. Put the rest through a fine sieve (to speed preparation, blend the fruit and then sieve). Put the cream and honey into a bowl and whisk to soft peaks. Cut the remaining strawberries into downward slices so that they retain the shape of the fruit. Fold the purée into the cream and stir in the slices. Spoon into a bowl and sprinkle with almonds. Serve chilled.

Gooseberry Fool

Serves 4–6

1 lb (450 g) gooseberries
¼ pint (150 ml) water
6 oz (150 g) sugar

2 teaspoons orange-flower
  water
¾ pint (450 ml) double cream

Gooseberries were traditionally eaten first at Whitsuntide, preferably following duck and green peas, because they all came into season at that time. Whitsun was always a time of celebration in the country, associated with processions connected with the church (everyone wore new white clothes), and such customs as dressing the wells. A fool was a popular dish for using this fruit, which was usually too hard and sour to be eaten raw.

Wash the berries, and top and tail them. Put into a pan with the water and sugar, and simmer until soft and pulpy. Leave until cold and then stir in the orange-flower water and cream. Serve very cold with small, sweet biscuits.

Boodles' Orange Fool

Serves 4

3 oranges
1 lemon
2 oz (50 g) caster sugar

½ pint (300 ml) double
  cream
4 trifle spongecakes

This fool is like a syllabub without alcohol, and it is spooned over pieces of spongecake, which absorb juices from the fruit. The name comes from a St James's Club formed in London in 1764.

Grate the rinds from 2 oranges and the lemon, and squeeze out the juice. Mix the rinds and juice with the sugar, and stir until the sugar has dissolved. Whip the cream to soft peaks and gradually beat in the juice until completely absorbed. Cut the spongecakes into ½ in (1.25 cm) slices and arrange in a single layer on the base of a serving dish and round the sides. Pour in the cream. Chill for 3 hours. Peel the remaining orange. Separate the segments and remove the skin from each piece. Arrange the orange segments on the cream just before serving.

Damson Fool

1½ lb (675 g) damsons
¼ pint (150 ml) water
3 oz (75 g) light soft brown
  sugar

1 pint (600 ml) egg custard
  (see Chapter 16 on sauces)
¼ pint (150 ml) double cream

The strong distinctive flavour and colour of damsons used to be very popular. The fruit makes a very good fool with custard and a sweetening of brown sugar.

Put the damsons, water and sugar into a pan and simmer until the fruit is very soft. Put through a sieve to remove the skins and stones. Mix the fruit purée with the custard until completely blended. Spoon into glasses and chill. Just before serving, whip the cream to soft peaks, and cover the tops of each fool.

4 Junkets and Syllabubs

Thou shall eat crudded cream
All the year lasting
And drink the crystal stream
Pleasant in tasting;
Whig and Whey while thou lust
And bramble berries,
Pie-lid and pastry crust,
Pears, plums and cherries.

Anon (17th century)

The very names junket and syllabub make us think of jollity and outdoor merrymaking, and indeed 'junket' has become associated with frivolous gatherings. Both dishes rose to popularity in Tudor times, when the cow became the most common animal for milking, gradually replacing goats and ewes for this purpose. Country people loved drinks of whey and buttermilk, and revelled in plentiful supplies of cream before it became too expensive.

Junket derived from an old French dish of renneted cream that was drained on a *jonquet* – a little basket made of *jonques*, or rushes – and formed a cheese curd known as a 'green cheese' because it was new and was not left to mature. The English junket was made with renneted cream and gradually changed from being a rich cheese to a sweetmeat sweetened with sugar and rosewater. According to C. Anne Wilson in *Food and Drink in Britain* (1973), this junket became known as 'fresh cheese' by the reign of Elizabeth I and was eaten with fresh cream. Another form had developed in which renneted cream was left to set, but not broken up and drained, and was flavoured with cinnamon or nutmeg, or with rosewater and sugar. The junket died out when more easily made syllabubs and fruit fools became popular with the eighteenth century gentry, who could afford cream. It lingered on in Devonshire and Cornwall, where it became a speciality served with thick clotted cream.

Originally, the rennet had to be prepared from a dried and salted calf's stomach, and even in nineteenth century London, junket made with this rennet was sold in mugs or glasses from stalls in the streets. Liquid rennet extract was in production from 1878 and junket returned to favour in private homes, but the introduction of the artificially coloured and flavoured junket tablet and powder turned it into a dreaded nursery pudding. A carefully-made Devon junket prepared with liquid rennet and flavoured with brandy is a revelation, with its accompaniment of thick cream.

The syllabub has a happier history and has returned to favour in the last few years. It was a festive drink originally, and the name is said to be Elizabethan – *bub* was a slang word for a bubbling drink, and *Sill* was the area in the Champagne country of France from which the wine Sill or Sille took its name. The drink was made by milking directly from the cow into ale, cider or wine so that a fine froth arose from the creamy and slightly alcoholic mixture. Charles II was so fond of the drink that he had cows kept in St James's Park so that he could have a drink whenever he was thirsty. (Perhaps the attraction was the milkmaids, always famous for their beauty and fine skin because milking gave them immunity from 'the pox'.)

As late as 1701 Katherine Windham of Felbrigg (Norfolk) included a recipe for 'Selibub from the Cow' in her notebook. Eighteenth-century cooks added lemon juice, often to homemade fruit syrup, or to currant wine, and used large quantities of cream instead of the earlier milk. Some traditional recipes were retained though, and a Newcastle farmer's recipe of 1812 recommends a cow be milked into a mixture of cider and strong beer spiced with nutmeg and sweetened. This was left for an hour and then decorated with currants that had been soaked with water in front of the fire to swell.

The most popular version, which is the one we make today, became known in the eighteenth century as Everlasting Syllabub because it would stand in the glass for some days after making. This was made with a mixture of sweetened wine laced with brandy and sometimes sherry, and sharpened by the juice of a lemon or Seville orange. Syllabubs were party dishes and were made pretty with sprigs of rosemary and curls of lemon peel. This popular whip later became the topping of the original trifle (see Chapter 5).

There were many local variations on syllabub, according to Mrs Copley's *The Housekeeper's Guide* (1834). London Syllabub used a bottle of port or white wine, sweetened with sugar and mixed with 4 pints of milk, flavoured with nutmeg. Devonshire Syllabub was similar but with clotted cream on top. Somersetshire Syllabub was a mixture of port and sherry, flavoured with sugar and nutmeg, and was left for 20 minutes to settle after milking, then covered with clotted cream. Staffordshire Syllabub used cider as the alcohol, strengthened with a glass of brandy. Hampshire Syllabub was made from strong old home-brewed beer, laced with a great deal of brandy. A rather grand Punch Syllabub contained lemon juice, rum and brandy, warm cream whipped with a chocolate mill to make a 'firm high froth'.

Devonshire Junket

1 pint (600 ml) creamy milk
2 teaspoons caster sugar
2 tablespoons dark rum or
   brandy

1 teaspoon liquid rennet
Cream
Ground nutmeg

For perfect results, use a cooking thermometer, as the milk should just heat to blood warm (98°–100°F). If this aid is not available, test the milk by dipping the tip of your little finger and you will only just be able to bear the heat. Use liquid rennet, and be careful to measure it carefully, as too much will make the junket taste salty. Junket should be set at room temperature, not put in a refrigerator, and it should remain undisturbed until needed. Make sure the milk used is rich and creamy – Channel Island milk is best.

Put the milk into a saucepan and bring to blood heat, but do not boil. Put the serving bowl in a place where it will not be disturbed and put the sugar, rum or brandy in the bottom. Stir until the sugar is dissolved. Pour in the warm milk and stir in the rennet gently. Leave undisturbed to set, which will take about 1 hour. Traditionally, it should be spread with clotted cream and then sprinkled with nutmeg. If clotted cream is not available, pour on thick cream, or lightly whipped cream. If preferred, the top may be simply sprinkled with a little sugar and ground nutmeg.

Damask Cream

1 pint (600 ml) single cream
3 teaspoons caster sugar
1 teaspoon liquid rennet
Ground nutmeg

5 tablespoons double cream
3 teaspoons rosewater
Fresh rose petals (pink or red)

This delicately flavoured eighteenth-century dish is made like junket, but with cream.

Heat the single cream to blood heat (see Devonshire Junket) and stir in the sugar. Pour into a serving dish and stir in the rennet gently. Leave until set and sprinkle with nutmeg. Sweeten the double cream with a little sugar to taste and stir in the rosewater. Just before serving, spoon the cream over the junket and decorate with rose petals.

Everlasting Syllabub

Serves 6

¼ pint (150 ml) white wine
1 tablespoon medium sherry
2 tablespoons brandy
Peeled rind and juice of 1 lemon
or 1 Seville (bitter) orange

¼ pint (150 ml) water
2 oz (50 g) caster sugar
½ pint (300 ml) double cream

The syllabub must be started the day before it is to be eaten, as the flavours of juice and wine must blend together overnight. The best wine to use is a slightly sweet one, like Sauternes. Use a large bowl to prepare the recipe: the liquid splatters everywhere and makes a mess when whipped.

Put the wine, sherry and brandy into a basin. Peel the fruit very thinly and reserve half the peel. Put the remaining peel into the wine with the strained fruit juice. Leave the wine mixture overnight, and then remove the peel. Cut the reserved peel into hair-thin strips and put into the water in a small pan. Bring to the boil and simmer for 2 minutes. Drain off the water and keep this peel for decoration. When ready to complete the syllabub, stir the sugar into the wine mixture. Add the cream and whip until the mixture forms soft peaks. Spoon into tall wine glasses and sprinkle the reserved peel on top.

Norfolk Whipped Syllabub

Serves 4–6

4 egg whites
4 oz (100 g) caster sugar
Pinch of nutmeg

Grated rind and juice of
  1 lemon
¼ pint (150 ml) white wine
½ pint (300 ml) double cream

This eighteenth-century recipe is close to Hannah Glasse's Lemoned Honeycomb (see p. 41), but has a much higher proportion of egg whites and makes a lighter mixture than the usual syllabub.

Whisk the egg white to stiff peaks. Add the sugar gradually and whisk until it is incorporated. Add the nutmeg, lemon rind and strained juice to the egg whites and whisk until mixed. Pour in the wine and cream and whisk well, skimming off the froth into glasses until the mixture is finished. Chill before serving.

Honey Syllabub

Grated rind and juice of 1
  lemon
3 tablespoons brandy
3 tablespoons medium sherry

1 pint (600 ml) double cream
6 tablespoons clear honey
1 oz (25 g) candied lemon peel

The distinctive taste of honey blends very well with the lemon in the mixture.

Put the grated rind and juice from the lemon into a bowl with the brandy and sherry, and leave to stand for 2 hours. Add the cream and honey and whisk until the mixture is thick and light. Spoon into tall glasses. Chop the candied lemon peel very finely and sprinkle on top. Chill before serving with sponge fingers.

Lemoned Honeycomb

Juice of 1 lemon
2 oz (50 g) caster sugar

1 pint (600 ml) double cream
1 egg white

Although we have a modern dish of Honeycomb, which consists of custard, jelly and egg whites and sets in three layers (see p. 20) Hannah Glasse's recipe from 1747 is rather like a syllabub without alcohol when made, but settles into a kind of sweetened curd.

Strain the lemon juice into a serving dish. Stir in half the sugar until dissolved. Put the cream into a bowl with the egg white and the remaining sugar. Whisk the mixture and as it froths, spoon off the froth and put it on the lemon juice. Continue whisking and skimming in this way until the cream mixture has all been placed on the lemon juice. Leave to stand in a cool place for 18 hours.

5 Tipsy Cakes and Trifles

All sorts of good things for supper - scalloped oysters, potted lobsters, jelly, a dish called 'little Cupids' (which was in great favour with the Cranford ladies, although too expensive to be given, except on solemn and state occasions - macaroons sopped in brandy, I should have called it, if I had not known its more refined classical name).

This description of a whimsical dish from Mrs Gaskell's *Cranford* gives some idea of the special social occasion on which alcoholic little trifles were served.

There seems to be no record of when the tipsy cake became popular, although the trifle appears so often in recipe books, but the two dishes have been closely connected for centuries until they have become totally muddled in one dish. It seems likely that the tipsy cake derived from the medieval 'sops', pieces of bread soaked in wine or almond milk. Breadcrumbs were also often used to thicken milk or able to provide delicious and nourishing eating possets. Richer people enjoyed these eating possets made with cream and sack or brandy, with the addition of eggs and grated spongecakes or ground almonds. It is not hard to see that a complete spongecake soaked in alcohol, spiked with almonds and surrounded by custard should eventually become a dish in its own right, and that the amount of alcohol used should be adequately described by the adjective 'tipsy'.

The trifle began life as a simple Elizabethan custard deriving from the flavoured almond milk of medieval times. The earliest trifle was made with thick cream sweetened with sugar and flavoured with ginger and rosewater, which was cooked gently like a custard and was grand enough to be presented in a silver bowl. At the beginning of the eighteenth century the cream was heated and lightly set with rennet to make it thicker, and was decorated with tiny sugar sweets called comfits.

By the middle of the century, cream thickened with eggs into a custard was being poured over broken sponge fingers, almond macaroons and little ratafia biscuits that had been soaked in sack. The association with the alcohol-soaked tipsy cake was gradually evolving, but the next stage was the addition of the newly-developed Everlasting Syllabub (see Chapter 4) piled on top of the custard.

There were endless variations, for such a 'trifling dish' was subject to the whims and fancies of the cook and the consumer. In 1747 Hannah Glasse composed her trifle from a simple mixture of broken sponge fingers, macaroons and ratafias lightly wetted with sack and covered with 'good boiled custard not too thick', over which went syllabub and a garnish of ratafias, currant jelly and flowers. The Dean's Cream, a contemporaneous favourite from Cambridge, was made with spongecakes spread thickly with jam and mixed with macaroons and ratafias before being soaked in sherry and covered with syllabub. The recipe sometimes appeared as King's Pudding, Easter Pudding, Victoria Pudding or Colchester Pudding, with the sponge soaked in wine, sherry or fruit juice, and a topping of whipped cream or egg white, often tinted pink. Eliza Acton, writing in 1855, described The Duke's Custard, which was made from brandied cherries rolled in sugar, covered with custard, garnished with macaroons or sponge fingers, and topped with rose-coloured whipped cream. Mrs Beeton in 1861 described a trifle made with raisin wine and topped with syllabub, but mounded up on a dish to look like tipsy cake.

Colonel Kenney-Herbert, writing under his pen-name of Wyvern in 1881, described the trifle as a 'time-honoured, excellent dish, so dear to the hearts of our elderly cousins and our maiden aunts'. Today it remains as the climax to celebration meals, particularly in the country. It is most important, however, that it should be made to time-honoured standards, and not debased into a horror of stale cake, mean jam, canned fruits, packet jelly and packet custard.

Tipsy Cake

Serves 4–6

1 moulded spongecake
¼ pint (150 ml) sweet sherry
6 tablespoons brandy

2 oz (50 g) blanched almonds
1 pint (600 ml) custard (p. 198)

This is Mrs Beeton's version of a tipsy cake that could be made with a spongecake, Savoy cake (a fatless sponge flavoured with lemon, orange or almond), or rice cake (similar to a Madeira cake but made with equal quantities of ground rice and flour). The cake was prepared in a decorative mould and soaked in sweet wine or sherry and brandy, before being spiked with almonds and surrounded by rich custard. Mrs Beeton indicated that the cake could be crumbled and soaked before being topped with whipped cream like a trifle. She also gave 'an easy way of making a Tipsy Cake', using stale small spongecakes, raisin wine, jam and custard, and cut preserved fruit for decoration, which seems to be a direct ancestor of today's cheap trifles.

Make up a basic Victoria sponge mixture and bake it in a domed cake tin (a small Kugelhopf mould will do). If this is not available, use an ovenglass pudding basin. Keep the cake for 3 to 4 days before using. Trim the base of the cake so that it will stand firmly on a serving dish, which should be a deeply rounded plate or cake stand, as the custard has to surround the cake. Make a hole in the centre of the cake with a skewer. Mix the sherry and brandy and spoon over the centre of the cake. Leave the cake to soak for 2 hours and then stick it all over with the almonds cut into narrow, lengthway strips. Pour the cold custard round the outside of the cake.

Tipsy Squire
Serves 6

8 trifle spongecakes
2 tablespoons strawberry jam
2 tablespoons apricot jam
2 tablespoons greengage jam
2 tablespoons marmalade
3 oz (75 g) ratafia biscuits
3 tablespoons brandy

8 tablespoons sweet sherry
2 oz (50 g) flaked almonds
1 pint (600 ml) milk
½ pint (300 ml) single cream
1 bay leaf
1½ oz (40 g) caster sugar
6 egg yolks

This pudding seems to come somewhere between the simple tipsy cake and the elaborate trifle. Its name makes me feel that it must have been a great favourite with yeomen farmers and the minor gentry.

Split the trifle sponges in half lengthways. Fill two of them with strawberry jam, two with apricot, two with greengage and two with marmalade. Put the ratafia biscuits in a layer on the base of a serving dish and sprinkle with brandy. Put half the filled spongecakes on top and sprinkle with half the sherry. Sprinkle with half the almonds. Top with remaining sponges and sprinkle with sherry. Put the milk, cream and bay leaf together in a bowl and put over a pan of hot water. Heat until the milk is just under boiling point and has taken the flavour of the bay leaf, which will take about 10 minutes. Whisk the sugar and egg yolks together and pour on the hot milk. Whisk well and then return to the bowl over hot water. Heat and stir gently until the mixture coats the back of a spoon. Cool slightly and pour over the spongecakes. Leave until cold. Spread the remaining almonds on a baking sheet and toast under the grill until golden. Sprinkle on top of the custard.

Mrs Toone's Apple Snow Trifle

1 lb (450 g) cooking apples
2½ oz (65 g) caster sugar
Strip of lemon peel
2 tablespoons water
½ pint (300 ml) milk

1 vanilla pod
2 eggs
4 trifle spongecakes
Glacé cherries
Angelica

This recipe from 1930, which comes from Leicestershire, shows clearly the way in which the English housewife continued to improve and to vary traditional dishes, with the foamy apple snow taking the place of the original whipped syllabub. With its lack of alcohol and cream, this is an economical dish that is also pleasant and refreshing, and far more interesting than stewed apples served with a biscuit.

Peel and core the apples and cut them into slices. Put into a saucepan with 2 oz (50 g) sugar, lemon peel and water. Simmer until the apples are soft. Remove the lemon peel and rub the apples through a sieve. Heat the milk with the vanilla pod just to boiling point. Remove the vanilla pod (washing and drying it for future use). Separate the eggs. Stir together the egg yolks and the remaining sugar. Pour on the milk and whisk well. Return to the pan and stir over low heat until the custard is thick and creamy.

Split the spongecakes in half through the centres and arrange on the base of a glass dish. Cool the custard slightly so that it will not crack the bowl, and then pour it over the spongecakes. Leave until cold. Whisk the egg whites to stiff peaks and fold them into the apple purée. Pile the apple foam on top of the custard and decorate with cherries and angelica.

Damson Trifle

1½ lb (675 g) damsons
3 oz (75 g) light soft brown sugar
7 in (17.5 cm) round Victoria
  spongecake

1 pint (600 ml) egg custard
  (see p. 198)
½ pint (300 ml) double cream
2 oz (50 g) chopped mixed nuts

While fruit is generally unattractive in trifle, this country version made from layers of sponge, damsons and custard is remarkably good. The original dish was finished with stiffly-whipped sweetened egg white, but this may not appeal to today's palates, and whipped cream may be more popular.

Put the damsons into a pan with the sugar and simmer gently until the fruit is tender. Cool and then carefully remove the stones from the fruit so that the fruit is not mashed up. Split the spongecake through the middle, and then cut each round into short slices. Arrange one half of sliced spongecake in the base of a glass dish and cover with half the damsons. Pour on half the custard. Top with remaining slices of spongecake, then remaining damsons and custard. Cover with a piece of film or kitchen foil and leave to stand for 8 hours. Whip the cream to soft peaks and spoon over the custard. Sprinkle with chopped nuts.

Whim Wham   *Serves 6*

1 pint (600 ml) double cream
2 oz (50 g) caster sugar
¼ pint (150 ml) white wine
Grated rind of ½ lemon

8 trifle spongecakes
8 oz (225 g) redcurrant jelly
3 oz (75 g) candied peel

This delightful name was applied to a little trifle, a sort of emergency pudding that could be assembled quickly from ingredients that were in the house. There are a number of versions, but this comes from Mrs Dalgairns' Practice of Cookery (1829). The contrast of redcurrant jelly with cream and spongecake is delicious. If liked, the layers may be arranged in individual glasses, but they look very attractive in a large glass bowl. Try to find some whole pieces of candied peel to cut for the decoration.

Put the cream, sugar, white wine and lemon rind into a large bowl. Whip the cream until light and fluffy. Put one-third cream into the serving bowl. Cut the sponges in very thin slices, and use half of the slices to cover the cream. Cover with half the redcurrant jelly. Put on another layer of one-third cream, then the remaining spongecake slices and jelly. Cover with the remaining cream. Cut the candied peel into very thin strips and sprinkle on the cream. Chill before serving.

Miss Jacob's Suffolk Trifle   *Serves 8*

6 large macaroons
¼ pint (150 ml) white wine
3 fl oz (75 ml) brandy
1 pint (600 ml) single cream
2 eggs
2 egg yolks
1 tablespoon cornflour
1 oz (25 g) caster sugar
4 oz (100 g) raspberry jam

3 oz (75 g) blanched almonds
3 oz (75 g) chopped mixed
   candied peel
Everlasting Syllabub (see p. 40)

Decoration

Candied peel, blanched almonds,
crystallized violets and roses

*This recipe from 1790 clearly shows the transitional stage between
the tipsy cake and syllabub combination and today's trifle. It will be
seen that the jam is placed on top of the custard instead of
underneath as in modern practice.*

Choose a large glass dish for the trifle. Put the macaroons in the
bottom and pour on the wine and brandy. Leave to soak and add a
little more wine if the macaroons remain dry. Make the custard
next. Bring the cream just to the boil. Meanwhile, beat together the
eggs, egg yolks and cornflour. Pour on the cream and whisk
together. Return to the pan and cook very gently without boiling.
Stir well until the custard is thick. Remove from the heat and stir in
the sugar. Cool slightly and then pour over the macaroons. Leave
in a cold place to set. Carefully spread the jam on top of the
custard, and sprinkle with almonds and peel. Make up the
syllabub recipe and put on top of the jam. Leave in a cool place
overnight so that the flavours blend together. Just before serving,
decorate with pieces of candied peel, blanched almonds or
crystallized flowers to taste.

Edwardian Trifle   *Serves 8*

8 trifle spongecakes
8 oz (225 g) raspberry jam
½ pint (300 ml) medium
   sherry
1 pint (600 ml) custard
   (see p. 198)
4 oz (100 g) ratafia biscuits

6 tablespoons brandy
¾ pint (450 ml) double
   cream
1 oz (24 g) caster sugar
Maraschino cherries
Blanched almonds

The prosperous Edwardians finally evolved the trifle in all its glory as we know it today. This version comes from a family recipe book and I always make it at Christmas time. It is very rich indeed, and must be made with egg custard.

Split the spongecakes lengthways and spread liberally with raspberry jam before putting together again. Arrange in a large glass serving dish, letting some of the spongecakes come up the side if necessary, but being sure that there is only one layer of cakes. Spoon over the sherry. Cover the dish and leave in a cool place overnight. Make custard with creamy milk and eggs and leave until cool. Spoon over the spongecakes. Arrange the ratafia biscuits in a layer on top and sprinkle with half the brandy. Whip the cream with the sugar and remaining brandy until it forms soft peaks. Spoon lightly over the ratafias. Drain the cherries very well and decorate the trifle with cherries and split almonds.

Brown Bread Trifle   *Serves 4-6*

6 oz (150 g) fine brown   1 pint (600 ml) double cream
  breadcrumbs   3 tablespoons brandy
2 oz (50 g) caster sugar   4 oz (100 g) crystallized fruit

Variations of this recipe appear in a number of handwritten books and I suspect that it was a simple way of using precious bread to make a simple but delicious dish. In one version the crumbs are mixed with 'moist juicy jam, such as strawberry' before being arranged in layers with whipped cream. Another version merely soaks the crumbs in jam and then covers them in cream, without the extra trouble of making layers. The following recipe is a little more delicate, but in common with all the other variations fine breadcrumbs are specified. In the old days these would have been sieved, but now it is easier to make them very fine in a blender or food processor.

A colourful mixture of fruit is the most attractive. I use pineapple, apricots, greengages and cherries if possible, and this is a good way of using the oddments sometimes left after Christmas.

Stir together the breadcrumbs and sugar. Whip the cream and brandy to soft peaks. Fold into the breadcrumbs and pile in a dish. Chop the fruit finely and sprinkle over the surface.

Floating Island

3 eggs

4 oz (100 g) caster sugar

4 oz (100 g) sifted flour

4 oz (100 g) raspberry jam

4 oz (100 g) apricot jam

4 tablespoons sweet sherry

¾ pint (450 ml) double cream

¼ pint (150 ml) white wine

4 tablespoons brandy

4 oz (100 g) icing sugar

Rosemary sprigs

Crystallized roses and violets

This bears little resemblance to the French dish of the same name, which consists of poached meringue arranged in little islands on a sweet liquid custard, although it is possible that the two versions have a common ancestry. The English dish was a side dish for grand dinners in the seventeenth century, and became fashionable in the eighteenth century when elaborate set-pieces were all the rage with the aspiring middle-classes. An island of filled spongecake was floated on a sea of fruit purée or syllabub, surrounded by billows of more syllabub or whipped cream, and then decorated with sprigs of rosemary and crystallized flowers. The earliest recipes used fine French bread (brioche) instead of sponge, and sometimes irregular pieces of the cake were arranged as jagged islands.

Put the eggs and sugar into a bowl over hot water and whisk until thick and creamy. Remove from the heat and fold in sifted flour. Put into two greased and base-lined sponge sandwich tins, measuring 7 in (17.5 cm) and 8 in (20 cm). Bake at 375°F/190°C/Gas Mark 5 for 20 minutes. Turn out and cool on a wire rack. Split each spongecake into three thin slices. Spread the larger sponge with raspberry jam and reassemble very lightly without pressing the sponges together. Assemble the smaller sponge in the same way with apricot jam, leaving a little jam to place one assembled sponge on the other. Sprinkle the top and sides with the sherry.

Put the cream, wine, brandy and sugar into a large bowl and whisk to soft peaks. Dip four or five rosemary sprigs lightly in the mixture. Spoon one-third of this mixture into a glass serving dish. Place the assembled spongecake in the centre. Spoon the remaining cream round the spongecake in billows, reserving a few spoonfuls to drop on the top like snow. Stick the rosemary sprigs into the spongecake like trees. Garnish with crystallized flowers.

6 Charlottes

There are many theories concerning the origins of the charlotte. In the fifteenth century there were charlets, consisting of finely chopped meat cooked in milk and sweetened, and that name is a combination of *chair* (flesh) and *laitée* (milked). It also has been suggested that the dish was named after the heroine of a Goethe novel, or that it is a misspelling of the Hebrew *schaleth* – a sweet, spiced purée with dried fruit and a crisp crust. Some people say that Carême (1784–1833), the great French chef, evolved the charlotte we know today from this Hebrew dish, but was unable to cope with the unfamiliar spelling.

Carême, known as the Cook of Kings and the King of Cooks, certainly invented the Charlotte Russe, so called because the dish made its first appearance at the tables of security and foreign ministers, although he preferred the name Charlotte Parisienne. The confection, consisting of a wall of sponge fingers surrounding a cream filling, appeared in upper-class English homes and achieved some popularity, often with the cream filling strongly-flavoured. Mrs de Salis in *Sweets à la Mode* (1889) gives recipes for one filled with a mixture of apricot purée and cream, and another flavoured with coffee (8 oz/225 g coarsely ground freshly roasted coffee beans to 2 pints/1.2 l cream). Perhaps this type of Charlotte never became truly popular in England because of the complications of making it perfectly, although Eliza Acton in 1855 gives an easy version made from sliced pound cake decorated with coloured icing or leaves of almond paste, and hollowed out to contain whipped cream – sadly, this version was known as a Gertrude, and the name was hardly endearing.

Carême was employed by the Prince Regent, and the legend is that he invented Apple Charlotte, replacing spongecake with bread and the cream filling with fruit. *Larousse Gastronomique* feels that this is in fact the earlier version of the dish, and it certainly seems close to the Hebrew *schaleth*, but it has been suggested that the dish was named in honour of Queen Charlotte.

A second and inferior version of the charlotte involves a mixture of breadcrumbs and fruit instead of the classic bread wall. I have always been struck by the fact that this is identical with a dish known as a Betty, which makes its appearance in some modern English cookery books as a country dish. It is, in fact, also very close to popular Danish and Swedish dishes, and has appeared in generations of American cookery books, possibly having been introduced by Scandinavian immigrants. Although we have attached the name of Charlotte to this dish, no good American would want to commemorate the queen of the hated George III.

When preparing the classic charlotte, some care is needed. Today's soft bread does not provide a satisfactory wall, and the pudding is better made with good bread from an individual baker or home-baked bread. The butter with which the bread is brushed, or in which it is fried, should be clarified so that the bread will remain clean and golden. Apples provide the classic filling, but any sharp fruit, such as rhubarb or gooseberries, may be used. The fruit should be cooked to a firm purée, with no surplus moisture to seep through the wall, which must be arranged with closely-fitting or slightly overlapping bread. Old-fashioned cooks often added apricot jam to the purée, and sometimes brandy. A hint of spice does not come amiss – cinnamon with apples, or ginger with rhubarb. Eliza Acton suggested that the charlotte should be left to stand for a few minutes before turning out, so that it became firmer, and could then be brushed with melted red jelly (redcurrant jelly is ideal).

Apple Charlotte   *Serves 4–6*

1 lb (450 g) cooking apples
2 oz (60 g) butter
6 oz (150 g) sugar
Grated rind and juice of
   1 lemon

1 teaspoon ground mixed spice
8 thin slices of bread from a
   large loaf
4 oz (100 g) clarified butter
1 oz (25 g) caster sugar

Some charlotte recipes suggest buttering the bread, and others dipping the bread in melted butter. An old lady from Staffordshire said that she always lightly fried the bread in butter, and this does produce a far superior version of the dish.

Peel and core the apples, and cut them into thin slices. Put into a pan with the butter, sugar, grated lemon rind and juice, and the spice. Simmer very gently until the apples form a soft purée with no surplus liquid. Remove crusts from the bread and cut each slice into three strips. Heat the butter and fry the bread slices until just golden and crisp. Line the sides and bottom of a straight-sided dish with bread slices. Put in the apple purée and cover with the remaining strips of bread. Sprinkle with half the caster sugar. Bake at 400°F/200°C/ Gas Mark 6 for 45 minutes. Turn out and sprinkle with remaining sugar.

Mrs Spurrell's Apple Charlotte

Serves 4–6

1 lb (450 g) cooking apples
2 oz (50 g) unsalted butter
6 oz (150 g) caster sugar
½ teaspoon ground nutmeg
Grated rind of 1 lemon

8 thin slices of bread from
large loaf
4 oz (100 g) clarified butter,
melted
3 oz (75 g) apricot jam

This recipe dates from 1865.

Peel and core the apples and cut them into thin slices. Put into a pan with the butter, sugar, nutmeg and lemon rind. Simmer very gently until the apples form a soft purée. Remove the crusts from the bread and cut each slice into three strips. Dip them into the clarified butter and arrange round the sides and bottom of a straight-sided dish. Put in the apple purée and hollow out a hole in the centre. Put the apricot jam into this hole, and then cover the top of the apples and jam with the remaining bread dipped in butter. Bake at 400°F/200°C/Gas Mark 6 for 45 minutes. Turn out onto a heated serving dish and serve with cream or custard.

Apricot Brown Betty

Serves 4–6

1 lb (450 g) ripe fresh apricots
8 oz (225 g) wholemeal bread
2 oz (50 g) melted butter
4 oz (100 g) light soft brown
sugar

Grated rind and juice of
½ lemon
½ teaspoon ground cinnamon
¼ pint (150 ml) boiling water

Cut the apricots in half and remove the stones. Chop coarsely and keep on one side. Remove crusts from the bread and make the bread into crumbs. Mix the crumbs with melted butter. Put a layer of crumbs into a greased baking dish and put in half the fruit. Sprinkle with half the sugar, half the lemon rind and juice, and half the cinnamon. Top with a layer of buttered crumbs. Repeat the layers. Pour on the water. Bake at 375°F/190°C/Gas Mark 5 for 45 minutes. Serve with cream or custard.

Gooseberry Charlotte with Sweet Cicely   *Serves*

1 lb (450 g) gooseberries
3 oz (75 g) butter
3 tablespoons water
4 tablespoons finely chopped
   sweet Cicely

2 oz (50 g) fresh white
   breadcrumbs
2 oz (50 g) shredded suet
2 oz (50 g) demerara sugar

Sweet Cicely is an easily-grown herb with delicate flavour. It has the effect of lightly sweetening fruit with which it is cooked – a valuable aid to those who wish to cut down on the amount of sugar they consume.

Top and tail the gooseberries. Melt 2 oz (50 g) butter in a saucepan. Add the gooseberries, water and sweet Cicely. Simmer gently until the berries are soft. Mix together the breadcrumbs, suet and sugar in a bowl. Grease an ovenware dish and put a layer of crumb mixture on the base. Add layers of gooseberries and crumbs, finishing with crumbs. Dot with flakes of the remaining butter. Bake at 350°F/180°C/Gas Mark 4 for 1 hour. Serve with custard or cream.

7 Ices and Iced Puddings

Plain food is quite enough for me;
   Three courses are as good as ten.
If nature can subsist on three,
   Thank heaven for three. Amen!
I always thought cold victual nice;
   My choice would be vanilla ice.

Many of us might have once echoed the words of Oliver Wendell Holmes, but today's commercial products have taken away our taste for this one-time treat. For centuries ices were considered very attractive, possibly because of the difficulty of obtaining ice, which made the frozen confections exclusive to those who could afford them.

Alexander the Great is supposed to have had a special fondness for iced drinks, and the Roman emperors enjoyed fruit juices frozen with ice and snow carried from the Alps by relays of slaves. Nero is said to have executed a general who failed to organize the necessary transport that would ensure that the snow remained unmelted when it reached Rome. At the same time, ices were being served at banquets in the East. Chinese, Indian, Persian and Arabian gentlefolk enjoyed fruit juices mixed with crushed ice, which were used as digestives between courses. The delicately flavoured iced Persian drinks were known as sherbets, later corrupted to sorbets as a name for sweetened water ices (the name sherbet is still used in America).

In the thirteenth century Marco Polo noticed the Eastern habit of eating frozen confections after meat, and brought back recipes which were developed all over Italy. Milk ices, cream ices and butter ices became very popular, and Catherine de Medici introduced them to France on her marriage to Henry II in 1533. Her son, Henry III, ate ices every day, but these confections remained the privilege of the few.

It is thought that the French introduced ice cream to the English in the reign of Charles I (in 1640 the King decreed that the recipe should always remain a royal secret). An ice-house was built in St James's Park soon after this, and there was even a poem of praise written on the subject.

Ice-houses were built in the grounds of many country houses, and instructions for designing them were printed. Basically they were underground caves constructed near the estate lake, from which ice could be cut in the winter. The ice was insulated with straw, and the ice-house was thickly thatched. *Gunter's Modern Confectioner* (1861) describes the way in which an ice-house should be prepared. By this time, it consisted of a well or tank decreasing in diameter as it went deeper into the ground, the object being to keep the ice compact as it gradually melted and sank. The ice-house had to be built on gravel or chalk, with a northerly aspect so that it did not catch the sun. Waste water would drain through the soil, but it was important to stop up the drain when not in use so that warm air would not pass upwards to melt the ice. The ice-house had to be built of perforated bricks, with a thickness of 18 inches, then covered with cement. There had to be at least six feet of earth on top of the arched roof, and shrubs on top to keep off the sun. The entrance, a slanting passage, or a few steps at the side, should have two doors and every aperture had to be padded with ice. It was no wonder that the ice-house was the prerogative of those with large country houses, but it was suggested that an ice-house could be built by the side of a dairy at the entrance to the kitchen quarters.

The ice had to be put in at a dry time and had to be refilled during the winter as the first lot of ice settled down. Ice had to be removed from the sides first, leaving the centre, which would last until midsummer. In the 1830s large ice-chests were coming into use, in which the ice was wrapped in a blanket, which saved the ice but not the food. By 1840 boxes were lined with tin or zinc and ice was transferred from the outdoor ice-house or delivered by the iceman. Ice was imported from America's Wenham Lake and sold in British towns, and ice-chests were still available from Harrods in 1890. Many inventors had experimented with cooling processes and 'artificial' ice since 1755, but refrigerators as we know them did not begin to appear until the final decade of the nineteenth century. The increasing use of gas and electricity, however, resulted in improved methods of refrigeration and these useful pieces of equipment began to appear in many homes in England in the 1920s.

Seventeenth-century ices were set in moulds in the ice-houses, and elaborate moulds of tin or pewter were used for simple confections of sweetened fruit juices, or plain or unsweetened cream. Hannah Glasse added a note on making ice cream to her *Art of Cookery* (1797) but without giving recipes, and her method of preparing ices was more suitable for the small domestic kitchen. Two pewter basins were used, one being larger than the other, and the smaller one having a close-fitting lid. Sweetened cream mixed with fruit was put into the smaller basin, which was set into the larger bowl containing a mixture of ice and salt. The ice cream was left to stand for 45 minutes, then stirred and frozen again. Mrs Dalgairns, writing in 1829, described a refinement of this method, in which the inner basin was turned round and round for 10 minutes during the initial freezing, then stirred and frozen.

Nancy Johnson is credited with the invention of the first ice-cream freezer in America, in 1864, which worked like a butter churn in the centre of a bed of ice and freezing salt. Some people say that the old crank method of freezing ice cream is still the best, and today we can use an equivalent in the electricity-driven *sorbetières* that fit into refrigerators or freezers.

Ices continued to be simple confections of cream or fruit juices until the Victorians discovered the enormous possibilities of moulded iced puddings for elaborate dinner and buffet parties in contrast to the light fruit ices served as digestives between courses. Pewter moulds were designed to resemble fruit, flowers, vegetables and fish, and *Gunter's Modern Confectioner* makes the point that pewter should always be used in preference to tin, as it was much thicker and prevented the contents freezing quickly into lumps so that it was not easy to mix the ingredients together thoroughly.

The queen of ices was Agnes Marshall, who founded a cookery school in 1857, wrote articles, gave lectures, and developed her own commercial range of cooking aids and ingredients. She first wrote a simple *Book of Ices* (1870) giving basic instructions and recipes, but by 1894 she was really into her stride with *Fancy Ices*. Here were ices in the shape of asparagus stalks, cucumbers, wheatsheaves, swans, melons and baskets of flowers. There was the Rosamond Timbal made of liqueur-flavoured almond paste, decorated with rose-coloured icing and whipped cream, and filled with alternate layers of chocolate, strawberry and maraschino ice cream, then covered with whipped cream and decorated with chocolates; or there were Sandringham Strawberries composed of a rich strawberry-flavoured ice set into a giant strawberry mould and surrounded by smaller strawberry shapes garnished with maidenhair fern.

These elaborate iced puddings remained in favour for about thirty years, as Lady Jekyll describes in *Kitchen Essays* (1922):

A blue-blooded and conservative marquis may be forgiven his temporary loss of self-control when the newly-engaged cook sent on its gay career round a decorous dinner-party of county neighbours a transparent and highly decorated pink ice pudding concealing within inmost recesses a fairy light and a musical box playing 'The Battle of Prague'. Words were spoken, and, like the chord of self in Locksley Hall, this over-elaborated creation 'passed in music out of sight'.

Shades of those 'subtleties' that delighted our medieval ancestors.

The elegant confections gave way to simpler ices that the

average housewife could prepare in her new refrigerator, but the death-knell of the ice cream was sounding with the introduction of commercially produced ices. In the second half of the nineteenth century, and until the Second World War, in tearooms such as Jolly's, Buszards and Gunter's, people were able to enjoy simple little ices made by old-fashioned methods with fresh ingredients, just as French and Italian ices still are today. Hokey-pokey, an Italian confection, was also sold from stalls, and this developed into the sale of ices from tricycles. There were simple fruit ices and cream ices sold in paper cones, scooped and moulded ices to be placed in cornets or between wafers, and blocks that could be turned into simple ice-puddings at home with sauces or fruit.

Sadly, the earlier commercial counterparts of homemade ices have declined so that today they are composed of non-milk fats, artificial flavourings and colourings, and a variety of additives that maintain the texture of ices during storage. On the other hand, we now have the advantage of very efficient refrigerators and freezers in our kitchens and there is no reason why we should not make some of the ices that pleased earlier generations. A refrigerator freezing compartment should be turned to the lowest setting for an hour before preparing ices. Many ices need beating during freezing to make them smooth and creamy, and this is easily achieved with an electric mixer, blender or food processor. Ices taste more delicious if put into the refrigerator for 30 minutes before serving, so that they have a chance to 'come to' after being solidly frozen.

Tea Cream Ice
Serves 4–6

2 oz (50 g) Earl Grey tea
1 pint (600 ml) water
3 eggs

½ teaspoon lemon juice
3 oz (75 g) caster sugar
½ pint (300 ml) double cream

Put the tea into a basin and pour on freshly boiling water. Leave to stand for 5 minutes. Strain and leave until completely cold. Beat the eggs with the lemon juice and sugar until white and thick. Add the cold tea slowly, whipping all the time. Whip the cream to soft peaks and fold into the tea mixture. Put into freezing trays and freeze for 3 hours, beating once during freezing.

Tea Ice

Serves 4

½ pint (300 ml) water
1 oz (25 g) Earl Grey tea
4 oz (100 g) caster sugar

Juice of 2 lemons
1 egg white

Fragrant tea makes a refreshing ice to end a heavy meal, although it originally would have been used to clear the palate between courses. I find a good blend of Earl Grey tea is best for this, with the necessary strength and a distinctive scent.

Boil the water and pour onto the tea. Leave to stand for 5 minutes and strain. Stir in the sugar and leave until cold. Stir in the lemon juice. Pour into an ice tray and freeze at lowest setting. Freeze for 1 hour and then scoop into a bowl. Whisk the egg white stiffly and fold into the tea mixture. Return to the ice-tray and continue freezing for 2 hours.

Simple Fruit Ice

Serves 4

10 oz (300 g) prepared fruit
4 oz (100 g) caster sugar

1 teaspoon lemon juice
¼ pint (150 ml) double cream

The earliest cream ices were simple mixtures of cream and fresh fruit, and they taste just as good today. Ripe soft fruit such as strawberries, raspberries, apricots, peaches, bananas, cherries and pineapple may simply be sieved and sweetened before adding to the cream. A little lemon juice helps the colour and flavour of the fruit, Currants are better lightly cooked in the minimum of water before sieving and mixing with the cream. To speed processing, fruit may be crushed in an electric blender and then sieved if necessary to remove pips.

Weigh the fruit after removing skins or stones if necessary. Rub through a sieve or purée in a blender. Stir in the sugar and lemon juice until the sugar has dissolved. Stir in the cream until evenly coloured. Pour into a freezing tray and freeze in the ice-making compartment of the refrigerator at lowest setting. Beat twice during freezing to ensure smoothness.

Blackcurrant Leaf Ice

1 pint (600 ml) water
6 oz (150 g) sugar

3 large handfuls young
    blackcurrant leaves
3 lemons

Blackcurrant leaves are very fragrant and scent this light and refreshing ice.

Put the water and sugar into a pan and heat gently until the sugar has dissolved. Boil for 5 minutes and add the blackcurrant leaves. Peel 2 lemons and squeeze out the juice from all 3 of them. Add the peel and juice to the pan, cover and remove from the heat. Leave until cold. Strain the syrup, pressing the leaves to extract all the liquid. Pour into an ice-tray and freeze at the lowest setting for 1 hour. Turn into a chilled bowl and beat well. Return to the tray and continue freezing for 2 hours.

Apricot Ice Cream

3 tablespoons apricot jam
1 oz (25 g) caster sugar
Juice of 1 lemon

½ oz (15 g) ground almonds
2 teaspoons rosewater
1 pint (600 ml) double cream

At the beginning of the nineteenth century cunning housewives devised fruit-flavoured ices that could be made when fresh fruit was not available. They flavoured cream with raspberry or apricot jelly or jam, lemon juice and sugar, and coloured the pale cream lightly. Sometimes ground almonds or rosewater were added, as in this recipe. The original version of 1829 goes into some detail about preparation and serving:

Put it into the freezing pot, cover it closely and place it in a bucket which has a small hole near the bottom, and a spigot to let the water run off, and which has in it plenty of ice broken small, and mixed with three or four handfuls of coarse salt – press the ice closely round the freezing-pot, turn it round and round for about ten minutes, take off the cover, and remove the frozen cream to the centre with a spoon, cover it again, and turn in till all be equally iced. Serve it in China ice pails, or put it into moulds, cover them tightly with wet bladder, and place them in a bucket with ice, as before, for an hour or more; dip the moulds into cold water before turning out, and serve them immediately.

Mix together the jam, sugar, lemon juice, almonds and rosewater. Whip the cream to soft peaks and fold in the other ingredients. Put into a mould, cover and freeze for 1 hour at lowest setting. Stir well and continue freezing for 2 hours.

Scented Gooseberry Ice Cream   Serves 4–6

12 oz (350 g) gooseberries   6 cottage geranium leaves
3½ oz (90 g) caster sugar   ¼ pint (150 ml) double cream
4 tablespoons water

Scented geraniums have been resident on cottage windowsills for generations. They are grown for their attractive foliage, as the tiny flowers are insignificant and quite unlike those of the flamboyant geraniums that appear in municipal parks. The foliage of cottage geraniums has a haunting scent of lemons, roses, oranges, peppermint or ginger (according to variety) as each leaf is bruised, and dried leaves are used in pot-pourri. Fresh leaves traditionally add a delicate flavour to apple jelly and to old-fashioned sponge-cakes, but I had never tried them in other dishes until I discovered this old recipe for ice cream, which seems to reflect the passing pleasures of a perfect English summer day. Rose-scented leaves are the best for this recipe.

Adjust the refrigerator to the lowest setting. Wash the gooseberries and top and tail them. Put the fruit into a pan with the sugar, water and 4 geranium leaves. Put on a lid and simmer the fruit to a pulp. Put through a sieve and discard the pips. Chill the gooseberry purée in the refrigerator. Whip the cream to soft peaks and fold into the cold purée. Put into an ice-tray and freeze for 1 hour. Scoop the half-frozen mixture into a bowl and whisk with a fork or beater until smooth. Rinse out the ice-tray and dry it thoroughly. Put the 2 remaining geranium leaves on the base of the ice-tray and put in the mixture. Leave to freeze for 3 hours. About 30 minutes before serving time, put the ice-tray into the refrigerator, and adjust the setting to normal. To serve, scoop the cream into individual glasses and serve with sponge fingers or shortbread.

Custard Ice Cream

¾ pint (450 ml) creamy milk
1 vanilla pod
2 egg yolks

2 oz (50 g) caster sugar
¼ pint (150 ml) double cream

A simple custard ice is not too expensive to make at home, and provides a useful base for other flavourings. Use pure flavourings for these ices, as synthetic essences do not react well to freezing.

Put the milk into a pan with the vanilla pod. Heat gently until the milk comes to boiling point. Beat the egg yolks and sugar in a bowl. Remove the vanilla pod and pour the milk onto the egg mixture. Put the bowl over a pan of hot water and stir over gentle heat until the mixture coats the back of a spoon. Leave until cold. Whip the cream to soft peaks and fold into the custard. Pour into a freezer tray and freeze at lowest setting for 1 hour. Scoop out into a chilled bowl. Beat until smooth and freeze for 1 hour. Repeat the process and continue freezing for 1 hour. This makes a basic vanilla ice cream. If the vanilla pod is split, the flavour will be stronger and the ice flecked with tiny black seeds.

Chocolate
Melt 2 oz (50 g) plain chocolate in the milk before adding to the pan.

Coffee
Scald 4 tablespoons freshly ground coffee with the milk and strain before adding to the egg yolks.

Christmas Ice
Soak 3 oz (75 g) mixed dried fruit, 1 oz (25 g) chopped mixed candied peel and 1 oz (25 g) chopped nuts in 3 tablespoons rum or brandy for 1 hour, and fold into ice before final beating.

Marmalade Ice Cream

1 pint (600 ml) single cream
3 egg yolks
4 oz (100 g) caster sugar

8 oz (225 g) dark chunky
    marmalade
¼ pint (150 ml) double cream

This is a delicious modern ice based on custard contrasting with dark orange marmalade. Thin, sweet marmalade is not suitable, as it makes the ice far too sweet.

Heat the single cream to just under boiling point. Whisk the egg yolks and sugar together, and whisk in the hot cream. Put over a pan of boiling water and stir over gentle heat until the custard thickens and coats the back of the spoon. Remove from the heat. Stir in the marmalade (if it is very stiff, warm it slightly first). Stir until the marmalade has completely melted into the custard and leave until cold. Whip the double cream to soft peaks, fold in, and put into two ice trays or a freezer container. Freeze at lowest setting for 3 hours, beating twice during freezing.

Mrs Marshall's Apple Sultan Sorbet   *Serves 6*

1¼ lb (675 g) cooking apples
6 oz (150 g) caster sugar
2 lemons
1 in (2.5 cm) cinnamon stick
1 pint (600 ml) water
3 tablespoons brandy
Green vegetable colouring
¼ pint (150 ml) double cream

Sauce
8 oz (225 g) sultanas
½ pint (300 ml) water
3 oz (75 g) caster sugar
1 bay leaf
Strip of lemon peel
2 tablespoons white rum

This recipe dates from 1894.

Peel and core the apples and cut them into slices. Put into a pan with the sugar. Peel 1 lemon and add the peel to the apples with the cinnamon and water. Simmer until the apples are soft. Stir in the juice from both lemons and put through a sieve. Cool and stir in the brandy and just enough vegetable colouring to tint the fruit purée lightly green. Pour into a freezing tray and freeze at the lowest setting for 1 hour. Turn into a chilled bowl and beat until smooth. Whip the cream to soft peaks and fold into the purée. Continue freezing for 2 hours.

   Put all the sauce ingredients into a pan and simmer until thick and syrupy. Take out the bay leaf and lemon peel and chill before serving with the ice.

Brown Bread Ice Cream

Serves 6

6 oz (150 g) wholemeal
   breadcrumbs
½ pint (300 ml) double cream
½ pint (300 ml) single cream

4 oz (100 g) light soft brown
   sugar
2 eggs
1 tablespoon rum

This brown bread ice cream was first popular at the end of the eighteenth century, and was a great favourite on Victorian tables. It is important to make the ice cream with coarse-textured wholemeal bread, not soft 'brown' bread, which cannot be made into the necessary coarse crumbs. A pretty Victorian decoration was a sprinkling of crushed crystallized violets.

Make the breadcrumbs by hand or in an electric blender. They should be coarse-textured. Spread them out on a baking tray and put into the oven at 325°F/170°C/Gas Mark 3 for 10 minutes until they are crisp and slightly browned. If you do not wish to use the oven, the crumbs may be toasted under a medium grill, but must be watched carefully so they do not become dark brown. Cool the crumbs completely. Mix the double and single cream and whip with the sugar to soft peaks. Separate the eggs. Beat the eggs lightly and add to the cream with the rum. Beat into the cream until just blended. Fold in the breadcrumbs until they are evenly mixed into the cream. Put into an ice tray and freeze for 1 hour at lowest temperature. Whisk the egg whites to stiff peaks. Scoop the half-frozen cream into a chilled bowl or blender goblet and mix until soft and well blended. Fold in the egg whites. Return to the ice tray and continue freezing for 2 hours. To serve, scoop into glasses or bowls.

Brown Bread and Honey Ice Cream

Serves 4–6

2 oz (50 g) fresh brown
   breadcrumbs
1½ oz (40 g) demerara sugar
½ teaspoon ground cinnamon

3 tablespoons clear honey
2 eggs and 2 egg yolks
4 oz (100 g) icing sugar, sieved
7 fl oz (200 ml) double cream

There is a legend that this was Queen Victoria's favourite ice cream, and it is certainly richly delicious.

Put the breadcrumbs, demerara sugar and cinnamon into a shallow fireproof dish (a foil pie plate is ideal). Stir them well so that the spice coats the crumbs and sugar. Heat under a medium grill, stirring occasionally, until the sugar begins to melt and caramelize. Remove from the heat and stir together again. Leave until cold and then break up the mixture by pressing with the back of a large spoon. Whisk the eggs and egg yolks together until well mixed. Add the icing sugar gradually and continue beating until the eggs are pale cream and double in volume. Put the cream into another bowl and whip to soft peaks. Stir the breadcrumb mixture into the cream. Warm the honey until it is runny but not hot. Mix it quickly into the eggs, then fold in the cream. Mix together quickly until completely amalgamated, and put into an ice-tray. Freeze for 3 hours without beating, as the mixture is very rich and does not develop pieces of ice during freezing. About 30 minutes before serving time, put the ice-tray into the refrigerator, and adjust the setting to normal. To serve, scoop the ice cream into individual glasses and serve with brandy snaps.

Country House Iced Pudding

Serves 6–8

1 Victoria spongecake, made in
  a loaf tin
½ pint (300 ml) double cream
½ oz (15 g) caster sugar
8 tablespoons brandy or
  medium sherry
4 oz (100 g) glacé cherries

Sauce
4 oz (100 g) apricot jam
2 tablespoons water
2 tablespoons Curaçao

The term 'iced pudding' is seldom used now, but frozen confections that were not necessarily ices were thus described in the days when ice-houses and ice-chests were available in large country houses, and the iceman delivered his wares to town houses. Iced puddings became very fashionable during the 1920s and 1930s when more households began to enjoy the benefits of a refrigerator in the kitchen. Chilled dishes provided an innocent way for the smart hostess to 'show off', and many women went overboard in their passion for the ice-box. Cookery books and menus of the period are packed with recipes for iced soups, savoury ices and fashionable American dishes, with little to recommend them but novelty.

Today's freezer enables us to make excellent iced puddings, but somehow the words 'frozen pudding' do not have the same flashy glamour as the original term. This easily made version was popular in a Sussex country house at the beginning of this century, and it really should be made with homemade spongecake and not today's sugary trifle sponges.

If glacé cherries are disliked, the pudding may be made with brandied cherries, which are suggested in the original recipe. These used to be obtainable in bottles, but are unlikely to be found in modern households. A good way of preparing a version of these cherries is to drain a can of black cherries, remove the stones, and soak the fruit in a few spoonfuls of brandy overnight. Drain before using and save the liquid for a sweet sauce, or use to sprinkle on the cake in this recipe.

Prepare and bake a Victoria spongecake in a 1 lb (450 g) loaf tin. Turn out and cool on a wire rack. Split the cake through lengthways to make three slices. Line the loaf tin with a piece of kitchen foil so that there are no gaps or joins. Whip the cream with the sugar and 1 tablespoon brandy or sherry to stiff peaks. Put one slice of the cake in the base of the loaf tin and sprinkle with one-third of the remaining brandy or sherry. Cover with half the cream and half the remaining brandy or sherry. Cover with the remaining cream and cherries. Top with the remaining spongecake and sprinkle with remaining brandy or sherry. Cover with a piece of foil and freeze for 3 hours.

While the pudding is freezing, prepare the sauce. Put the jam and water into a small saucepan and heat gently until melted and liquid. Put through a sieve and stir in the Curaçao. Chill in the refrigerator. To serve, turn out the pudding and pour the sauce over it. Cut the pudding with a sharp knife dipped in hot water.

8 Fruit

The first fruits to be eaten in England were wild apples and nuts gathered by prehistoric people, but there is no evidence that these were cultivated. Certainly during the Bronze Age there were also wild raspberries, blackberries, strawberries, bilberries, sloes and elderberries, which can be judged from archaeological research. The Romans were experienced gardeners, and introduced good eating apples, cherries and vines from their warmer climate. They used these fruits for cooking as well as for the making of wine and vinegar. Although the Roman agricultural system died out in Britain after their withdrawal, succeeding invaders continued growing fruit, so it must have been of some importance in their diet. The Saxons cultivated apple orchards, but also enjoyed quinces, medlars, plums and pears, and when the Normans arrived, they brought many new varieties of apples and pears. By the thirteenth century, peaches, cherries and gooseberries were being planted, and the Roman methods of grafting fruit trees were being taken up again by gardeners.

At the same time, exotic fruit, such as oranges, lemons and pomegranates, was being imported from southern Europe. It is thought that the Crusaders had enjoyed citrus fruit in the Near East early in the twelfth century, but the first consignments did not arrive in England for another hundred years. Lemons and Seville oranges remained in use at Court and in grander houses, but for poorer families citrus fruit was still only an occasional winter treat until well into the twentieth century. Many people can still remember the 'bun and an orange' given as a going home gift from Sunday School parties, and a tangerine in the toe of a stocking remains a traditional Christmas gift. Along with the citrus fruit, dried figs, prunes, dates, raisins and currants began to arrive and were very popular for sweetening when few people could afford rare sugar. They were used widely in rich houses, but poorer people looked on them as another Christmas treat to sweeten pottages.

The most important fact that affected the consumption of fruit in England was that raw fruit was considered extremely unhealthy. At banquets it was permissible to start the meal with raw plums, damsons and cherries, which were considered to be 'openers' for the stomach, while apples, pears, strawberries, and nuts accompanying cheese might be eaten at the end to 'close' it – a forerunner of the habit of serving dessert. Poorer people tended to stuff themselves with raw fruit that was sold in the streets, and their subsequent illnesses gave rise to the belief that the fruit was dangerous when raw. Fruit was therefore cooked into a purée for tarts or eaten in pottages. The superstition about raw fruit has died hard. There are still many people of the older generation who refuse raw fruit and will even stew strawberries and raspberries before eating them.

Fruit cultivation improved from the sixteenth century onwards, with subsequent improvement in native varieties and the introduction of apricots and currants. Culinary (rather than medical) rhubarb became a favoured ingredient in pies, puddings, custards and creams. However, it was still carefully cooked, since the doctors encouraged the belief that it affected the blood and was also a danger in times of plague. Consequently, fruit was pre-cooked before being added to dishes that were then cooked again. By the eighteenth century some of the berry fruits were eaten raw, and there was some improvement in 'stewing' fruit. The fruit was placed in a gallipot of earthenware which was placed in a pan of boiling water over the fire or in the bread oven. Little water was added to the fruit, and it was thus allowed to cook gently in its own juices and sweetening, with far more delicious results.

An adaptation of this method is still useful today to avoid the horrid traditional 'stewing', which results in pallid, stringy fruit in thin, sweetened water. Apples, pears, plums and damsons taste very good if layered in a casserole with sugar or honey and a little liquid in the form of water, cider or wine. Gently cooked in a low oven, the fruit will retain its shape, colour and flavour. Complementary flavourings are important to fruit: try a pinch of cinnamon with blackcurrants or raspberries, ginger or cloves with apples or pears. Apricot jam gives flavour to apples, and redcurrant jelly to the plum family or to cherries. A hint of liqueur is another enhancer of flavours, the fruit-flavoured brandies being particularly useful: try cherry brandy with cherries, or apricot brandy with apples.

Sadly, the range of fruit available is now becoming extremely limited unless we can grow our own. While the shops are full of imported exotics, where can we find English apricots, quinces, medlars, mulberries or even cherries? Even simple blackcurrants, redcurrants, raspberries and gooseberries are difficult to find, although there is sometimes a chance to pick-it-yourself for the freezer. What has happened to those deliciously sticky greengages of my youth, the enormous golden eating gooseberries, and the huge bowls of Kent cherries? All of these can be grown easily in private gardens, and some may be found in fruit areas such as Worcestershire and Kent. The following recipes will help to make the best of those we do not want to eat raw. Other fruit recipes are, of course, included throughout the book in appropriate chapters.

Fresh Fruit Salad

Serves 4

2 oranges
3 eating apples
2 bananas
Juice of 1 lemon

4 oz (100 g) white grapes
½ pint (300 ml) water
4 oz (100 g) sugar

Any mixture of fruit may be made into a salad, but it is important to get some variety of textures and colours. The liquid may be simple sugar syrup, but it is improved if a glass of light sweet wine is poured over the fruit before the syrup is added. Freshly-squeezed orange juice also improves the syrup, or you can add a little fruit-flavoured brandy. I find that a little gin gives an excellent flavour, particularly if the fruit salad is orange-based.

Peel the oranges and divide into segments. Skin the segments and put them into a serving bowl. Peel and core the apples and cut into thin slices. Put into a bowl with thinly sliced bananas and sprinkle with the lemon juice. Peel and pip the grapes and add to the oranges. Heat the sugar and water together gently until the sugar has dissolved, and then boil for 3 minutes. Cool and pour over the oranges and grapes. Stir in the apples and bananas and chill lightly before serving. In the summer, sections of peach or melon may be added, or some fresh strawberries. In the winter, stoned dates and walnut kernels are good additions.

Winter Fruit Salad

Serves 6

1 lb (450 g) dried fruit
1 pint (600 ml) freshly made
   China tea

1 cinnamon stick

Dried fruits such as prunes, apricots, apple rings, pear and peach halves make a lovely winter fruit dish that may be served hot or cold with cream. Single types of fruit or mixtures taste far better if soaked and cooked in tea rather than plain water.

Put the dried fruit into a bowl and pour the hot tea over it. Leave to stand overnight so that the fruit swells. Put the fruit and liquid into a pan with the cinnamon stick and simmer until the fruit is just

72

tender, which will only take about 15 minutes if the fruit is of high quality and not very old and dry. Serve hot or cold, taking out the cinnamon stick just before serving. Sugar may be cooked with the fruit, but it should not be necessary. A few drops of rosewater stirred into the cold fruit after cooking gives a delicious flavour.

Summer Fruit Bowl   *Serves 4–6*

1 lb (450 g) gooseberries	¼ pint (150 ml) water
4 oz (100 g) redcurrants	4 oz (100 g) raspberries
4 oz (100 g) blackcurrants	6 oz (150 g) caster sugar

A delicious dish may be made by layering fresh blackcurrants, redcurrants, strawberries, raspberries and stoned black cherries in a bowl. Each layer should be lightly sprinkled with sugar (and a little liqueur if liked) and then the bowl chilled for 4 hours before serving the fruit with thick cream. If the fruit is not quite so perfect, try this mixture instead, cooking some of the fruit.

Top and tail the gooseberries. Remove stems from the currants. Put into a pan with the sugar and water. Bring slowly to the boil and simmer for 5 minutes so that the fruit does not break. Cool to lukewarm and stir in the raspberries. Pour into a serving dish and chill before serving with cream.

Spiced Cherries   *Serves 4*

1 lb (450 g) red eating cherries	½ teaspoon ground nutmeg
4 tablespoons water	Pinch of ground cloves
4 oz (100 g) caster sugar	4 oz (100 g) redcurrant jelly
½ teaspoon ground cinnamon	

Use firm, red eating cherries for this dish, which is very good served with cream or ice cream.

Stone the cherries and put the fruit into a pan with the water, sugar and spices. Cover and simmer for 10 minutes. Lift out the cherries with a slotted spoon and put into a serving dish. Add the redcurrant jelly to the cooking liquid and simmer until syrupy. Pour over the cherries and chill.

Baked Pears in Cider

Serves 6

2 lb (900 g) cooking pears (or
  hard eating pears)
4 oz (100 g) caster sugar
½ pint (300 ml) sweet cider

½ pint (300 ml) water
Piece of lemon peel
1 oz (25 g) shredded almonds

*Pears used to grow in many country gardens, but they were often
'wardens', or hard cooking pears, and many preserves and sweet
puddings were devised to make use of them. They take a long time
to soften, so are traditionally cooked in a slow oven with cider or
wine, which soaks into them, giving colour and flavour, and
producing a delicious syrup at the end of cooking.*

Leave the stems on the pears, but peel the fruit thinly. Arrange the
pears upright in a deep casserole. Sprinkle on the sugar. Mix the
cider and water and pour over the pears. Put in the lemon peel.
Cover and cook at 300°F/150°C/Gas Mark 2 for 4 hours. The pears
should be tender but not broken, and a fork should go in easily. If
they are still firm continue cooking for another hour. Leave to cool
in the liquid. Remove the pears to a serving bowl, and arrange them
close together so that they remain upright. Put the cooking liquid
into a saucepan and simmer until reduced to half, and the liquid
forms a thick syrup. Meanwhile, stick the almonds all over the
pears. Pour the syrup over the pears. Serve chilled with thick
cream.

Baked Apples

Serves 4

4 Bramley Seedling apples
3 oz (75 g) unsalted butter
Pinch of ground ginger or
  cinnamon

4 oz (100 g) light soft brown
  sugar

*This is one of the classics of the English kitchen, yet so often it is
boring and sharp-tasting. The secret lies in cooking the apples with
butter and brown sugar, but no other liquid. Some people like to
stuff the centres with fruit mincemeat or dried fruit, but I prefer the
simple flavour of apples, butter and sugar, lightly spiced.*

Wipe the apples and take out the cores with a corer. Cut around the circumference of the apple skins with a sharp knife, cutting just into the skin (this ensures that the apples will not burst and will retain a nice round shape). Butter a shallow ovenware dish thickly and place the apples close together so that they are almost touching. Try to find a dish that will just fit them neatly. Put a little piece of butter in the bottom of each apple. Add a pinch of the chosen spice and fill up with sugar. Dot the tops of the apples with remaining butter. If you have too much sugar and butter to fit into the apple cavities, distribute them in the bottom of the dish. Bake at 350°F/180°C/Gas Mark 4 for 30 minutes until the centres of the apples are soft and fluffy, and the butter and sugar have turned into a thin toffee. Serve very hot with chilled thick cream as a contrast.

Apple Snow   *Serves 4*

1 lb (450 g) cooking apples   Grated rind and juice of
3 oz (75 g) caster sugar   1 lemon
                                            2 egg whites

It was difficult to beat eggs before the acceptance of the fork, in common use late in the seventeenth century, but egg whites were whisked with birch whisks. The first 'snow' was a favourite Elizabethan dish made from whipped cream and sugar piled onto an apple, with a large rosemary sprig to look like a snow-covered tree. Often the snow was gilded for a more spectacular effect. By the middle of the seventeenth century, egg whites were beginning to be whisked into cream for a dish of 'snow cream', which remained popular until the eighteenth century. Apple purée was added to make Apple Snow, but other seasonal fruits were sometimes used.

Be sure that the apples are those, such as Bramley Seedling, that become light and fluffy when cooked.

Peel and slice the apples and remove the cores. Put the slices into a pan with the sugar. Add the lemon rind and juice to the pan and simmer over low heat, stirring often until soft. There should not be surplus liquid in the purée, which should be about the thickness of whipped cream and slightly dry. Continue simmering the apples until this texture is obtained. Put the mixture through a fine sieve or whirl in an electric blender until light and fluffy. Whisk the egg whites to soft peaks and fold into the apple purée. Spoon into glasses and chill before serving with small sweet biscuits.

Apple Hog

4 eggs
4 oz (100 g) caster sugar
12 oz (350 g) ground almonds
7 fl oz (200 ml) sweet sherry
2 large eating apples

2 teaspoons lemon juice
4 oz (100 g) fresh white
  breadcrumbs
½ pint (300 ml) double cream

The little hedgehog has always been a favourite animal in the country. They were reputed to suck milk from the cows' udders as they lay sleeping in the fields, and certainly hedgehogs are very fond of milk. Country people used to put bowls of bread and milk out for them, and took great pleasure in watching the prickly little animals scuttle across the garden to eat. By happy coincidence, the hedgehog's shape was easy to copy for those representational puddings so much favoured by past generations. In medieval times they were shaped in marzipan with the prickles represented by almonds; the Georgians and Victorians were very fond of a stiff fruit cheese made from apples which could be likewise decorated and was often known as Apple Hedgehog (see Victorian Apple Jelly, p. 17). The recipe was given to me by a French girl who said that it had been in her family since the seventeenth century, and it certainly seems to derive from those early marzipan 'hogs'. This version is very rich and delicious, but is not firm enough to turn out and decorate in traditional style.

Separate the eggs and whisk the yolks and sugar together until very light and pale. Stir in the almonds and sherry. Peel and core the apples and grate them finely. Sprinkle with lemon juice to prevent discolouring. Stir into the almond mixture with the breadcrumbs and mix very well. Whip the cream stiffly and fold into the almonds. Finally, whisk the egg whites to stiff peaks and fold into the mixture. Pile into a bowl and chill before serving.

Gooseberry Amber

1 lb (450 g) gooseberries
2 oz (50 g) unsalted butter
11 oz (275 g) caster sugar

8 oz (225 g) fresh white
  breadcrumbs
3 eggs

Fruit 'ambers' seem to have a very close connection with that favourite old dish, the tansy, a kind of omelette composed of fruit purée, breadcrumbs and eggs, fried in butter and flavoured with the bitter herb, tansy. Perhaps the amber was a natural transition of a favourite dish from the open fire to the oven when the latter became a common fixture in households, and the economical housewife used up the egg whites for a meringue topping. Sometimes the fruit goes into a pastry case, but this lighter version is more delicious.

Top and tail the gooseberries and put into a pan with the butter and 5 oz (125 g) sugar. Cook very gently until the fruit mixture is soft and thick. Rub the breadcrumbs through a sieve, or prepare them in a food processor so that they are very fine. Stir into the fruit mixture. Separate the eggs and beat the yolks into the fruit. Pour into a greased pie dish and bake at 350°F/180°C/Gas Mark 4 for 30 minutes. Whisk the egg whites to stiff peaks. Add half the remaining sugar and beat until the mixture is thick and shiny. Fold in the remaining sugar and spoon the mixture over the pudding. Bake for 10 minutes and serve at once.

Damson Cheese

4 lb (1.8 kg) damsons	Sugar
Water	3 oz (75 g) blanched almonds

Fruit cheeses are a type of preserve made from fruit pulp and sugar cooked until thick. Traditionally, they were poured into straight-sided jars and tied down with brandy-soaked paper so that the preserve could keep through the winter. The 'cheese' could be used as a spread, but was more commonly turned out (hence the straight-sided container) and served sliced with milk puddings, or with cream. Apricots, blackberries, sloes, cherries and gooseberries all make good cheeses, but damson cheese seems to have been the greatest favourite. In common with many other dishes, fruit cheese was sometimes set in oval moulds or dishes, turned out and stuck with almonds like a hedgehog.

Put the damsons into a preserving pan and just cover with water. Simmer until the fruit is tender. Put through a sieve and weigh the pulp. Allow 12 oz (350 g) sugar to each 1 lb (450 g) fruit pulp. Heat the pulp and sugar together gently until the sugar has dissolved, stirring well. Bring to the boil and cook for about 30 minutes until the mixture is thick enough to hold the impression of a spoon. Cut the almonds into strips and stir into the mixture. Pour into hot straight-sided jars and cover as for jam.

Summer Pudding

1½ lb (675 g) mixed soft fruit
4 tablespoons water
6 oz (150 g) sugar

6 thin slices of bread from
large loaf

Summer fruit encased in juice-soaked bread is one of the best English native puddings. I like to fill mine with a mixture of raspberries and blackcurrants and a few stoned black cherries, but the choice may have to depend on the fruit available. It is important to make the bread casing from homemade bread or a loaf from an individual baker – the factory-baked variety just turns into a slimy sponge when soaked in fruit juice. Quite often there is some surplus fruit and I like to turn this into a glossy sauce to serve with the pudding and its accompaniment of cream.

Put the fruit into a pan with the water and sugar, and simmer until just soft. Trim crusts from the bread. Arrange the bread to cover the bottom and sides of a pudding basin so that the slices only just overlap, reserving one slice. Cool the fruit to lukewarm and pour into the bread-lined basin until it comes to the top. Cover with the remaining bread. Put a saucer on top and a heavy weight (a can of food can be used as a weight). Leave to stand in a cold place for 24 hours. Turn onto a deep plate and leave to stand for 5 minutes before removing the bowl. Serve with cream.

If a sauce is liked, put any surplus fruit and juice into a pan and add ¼ pint (150 ml) water. Simmer until the fruit is very soft and put through a sieve. Sweeten to taste and simmer until the liquid is slightly syrupy. Chill and pour over the pudding when it is turned out.

Blackberry Autumn Pudding
Substitute 1 lb (450 g) blackberries and 2 eating apples for soft fruit. Cook them in ½ pint (300 ml) medium cider instead of water.

9 Milk Puddings

A mixture of broth and cereals, sometimes with a little meat and vegetables, was introduced into Britain by the Saxon invaders. This pottage remained a staple part of the British diet, and developed in many ways as soups and stews as well as puddings. The pottage that contained a high proportion of cereal developed into such dishes as porridge and a variety of sweet puddings such as blancmange and frumenty. Bread, ale and cereal pottage were three vital elements in English meals until the sixteenth century. Sometimes these cereal mixtures were improved with milk or cream, and occasionally eggs were added.

In the middle of the eighteenth century Hannah Glasse gave a number of recipes for the kind of milk pudding we would recognize today, but she obviously considered that the bland grains needed quite a lot of help to make them acceptable to sophisticated palates. Sago, for instance, was boiled in new milk flavoured with cinnamon, then mixed with a large quantity of butter, eggs, sweetening and sack. Currants then had to be plumped in more sack and rosewater before being added to the pudding, which was finally covered with puff pastry and baked.

Rice and barley received the same sort of treatment, as did millet, now considered as bird food. Charles Lamb remembered his schooldays at Christ's Hospital thus: 'the Wednesday mess of millet (we had three banyan to four meat days in the week) was endeared to the palate with a lump of double-refined sugar, and a smack of ginger (to make it go down the more glibly) or the fragrant cinnamon'. The value of filling cereals combined with nourishing milk was recognized early by schools and other institutions, and so began the long decline from the richness of Hannah Glasse's recipes to the horrors of schoolchildren's 'frog-spawn', 'frog's eyes' and 'nose bleed' (the inevitable name for that dreaded blob of jam on semolina). The earlier delectable eighteenth-century pudding became staple nursery fare, much disliked by small children well into this century, as A. A. Milne's Mary Jane knew to her cost. Mrs Beeton's milk puddings were less rich than Hannah Glasse's, and she also prepared the newly-fashionable pasta in sweet puddings. Her horrific recipe for macaroni pudding echoes the earlier treatment, however, with the macaroni cooked in a pint of sherry with lemon juice, then added to a little milk, a lot of eggs, raisins, sugar and spice before being covered with puff pastry.

Perhaps children long ago found the bland sweetness of milk puddings a happy contrast to the salt meat and dark bread, which was a family's daily diet. My favourite milk pudding recipe comes from the touching entry in the handwritten book kept by Katherine Windham of Felbrigg, Norfolk in 1707, 'To Make my Sons Rice pudding'. The simple mixture of rice and milk was first boiled to soften the rice, then mixed with a lot of butter and fine sugar, and flavoured with nutmeg before being baked for two hours – just the way a good rice pudding should be made. A knob of suet was often stirred into a milk pudding for enrichment, but butter gave a better flavour, of course.

Sadly, a modern milk pudding is often just a mixture of grain and milk with sweetening, but the addition of butter and/or eggs in the old style adds to the flavour and richness, and gives that creamy golden skin that some people find the best part of the dish. My father heartily disliked this feature of a milk pudding, and always preferred rice plainly boiled in water but eaten with plenty of butter and brown sugar. Brought up in a Victorian household, he echoed an earlier Tudor custom of eating cereals with butter, sweetening and spice (the prepared cereals were sold in the streets and dressed by the vendors). Another favourite way of serving milk puddings, which still lingers on in country districts, is with stewed fruit, fruit pies, jam tarts or mince pies, but this is somewhat overwhelming for modern appetites.

However one prefers to eat puddings made with grains, and whichever grain is preferred, there are one or two simple rules for achieving a delicious result. Be sure to use creamy milk and enrich the pudding with butter and/or eggs, and be careful that you do not over-sweeten. The grain may be first boiled to soften the grain and then baked with the enriching ingredients. If the milk is warmed with a little lemon rind, cinnamon stick or mixed spice, the flavour of the pudding will be improved. A bayleaf gives a subtle flavouring and combines well with the nutmeg usually sprinkled on the pudding before baking. It is most important that milk puddings should be cooked slowly and gently to achieve creaminess – additional milk or cream may be stirred into the pudding during cooking if it is becoming dry.

Mrs Spurrell's Tapioca Pudding *Serves 4–6*

1 pint (600 ml) milk
1 piece lemon peel
Pinch of ground cinnamon
2 oz (50 g) sugar

2 eggs
1 oz (25 g) butter
2 oz (50 g) tapioca

This is a good basic farmhouse way of enriching a milk pudding with eggs and butter, and it is delicious with jam or marmalade and cream. It dates from 1865.

Put the milk, lemon peel and cinnamon into a saucepan. Heat gently until the milk comes to boiling point. Remove from heat and leave until lukewarm. Take out and discard the lemon peel. Add the sugar, eggs and butter to the milk and beat with a fork to mix well. Stir in the tapioca. *Either* return to the saucepan and simmer for 1 hour, *or* pour into a greased pie dish and bake at 325°F/170°C/ Gas Mark 3 for 1 hour.

Mrs Spurrell's Macaroni Pudding
Make in the same way, substituting 2 oz (50 g) macaroni for the tapioca. Blanch the macaroni in water for 10 minutes before simmering the pudding.

Rice Pudding

Serves 4

2½ oz (65 g) round pudding rice

2 pints (1.2 l) creamy milk

1 oz (25 g) butter

2 oz (50 g) sugar

Pinch of ground nutmeg

Rice pudding had long held a reputation as being soothing and strengthening. In the sixteenth century rice soaked in milk with white breadcrumbs, fennel and sugar was given to nursing mothers to improve their milk supply. Rice from India was known to the Romans, but was little used in their cooking. It was discovered, however, that rice pottage made from boiled rice mixed with goats' milk and cooked slowly to a pudding was soothing for stomach upsets (even now, plain boiled rice is recommended by those who have lived in the East to those who are suffering from the unpleasant side-effects of hot weather and unsuitable food or infected water).

Rice was hardly known in Britain until the Arabs cultivated it in the Mediterranean lands, from where it spread to Sicily, parts of Spain and the Lombardy area of Italy. Medieval recipes used 'Lombardy rice' for pottages to be enjoyed by the wealthy, for rice was imported with spices and considered just as valuable. In the thirteenth century wealthy families used it mainly for Lenten dishes. The simplest pottages were made with rice boiled in broth, finished with almond milk and sweetening, and coloured with saffron. For fast (meatless) days the rice was cooked with almond milk only and then sweetened. It is easy to see how rice became an everyday sweet pudding, and also why old-fashioned cooks sometimes stirred a piece of suet and/or egg in for extra nourishment. A true rice pudding must be made with round pudding rice, creamy milk and a knob of butter to give a creamy skin. A flavouring of ground nutmeg is a popular finish, and the pudding is best served with plenty of thick cream. Some people like a spoonful of dark orange marmalade with it too.

Put the rice and half the milk into a pie dish and stir in the butter and sugar. Cook at 275°F/140°C/ Gas Mark 1 for 1 hour. Stir in the remaining milk and continue cooking for 1 hour. Stir again and sprinkle with nutmeg and continue cooking for 1 hour.

Caramel Rice

Serves 6

2 pints (1.2 l) milk
3 oz (75 g) pudding rice
1 vanilla pod
1 oz (25 g) unsalted butter
2 oz (50 g) granulated sugar
3 eggs

Caramel
4 oz (100 g) caster sugar
¼ pint (150 ml) water

Put the milk into a pan and heat to boiling point. Add the rice, vanilla pod and butter, and simmer, stirring often, until the rice is tender and the liquid has thickened, which will take about 1 hour. Remove the vanilla pod. Stir in the granulated sugar. Make the caramel by heating the caster sugar and water in a thick pan over low heat until the sugar melts. Do not stir but heat until the sugar becomes golden brown. Stir this caramel into the hot rice until it has coloured the rice. Cool for 15 minutes. Separate the eggs and beat the yolks into the rice. Whisk the egg whites to soft peaks and fold into the rice pudding. Pour into a greased pie dish. Bake at 375°F/190°C/Gas Mark 5 for 25 minutes.

Golden Rice Pudding

Serves 4–6

1 pint (600 ml) creamy milk
2 oz (50 g) pudding rice
3½ oz (90 g) caster sugar

4 oz (100 g) dark coarse-cut
   marmalade
2½ oz (65 g) unsalted butter
5 egg yolks

Marmalade has a curious affinity with rice pudding, providing a contrast between the dark slightly bitter chunks of the really old-fashioned preserve and the smooth, creamy sweetness of the cereal. Use the very best homemade or commercial coarse-cut marmalade for this rich recipe.

Put the milk into a saucepan and bring just to the boil. Add the rice, stir well and simmer for 30 minutes until the rice is tender. Stir in 1 oz (25 g) sugar, and put the rice mixture into a greased pie dish. Spread the marmalade lightly over the top and hollow the centre slightly with a spoon. Melt the butter until just soft, and beat in the remaining sugar and then the egg yolks. When the mixture is creamy, pour it over the pudding. Bake at 350°F/180°C/Gas Mark 4 for 30 minutes.

Mrs Spurrell's Bishop Pudding

Serves 6

2 pints (1.2 l) milk
3 oz (75 g) pudding rice
4 oz (100 g) sugar
2 oz (50 g) butter
24 blanched almonds

4 eggs
1 tablespoon brandy
1 tablespoon sweet white
  wine

This pudding originated in 1865.

Put the milk into a large saucepan and bring to the boil. Add the rice and simmer for 30 minutes until the rice is just tender. Remove from the heat and leave until lukewarm. Stir in the sugar and butter. Chop the almonds very finely and add to the rice. Whisk the eggs lightly with a fork to mix them. Add to the rice with the brandy and wine. Pour into a greased pie dish and bake at 325°F/170°C/ Gas Mark 3 for 1 hour. Serve hot with cream.

Mrs Hingston's Chocolate Rice

Serves 4-6

1 pint (600 ml) milk
2 oz (50 g) pudding rice
1 oz (25 g) sugar
2 oz (50 g) plain chocolate

2 eggs
¼ pint (150 ml) single cream
2 oz (50 g) caster sugar

This recipe dates from 1930.

Put the milk, rice and sugar into a basin. Stir well and bake at 300°F/150°C/Gas Mark 2 for 1½ hours. Leave to stand for 30 minutes, and remove the skin from the pudding. Grate the chocolate coarsely and stir into the pudding. Separate the eggs and beat together the yolks and cream until thoroughly mixed. Stir into the pudding. Return to the oven for 1 hour. Whisk the egg whites to stiff peaks and fold in the caster sugar. Spoon over the top of the pudding and bake for 15 minutes. Serve hot.

Rice Snowballs

Serves 4-6

¾ pint (450 ml) creamy milk
1 vanilla pod
2 oz (50 g) short-grain rice

1 oz (25 g) sugar
Jam
Custard

These amusing little puddings may reconcile children to liking rice pudding. The mixture is slightly stiffer than conventional milk pudding and is set in cups. These should be old-fashioned well-rounded cups to give a good shape.

Put the milk into a pan with the vanilla pod. Bring to boiling point and add the rice and sugar. Simmer until the milk has just been absorbed. Remove the vanilla pod. Rinse 4–6 cups (depending on size) with cold water and press in the rice. Leave in a cold place until set. Turn out on a serving dish, put a blob of jam on each, and pour custard round.

Hasty Pudding
Serves 4–6

1 pint (600 ml) milk
2 oz (50 g) plain flour
1 oz (25 g) butter
2 oz (50 g) sugar

3 eggs
Pinch of ground nutmeg
2 oz (50 g) jam or marmalade

As its name implies, this recipe can be prepared very quickly. It was popular in Victorian recipe books, when the thickening ingredient could be flour, oatmeal, sago or tapioca. The version with flour was often known as Farmer's Rice, and could be served with an accompaniment of black treacle, butter, sugar or cream. The simplest form of Hasty Pudding contained only milk thickened with flour and seasoned with a pinch of salt, but richer versions had the addition of butter and eggs. The most basic pudding was the boiled mixture of milk and thickening, served at once with an accompaniment, but a more attractive version was baked after the initial boiling.

Reserve 4 tablespoons milk, and put the rest into a saucepan. Mix the reserved milk with the flour to a smooth paste. Bring the milk to the boil, and pour slowly onto the flour mixture, stirring well. Return to the pan and stir over a low heat until the mixture is smooth and thick. Remove from the heat and stir in the butter and sugar. Leave until cool and then add the well-beaten eggs and nutmeg. Spread the jam or marmalade in a greased pie dish and spread the pudding mixture on top. Bake at 350°F/180°C/Gas Mark 4 for 30 minutes. Serve hot with black treacle or golden syrup, jam or thick cream.

Gloucestershire White Pot

Serves 6–8

2 pints (1.2 l) creamy milk
4 oz (100 g) plain flour
1 tablespoon soft brown sugar
5 oz (125 g) black treacle

4 eggs
¼ teaspoon ground nutmeg
4 fl oz (100 ml) cold water

There are two or three versions of this dish, traditionally eaten at village 'revels' or feasts in west Gloucestershire, and particularly at Whitsuntide. They are all typical of a simple milk and cereal dish that might be eaten every day, but which was flavoured with sugar and spice for special occasions. The pudding was baked in a deep earthenware dish in a farmhouse bread oven. The cold water forms a white jelly in the pudding. When baked, the pudding should be set, not firm, as it becomes thicker on cooling.

Put the milk into a pan, reserving 6 tablespoonfuls. Mix the reserved milk with flour, sugar and treacle. Boil the remaining milk and stir into the flour mixture. Beat in the eggs and nutmeg. Put into a greased 3 pint (1.5 l) pie dish and pour the cold water into the centre, without stirring. Bake at 325°F/170°C/Gas Mark 3 for 4 hours. Eat warm or cold.

Apple Milk Pudding

Serves 4

1 pint (600 ml) creamy milk
2 oz (50 g) pudding rice
2 eating apples
2 oz (50 g) sugar
Pinch of ground cinnamon

Grated rind of ½ orange or
  lemon
1 oz (25 g) butter
Pinch of ground nutmeg

Milk puddings are often accompanied by stewed apples, and somehow the combination of creamy cereal and watery sharp fruit never seems quite right. I feel that this is, in fact, a poor relic of a dish that appears in various forms in handwritten books through the centuries in which the fruit is actually incorporated in the pudding. The combination is much more attractive when highlighted with spices. Rice or tapioca were the cereals most often used in this way, but the fruit can even help sago or semolina.

Put the milk into a pan and bring just to the boil. Stir in the rice and simmer for 20 minutes. Peel and core the apples and chop the flesh finely. Add to the milk and continue simmering for 15 minutes. Remove from the heat and stir in the sugar, cinnamon, grated rind and butter. Pour into a greased pie dish and sprinkle with nutmeg. Bake at 325°F/170°C/Gas Mark 3 for 45 minutes. Serve with thick cream.

Clipping Time Pudding   *Serves 4–6*

1 pint (600 ml) creamy milk	1 oz (25 g) raisins
2 oz (50 g) short grain rice	1 oz (25 g) currants
1 in (2.5 cm) cinnamon stick	1 egg
2 oz (50 g) sugar	1 oz (25 g) shredded suet

Clipping time, or sheep shearing, was often celebrated with special food in the country, perhaps because it signalled the selling of fleeces and the comparative prosperity of the farmer for a short time. In Lincolnshire, they celebrated with a Firmity (frumenty) Tea, and in Cumberland a milk pudding was also part of the celebration, but this time made with rice. Bone marrow was traditionally used for enrichment, but suet may be used instead.

Put the milk into a saucepan and bring to the boil. Add the rice and cinnamon stick and simmer for about 25 minutes until the rice is tender. Remove the cinnamon stick. Stir in the sugar and dried fruit. Beat in the egg and stir in the suet. Put into a greased pie dish and bake at 325°F/170°C/Gas Mark 3 for 45 minutes.

Frumenty

8 oz (225 g) wheat grains	4 oz (100 g) raisins
¼ teaspoon salt	¼ teaspoon ground nutmeg
3 pints (1.5 l) water	2 oz (50 g) sugar
2 pints (1.2 l) milk	2 eggs (optional)

> With sev'rall dishes, standing by,
> As here a Custard, there a Pie
> And here all tempting Frumentie.

Thus Robert Herrick (1591–1674) sang merrily of one of the great milk puddings that has only recently been lost to us. The dish occurred in Yorkshire, Staffordshire, Lincolnshire, Suffolk, Leicestershire, Derbyshire, Wiltshire and Hampshire, and is still remembered by many people. It was formerly eaten at royal banquets as an accompaniment to savoury meats such as venison and porpoise, and it featured at the marriage feast of Henry IV and at the coronation feast of Henry VII. It was a favourite festive dish, eaten on Christmas Eve with cheese and gingerbread in Yorkshire, where it heralded the decoration of the house and the lighting of the Yule log. In Lincolnshire, the dish was eaten at Firmity Teas, which celebrated sheep-shearing and harvest, and in Wiltshire it was a Mothering Sunday dish. In Suffolk Ferminty or Thruminty (the spelling was variable) was eaten during the twelve days of Christmas, and a plateful was placed outside the door at night for the 'Pharisees' (fairies). The Suffolk version was flavoured with cinnamon and sweetened with honey, and was sometimes mixed with currants and apple as a filling for pasties to be eaten in the harvest field.

Fine wheat was given by grocers to favoured customers for preparation of this dish and in Yorkshire, bakers set aside special days to 'cree' or pre-cook the wheat. The completed dish was sometimes for sale in dairies, was sold in the streets of Leicester, Derby and Boston (Lincolnshire), and was offered by cottagers to weary Leicestershire huntsmen.

The origins of the dish are extremely puzzling. I had assumed that it was simply a rich form of the grain porridge eaten in Saxon times which could be easily prepared from stored grain, but I suspected that there was some deeper, primitive connection with the celebration of fertility (and therefore luck and happiness) through cereals that accounted for its appearance at farming festivals and at times of rebirth, such as Christmas and the springtime Mothering Sunday. A clue appeared in an article by Maria Kaneva-Johnson in Petits Propos Culinaires *(February 1979) describing the preparation and eating of boiled wheat in Bulgaria in association with burial rites and All Souls' Day. The cooked wheat was mixed with ground walnuts, sugar, lemon juice and spices. In answer to my query about whether boiled wheat had some special religious significance, Professor Robert Smith of the University of Birmingham told me that in the twelfth century, Russian princes and warriors prayed and made vows to God and the Blessed Virgin Mary, some with charitable contributions to the poor or to monasteries, and some with kut'ya. This was a kind of porridge made with the whole grain of wheat (sometimes with barley or imported rice) flavoured with honey-water and raisins. It was eaten at feasts in commemoration of the dead and on Christmas Eve, and was blessed by a priest. There were certain prohibitions associated with kut'ya, as it was forbidden to set water by it, or to place eggs on it. Unsanctified people were not allowed to present the wheat grains at the altar in 1499, and the practice of offering it as propitiation began to die out. The whole grain, which is the seed, indicates its symbolic importance, implying the possibility of growth, and it is linked with the cult of dead ancestors. The old Suffolk habit of putting out a bowl for the mysterious spirits seems in accordance with these ancient beliefs.*

The preparation of frumenty takes time, but it is not difficult, and it seems sad that this ancient dish is only a memory. The cleaned wheat kernels (sometimes known as kibbled wheat) may be bought at health food stores, as they are often sprinkled on wholewheat bread. The wheat has to be put into water in a covered dish and cooked in a low oven for about 8 hours (old cooks used to leave it in the cooling bread oven for 24 hours) until the grains have burst and the pan contains a thick jelly. The simplest frumenty was just this soft wheat mixed with milk and honey or treacle. It could also be cooked again with milk and thickened with flour before spicing. Raisins, a bayleaf or lemon peel were sometimes added, while eggs and cream were used for enrichment, and brandy or rum might be stirred in for special occasions. When dried fruit was added, it was boiled first 'to the point of bursting'. Here is a modern version of this ancient dish.

Rinse the wheat in a sieve under running water. Put into a large casserole with the salt and water. Cook at 250°F/130°C/Gas Mark ½ for 8 hours until the wheat is a soft jelly. If the grains have not burst, simmer for a few minutes on top of the stove. Drain off any surplus liquid. Stir in the milk, raisins, nutmeg and sugar and continue simmering for 2 hours on top of the stove. If used, beat the eggs and stir in just before serving. Stir in some brandy or rum if liked, and serve with cream.

10 Pancakes, Fritters and Fraises

It might be thought that some culinary genius had discovered the marvellous effect of hot fat on creamy batter, but the fried puddings we know today derive from simple tricks of the medieval kitchen. A favourite dish was a mixture of egg whites, milk, flour and barm (ale yeast) beaten, strained and seasoned with sugar and salt. The cook dipped his hands into the batter and let it drop from his fingers into a pan of boiling fat. When the pieces ran together, they were lifted with a skimmer, drained and sugared to make the delicious Cryspey detailed in the Harleian Manuscript of 1430. Another favourite trick was to spear dried and fresh fruit on a spit and baste with batter as the spit turned. The batter thickened and became crisp, and the resulting fritter was served with spiced sugar.

Originally, the eggs of wild birds were eaten, but in Roman times, domestic fowl were kept and there was an increasing use of eggs, which were eaten boiled, roasted or fried, or used to thicken sauces. An early dish was borrowed from the Greeks and consisted of a kind of fried custard of eggs and milk, served with honey and pepper. The Romans also discovered that sweet and savoury mixtures could be bound with eggs and fried rather like an omelette or cooked gently like scrambled eggs. Sometimes a sweet version was made with roses or pears.

While hens were still kept in Britain when the Romans left, there are no details of egg cookery, except that the Saxons either roasted or fried them. By Chaucer's time, eggs were added to other dishes to give nourishment, and were allowed on ordinary fasting days, but not in Lent. More complex dishes began to evolve under the influence of the Norman French and were closely connected with the early Roman dishes. There was, for example, a dish called Chardewardon that consisted of mashed boiled pears, sweetened and spiced and thickened with egg yolks and was like the Roman sweet omelette. In its turn, it became the ancestor of our fraises and tansys.

The French devised an omelette of eggs seasoned with herbs and ginger, and often finished with cheese. This was copied and became an amulet by the mid-eighteenth century, but the English only seemed to enjoy savoury versions containing vegetables, meat or cheese. An alternative was the English herbolace, a mixture of eggs and milk flavoured with herbs. From this came the tansy, a simple dish of eggs flavoured and coloured with the juice of tansy and other herbs (see recipes), which was sometimes simmered and sometimes fried.

Flour-thickened egg and milk batters were not considered grand enough to be included in recipe books, but rapidly increased in popularity as wheat flour became more widely available. They took the form of pancakes, but the early ones were thick and soft, rather like today's drop scones. By the eighteenth century the additions of cream and sack made them thin and delicious. The thicker batter was also used for the fraise, cooked in a frying-pan and consisting of two layers of batter enclosing bacon or sweet fruit.

The batter was also used for coating fruit, following the early spit-fritters. Apples were a popular filling, but so were sweet vegetables like parsnips. The fritters were often given extra rising power with barm (ale yeast) or ale, until the lightening powers of whisked egg whites began to be appreciated at the beginning of the eighteenth century.

The remaining medieval fried confection was the lozenge, made of a sweetened and spiced flour paste rolled out thinly and cut into shapes before being fried in oil and eaten with a sauce of wine, sugar, dried fruit and spices. Although this was said not to have survived into Tudor times, one can see the ancestry of the little fried pastries and fried bread dishes served with spiced sugar and white wine that continued through the centuries.

Quire of Paper

Serves 4

4 oz (100 g) unsalted butter
½ pint (300 ml) single cream
3 oz (75 g) plain flour
1 egg

2 tablespoons medium sherry
1 teaspoon orange-flower water
Pinch of ground nutmeg

Sometimes known as Thin Cream Pancakes, these were a favourite of early eighteenth-century cooks. The pancakes are meant to be paper-thin (hence the name), and should be piled up flat with a sprinkling of sugar in between. Mary Kettilby (1719) and Hannah Glasse (1747) used sack in this recipe, and today medium sherry makes a good substitute. Eighteenth-century pancakes were sometimes made with equal quantities of cream and sack, or a glass of brandy was added to a milk batter, and the pancakes were often well spiced with ginger, cinnamon or nutmeg. Mary Kettilby's recipe gives 1 pint (600 ml) of cream and 8 eggs to the rest of the ingredients below, but even allowing for the smaller eggs she would have used, this gives a very thin batter that is difficult to handle, and the modern proportions are easier to use. This quantity of batter should make 10 thin pancakes.

Melt the butter over low heat. Remove from the heat and beat with the other ingredients to a batter. This will look a little thicker than normal pancake batter as the butter cools, but it will melt again in cooking and thin the mixture. Grease a 6 in (15 cm) omelette pan with butter, and pour in just enough batter to coat the base very thinly. As soon as set, turn carefully with a knife, as the edges are very delicate. Pile onto a warm plate with sugar between the pancakes. The mixture is rich and the pan should not need greasing again.

Pancakes

Pinch of salt

3 oz (75 g) plain flour

3 eggs

½ pint (300 ml) milk

1 oz (25 g) melted butter

Lemon juice and caster sugar

Like Frumenty (see p. 88), pancakes were used as offerings to dead souls and today we still connect a religious festival with them. They were a favourite medieval dish made from flour and eggs, but they were rarely recorded in recipe books, except for the pale 'crisps' made from whites of eggs (the name derived from the Norman French crespes*), which were served sprinkled with sugar. The batter was made with flour, eggs, ground spices, and either milk or water. Gervase Markham, writing in 1615, said that new milk or cream made the pancakes tough and cloying, not crisp, pleasant and savoury as they were when mixed with water. By the eighteenth century, milk was generally used and some cooks even included cream and wine.*

The pancake is today particularly enjoyed with lemon juice and sugar, and is always associated with Shrove Tuesday, the day before the beginning of Lent, when in the past ingredients such as eggs had to be used up before fasting began. A number of towns in England, notably Olney in Buckinghamshire, stage pancake races on this day. The Olney Race is said to have been first run in 1445 and has taken place intermittently ever since. Competitors must be housewives who are inhabitants of Olney or nearby Warrington, and they have to wear aprons and a hat or scarf. They run just over 415 yards from the village square to the church and are warned by a pancake bell. This rings twice before the race to warn the women to start making the pancakes, and then to assemble in the square. Each woman carries a frying pan containing a pancake, and the bell is rung to start them running. The pancakes have to be tossed three times during the race, and the vicar rewards the winner and runner-up with a prayer-book. The verger can claim a kiss from the winner. All the frying pans are laid around the font and there is a short service of blessing.

The Pancake Greeze held at Westminster School involves a scramble for a pancake tossed by an official, and the winner receives a guinea. The cook is also rewarded, as the pancake has to be tossed about 16 feet above the ground over an iron bar.

Add the salt to the flour. Mix in the eggs and gradually beat in the milk. There is no need to leave the batter to stand as some old recipes recommend. Just before cooking, stir in the cool, melted butter. Grease an 8 in (20 cm) frying pan lightly with lard or butter and make it smoking hot. Pour about 3 tablespoons of the batter into the centre of the pan and twist the pan so that the mixture spreads over the surface. Cook until the batter has just set and then turn carefully with a palette knife or spatula. Cook until golden brown on the base (about ½ minute each side). Fold in three and serve hot with lemon juice and sugar.

Snow Pancakes
These pancakes used to be popular in the winter. It is best to omit ¼ pint (150 ml) of milk from the recipes and to stir in ¼ pint (150 ml) clean, freshly fallen snow just before frying the batter. The snow melts in cooking to make holes and light pancakes.

Saucer Pancakes   *Serves 4-6*

2 oz (50 g) butter	½ pint (300 ml) milk
2 oz (50 g) caster sugar	8 tablespoons jam
2 eggs	Caster sugar for sprinkling
2 oz (50 g) self-raising flour	

Sometimes known as French Pancakes, these are more puffy than the fried kind. They used to be made in large old saucers, but may be baked in large individual Yorkshire Pudding tins. A flavouring of grated lemon or orange rind is delicious and the puddings may be served flat with syrup instead of folded over jam.

Set the oven at 375°F/190°C/Gas Mark 5. Grease 8 saucers and put them into the oven to heat just before the batter is ready to cook. Cream the butter and sugar until soft and light. Beat in the eggs one at a time with a little of the flour. Beat in the remaining flour. Heat the milk until hot, but not boiling. Pour into the flour mixture and beat well. Pour into the warm saucers and bake for 20 minutes until risen and golden. Put a spoonful of jam on each pancake and fold in half. Sprinkle with caster sugar and serve at once.

Fruit Fritters

Serves 4–6

4 oz (100 g) plain or self-
raising flour
Pinch of salt
2 eggs

2 tablespoons milk
Fruit
Deep fat for frying

Fritters have always been a popular dish, with their combination of crisp crunchy exterior and tasty interior. Hannah Glasse in the mid-eighteenth century gave recipes for vegetable and apple fritters similar to those we eat today, although the batter for fruit fritters included large quantity of cream, wine, eggs and ale, which provided a raising ingredient in the place of the earlier yeast. In addition, there were fritters made with curds (similar to today's drop scones, which can be made with cottage cheese), ground rice fritters, fritters containing sage leaves or vine leaves, hasty fritters, and syringed fritters, which were piped into the hot fat in the shape of true lovers' knots. Most of us now think of fritters as containing fruit, which may be fresh or canned. Apples, bananas, apricots, peaches and pineapple rings make good fillings, but they must be as dry as possible when dipped into the batter, or the coating will be too thin. The food should be completely covered in batter, and may be cooked in hot lard, cooking fat or oil until crisp and golden. Fritters should be thoroughly drained on crumpled absorbent paper and then served at once. A sprinkling of spiced sugar is an excellent finish, or they may be served with cream, warm syrup, or Jam Sauce (see p. 203).

The amount of batter given here is enough to coat 1 lb (450 g) canned pineapple rings or 3 bananas cut in chunks, or 1 lb (450 g) apples cut in ½ in (1.25 cm) rings, or 1 lb (450 g) canned peach halves.

Sift the flour and salt into a bowl. Add the eggs and milk, and beat with a wooden spoon until the mixture is smooth. Dip in fruit to coat completely with batter. Fry in deep fat or oil until crisp and golden. Drain well and serve at once.

Pineapple

Drain pineapple rings. Add 2 tablespoons pineapple syrup and ½ teaspoon grated orange rind to the batter.

Banana
Cut into 2 in (5 cm) chunks. Add 2 tablespoons milk, 1 tablespoon icing sugar and ½ teaspoon ground mixed spice to the batter.

Apple
Peel and core apples and cut into ½ in (1.25 cm) thick rings. Prepare batter as for bananas, but substitute cinnamon for mixed spice.

Peaches
Drain peach halves. Add 1 tablespoon milk, 1 tablespoon sherry and 2-3 drops almond essence to the batter.

Pateley Fritters   *Serves 6-8*

¾ oz (20 g) fresh yeast	½ teaspoon grated lemon rind
1 pint (600 ml) milk	1 tablespoon sugar
12 oz (350 g) plain flour	Pinch of salt
1 oz (25 g) lard	Pinch of ground cinnamon
3 oz (75 g) currants	1 large eating apple
1½ oz (40 g) raisins	Dripping or lard for frying

The days immediately before Lent were traditionally associated with special foods. Collop Monday was celebrated with eggs and collops (thick slices of meat); this was followed by Shrove or Pancake Tuesday, Fritter or Frutas Wednesday, and Bloody Thursday when black puddings were eaten. These yeast fritters, which are really little pancakes, were eaten on Ash (fritter) Wednesday and come from Pateley in Yorkshire.

Put the yeast into a bowl. Heat the milk to lukewarm and mix a little into the yeast to start it working. Put the flour into a warm bowl and rub in the lard. Stir in the milk and the yeast, and mix well. Leave to stand for 5 minutes and then mix in the currants, raisins, lemon rind, sugar, salt and cinnamon. Peel the apple and chop the flesh finely. Add to the flour mixture and beat well. Cover and leave in a warm place for 1 hour to rise. Heat dripping or lard in a frying pan so that it is about 1 in (2.5 cm) deep. Put in large spoonfuls of the batter and cook on each side until golden. Serve at once.

Ellen Connor's Apple Fritters

Serves 4

4 eating apples
1 oz (25 g) icing sugar
5 tablespoons brandy
4 oz (100 g) plain flour
¼ pint (150 ml) water

1 tablespoon salad oil
2 egg whites
Oil for shallow-frying
Caster sugar

In 1890 Ellen Connor used lard to fry her fritters, but today's frying oils give a lighter and crisper result. The fritters may be eaten with cream, but the best sauce is made with a little apricot jam heated with the remaining brandy in which the apples were soaked.

First core the apples and then peel them (this prevents breakage of the fruit). Cut each apple across into four rings. Put the apple rings into a shallow bowl and sprinkle with icing sugar and brandy. Leave to stand for 3 hours, turning the apple rings occasionally.

Make the batter by whisking the flour and water together until creamy. Stir in the oil until it is completely mixed into the batter. Whisk the egg whites to stiff peaks and fold lightly but thoroughly into the batter. Dip each apple slice into the batter and fry on both sides in hot oil until the batter is puffy and crisp. Drain on a rack and sprinkle with caster sugar. Serve at once.

Almond Fraze

Serves 4–6

8 oz (225 g) ground almonds
½ pint (300 ml) single cream
4 eggs and 2 egg yolks
2 oz (50 g) caster sugar

2 oz (50 g) fresh white
  breadcrumbs
3 oz (75 g) unsalted butter
Caster sugar for sprinkling

This Victorian version of the fraze must be very close to the medieval original, with its mixture of almonds, cream, eggs, sugar and bread fried in butter. It is expensive to make these days, but filling, so a number of people may be served with small portions.

Put the almonds and cream into a bowl and leave to stand for 2 hours. Beat in the eggs, egg yolks, sugar and breadcrumbs until well mixed. Heat the butter in a frying pan until just melted and put in the mixture. Fry until the base is golden and the top is firmly set. Turn onto a warm serving dish and sprinkle with caster sugar.

Apricot Fraise

Filling
1 lb (450 g) ripe fresh apricots
3 oz (75 g) butter
2 oz (50 g) caster sugar

Batter
8 oz (225 g) plain flour
1 oz (25 g) caster sugar
Pinch of salt
8 eggs
2 oz (50 g) melted butter
½ pint (300 ml) milk

A fraise, froise or frayse appears to have been a kind of fried batter. Recipes go back to the fifteenth century, when they consisted of bacon, fruit, meat or vegetables fried in butter, then enclosed in two layers of fried batter. A seventeenth-century handwritten Suffolk recipe indicates that a 'froise' could be a rich dish that consisted of six beaten eggs with enough fine flour to make a thick batter, salt, spice and 2 pints (1.2 l) of thick cream, all fried in butter. This lighter modern version contains apricots, but is equally good made with slices of juicy eating apple.

Cut the apricots in half and remove the stones. Cook them gently in half the butter in a frying pan for 3–4 minutes until they begin to soften. Remove the apricots to a dish and sprinkle on the sugar. Put the remaining butter in the pan. Make up the batter by whisking together the flour, sugar, salt and half the eggs. Separate the remaining eggs. Beat the yolks into the batter with the butter and milk. Whisk the egg whites to stiff peaks and fold into the batter just before using. When the butter in the pan is hot, pour in half the batter and cook until the top just sets. Spoon on the apricots and top with the remaining batter. When the bottom of the batter is golden brown and firm, turn the fraise onto a plate. Add a little more butter to the pan if necessary so that the batter will not stick. Slide the fraise back into the pan so that the other side cooks until golden brown. Serve very hot.

Friar's Omelette

8 cooking apples	4 eggs
2 tablespoons water	2 oz (50 g) fine white
4 oz (100 g) unsalted butter	breadcrumbs
4 oz (100 g) sugar	Caster sugar for sprinkling

The name of this dish is misleading, as one suspects that it has little to do with friars and everything to do with the medieval fraise, sometimes known as an omelett (or to Hannah Glasse in the eighteenth century as an amulet). This delicious version came from Warwickshire in the 1930s.

Peel and core the apples and cut the flesh in slices. Put into a pan with the water. Simmer until the apples have collapsed into a purée and continue simmering until surplus liquid has evaporated. Stir in the butter and sugar and leave until cold. Beat the eggs to mix the yolks and whites, and then beat into the apples until completely mixed. Butter a shallow ovenware dish thickly and sprinkle half the breadcrumbs on the base and sides. Put in the apple mixture and sprinkle the remaining crumbs on top. Bake at 350°F/180°C/Gas Mark 4 for 30 minutes until set. Turn out on a hot serving dish and sprinkle with caster sugar. If you have doubts about turning out the omelette, sprinkle sugar on top and serve straight from the dish.

Somerset Gooseberry Tansy

1 lb (450 g) gooseberries	4 oz (100 g) fresh white
4 oz (100 g) unsalted butter	breadcrumbs
4 oz (100 g) granulated sugar	1 teaspoon rosewater
4 eggs	

Although this recipe comes from Somerset, the tansy was a favourite dish in other areas, originating in the fourteenth century. The herbolace was a British variation of the French omelette of the period, and consisted of eggs and herbs baked in a buttered dish, which often included milk and cheese, and was similar to modern scrambled eggs. An alternative was a more delicate tansy, the eggs being flavoured with the juice of tansy and other herbs before straining and cooking in 'fair goose grease'. The edges of the eggs were turned and gathered with the edge of a saucer as they cooked, in a similar way to our method of cooking omelettes.

This form of tansy remained until the beginning of the seventeenth century, when it began to change into the kind of sweet pudding that was becoming more popular. A scattering of breadcrumbs was added with spices and cream, and a sprinkling of sugar on the finished dish. Later in the century the pudding was made sweeter, more bread or spongecake crumbs were added, and the bitter tansy herb was gradually left out, colouring being supplied by spinach juice. In addition to the tansy, the dish had included violet and strawberry leaves and even the buds of walnut trees, which gave a delicate flavour. These were replaced by cowslips, primroses or violets, or even fresh rose petals with the additional flavouring of rosewater and nutmeg. Pieces of fruit were also introduced and this kind of tansy seems to be the only one that has survived in a few areas. Other soft fruits may be used instead of gooseberries – ripe blackberries are particularly delicious.

Top and tail the berries and put them into a thick-bottomed pan with the butter and sugar. Simmer until soft and take off the heat. Beat the eggs together and add gradually to the fruit pulp, beating well. Add the rosewater. Put the pan over low heat and stir gently and continuously, adding a few crumbs at a time until the mixture thickens like custard. The amount of breadcrumbs necessary varies, according to how much juice runs from the fruit. If too many crumbs are added at first, the dish will become too dry. More may be added when the custard has thickened. The tansy may be served at this point, traditionally with warm cider and crushed loaf sugar sprinkled on top. Alternatively, the mixture may be lightly fried on both sides in butter and served with sugar and cream.

Apricot Tansy

Serves 4

1 lb (450 g) ripe fresh apricots
2 oz (50 g) butter
3 oz (75 g) caster sugar
4 eggs and 2 egg yolks
2 tablespoons double cream

3 oz (75 g) fine white
   breadcrumbs
Pinch of ground nutmeg
Caster sugar for sprinkling

Cut the apricots in half and remove the stones. Cut each piece in half again and fry in butter in a heavy frying pan. Cook gently until the fruit is soft, but not coloured, and then sprinkle with 2 oz (50 g) sugar. Beat together the eggs, egg yolks, cream, breadcrumbs and nutmeg, and the remaining sugar. Pour over the apricots, stirring them into the mixture. Cook gently until golden brown underneath. Turn onto a plate and put a little more butter into the pan. Return the mixture to the pan so that the other side cooks until golden brown. Turn onto a warm plate and sprinkle with extra sugar. Serve with cream.

Poor Knights of Windsor

Serves 4–6

6 × ½ in (1.25 cm) slices
   day-old bread
4 tablespoons single cream
2 eggs
1 tablespoon medium sherry

Clarified butter for frying
2 tablespoons caster sugar
1 tablespoon ground cinnamon
Jam Sauce (see p. 203)

Pain perdu, or 'lost bread', was a favourite medieval French and English dish, possibly derived from a similar dish described in the Roman cookery book of Apicius. This was made by dipping slices of pandemain (the most delicate bread made from the finest flour) or manchet (good white bread) into beaten egg yolk before frying in butter and sprinkling with sugar. The recipe remained a favourite until the early seventeenth century, when the eggs were well spiced and sweetened. Later, cream was added to the eggs, and the recipe appeared as Pan Perdy, Cream Toast, Fried Toast or Poor Knights of Windsor (the Americans still love the dish under the name of French Toast). The Knights could not have been particularly poor, as originally the recipe specified the finest bread and clarified butter for frying, but like so many good dishes, this one deteriorated into a way of using up bread. Sometimes stale bread was just dipped in milk and fried before serving with jam. Lady Sysonby restored the balance in her 1935 recipe by soaking the bread in white wine and sugar before dipping the pieces in egg yolk and frying in butter. The bread slices were then finished with a sprinkling of cinnamon and sugar and eaten hot with more white wine poured on top, which seems much nearer the original dish. My family version combines the best of old and new recipes.

Remove the crusts from the bread. Cut each bread slice in three wide slices. Beat the cream, eggs and sherry together with a fork until well blended. Dip the bread into the mixture and fry in hot butter until crisp on both sides. Mix the sugar and cinnamon together. Pile the bread onto a hot serving dish, and sprinkle with cinnamon sugar. Serve with warm Jam Sauce.

11 Boiled and Baked Batters

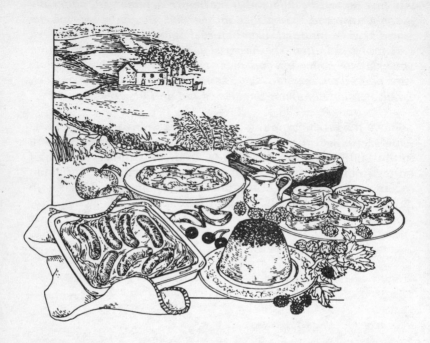

There seems to be no record of when batters were boiled rather than fried, but certainly a boiled batter was lighter than most of the boiled suet and bread mixtures or cereals that were the earliest bag puddings. Samuel Pepys in his seventeenth-century diary records his delight in a Shaking Pudding, another name for the Quaking Pudding that was a test of the skills of cooks until the nineteenth century. This fragile pudding is little more than a custard mixture, lightly thickened with flour or breadcrumbs, and was perhaps another way of preparing the earlier custards that dated from Roman times. More flour was introduced to the boiling batter in the middle of the eighteenth century and sometimes the eggs were omitted; it was cut and served with gravy or butter and sugar. It was extremely popular in Dickens's England and was certainly eaten until the 1940s.

The more solid boiled batter could support dried or fresh fruit and was then boiled in a mould, but Eliza Acton wrote in 1855 that a batter boiled in a cloth was much lighter and had room to swell, instead of being confined in a mould. The cloth had to be wrung out in water and then thickly floured, and it was essential that the pudding was served quickly so that it did not become heavy and solid. Mrs Roundell in her *Practical Cookery Book* (1898) suggested that a boiled batter made a better topping than suet pastry to accompany apricots, gooseberries, currants, cherries, damsons or apples. Her batter was simply poured over the prepared fruit in a bowl and boiled for about 1¼ hours, but no sugar was added to either fruit or batter until the pudding was done, as she considered that this made the batter heavy.

Crisp baked batter was introduced at the beginning of the eighteenth century, when it was placed in a pan under the meat roasting before an open fire and was bathed in the rich meat juices. This has come down to us as the ever-popular Yorkshire Pudding, or as batters poured over savoury or sweet fillings.

Quaking Pudding

Serves 6–8

1 pint (600 ml) double cream
4 eggs
Pinch of ground nutmeg
4 oz (100 g) caster sugar
1½ oz (40 g) plain flour
3 tablespoons very fine white breadcrumbs

Sauce
3 oz (75 g) unsalted butter
1 oz (25 g) caster sugar
6 fl oz (175 ml) white wine or claret

This pudding, sometimes known as a shaking pudding, is a rather special version of the more solid boiled batter. It looks solid but shakes like a jelly when turned out and very quickly cracks. The recipe appears in many cookery books from the sixteenth century onwards, and most versions use only a little flour to thicken the eggs and cream. A recipe of 1680 adds a few fine breadcrumbs, and this gives a slightly more stable result. The traditional accompaniment was melted butter, sugar and white wine or claret.

Heat the cream just to boiling point and then cool. When almost cold add to the beaten eggs. Beat in the nutmeg, sugar, flour and breadcrumbs so that the mixture is like soft butter. Grease a pudding cloth and dust it with flour. Put in the pudding and tie tightly. Immerse in a pan of boiling water and boil in a covered pan for 1½ hours, adding more boiling water if necessary to prevent boiling dry. Turn out very carefully. Serve with the sauce made by mixing together melted butter, caster sugar and white wine or claret.

Yorkshire Summer Batter
Serves 4

5 oz (125 g) plain flour
1 pint (600 ml) milk
2 eggs

4 oz (100 g) sugar
8 oz (225 g) summer fruit
Caster sugar for sprinkling

A boiled batter is particularly attractive when made with summer fruit. It is important that the fruit should be ripe and sweet. Blackcurrants, redcurrants, eating gooseberries, raspberries or stoned black cherries are ideal, or a mixture of fruit may be used.

Mix the flour with enough of the milk to give a smooth paste. Bring the remaining milk to the boil and gradually add to the flour mixture. Return to the pan and boil the mixture for 5 minutes, stirring all the time. Cool to lukewarm and then beat in the eggs and sugar. Beat thoroughly and stir in the fruit. Put into a greased pudding basin. Cover with a piece of greased greaseproof paper and foil, and tie with string. Put into a pan with boiling water to come halfway up the sides of the basin. Cover and boil for 1½ hours, topping up with more boiling water to prevent the pan boiling dry. Turn out on a warm serving dish and sprinkle with sugar. Serve with cream.

Blackcap Batter Pudding
Serves 4–6

4 oz (100 g) plain flour
Pinch of salt
1 egg

½ pint (300 ml) milk
2 oz (50 g) currants
2 oz (50 g) melted butter

The black cap of currants on this boiled batter gives the pudding its name. Like many batters, it was traditionally served with melted butter.

Sieve the flour and salt and work in the egg and milk to make a creamy batter. Leave to stand for 1 hour. Grease a pudding basin and sprinkle the currants on the bottom. Pour in the batter. Cover with greased greaseproof paper and foil and tie with string. Put into a pan with boiling water to come halfway up the sides of the basin. Cover and boil for 1 hour, adding a little more boiling water if necessary to prevent the pan boiling dry. Turn out on a hot dish and pour the melted butter on top.

Northallerton Sweet Baked Batter

Serves 4

4 oz (100 g) plain flour
1 egg
1 oz (25 g) caster sugar

½ pint (300 ml) milk
2 drops of vanilla essence
1 oz (25 g) lard

Eliza Acton's recipe of 1855 gives a similar batter, but without sugar, which makes it lighter. She served it with jam or stewed fruit, and said that the batter might also be baked in buttered cups for 20 minutes. She noted that in some countries a little very finely minced suet was added to baked batter puddings, which enriched them, but she did not feel this addition was an improvement.

Sieve the flour into a mixing bowl and make a well in the centre. Work in the egg and sugar and gradually beat in a little milk to make a paste. Add the essence and then beat in the remaining milk until small bubbles rise to the surface. Put the lard into a 12 × 8 in (30 × 20 cm) baking tin. Put into the oven set at 425°F/220°C/Gas Mark 7 until the lard is smoking hot, about 3 minutes. Pour in the batter and bake for 30 minutes. Serve at once with golden syrup and cream.

Apple Batter Pudding

Serves 4–6

1 lb (450 g) eating apples
4 tablespoons brandy
Pinch of ground cinnamon
1 oz (25 g) butter

2 oz (50 g) light soft brown sugar
3 eggs
5 oz (125 g) self-raising flour
4 tablespoons milk

Apples are a popular filling for batter, but chopped rhubarb may be used instead. Omit the brandy and flavour the rhubarb with ginger – a little more sugar may be needed. Sultanas or chopped dates may be added to the fresh fruit.

Peel and core the apples and chop them coarsely. Put into a bowl with the brandy and cinnamon and leave to stand for 1 hour. Use a little of the butter to grease an ovenware dish. Put in the apples and brandy and sprinkle with the sugar. Dot with flakes of butter. Put the eggs, flour and milk into a bowl and beat to a thick cream. Pour over the fruit and bake at 425°F/220°C/Gas Mark 7 for 35 minutes until the batter is crisp and golden. Serve very hot with cream.

Baked Cherry Batter

Serves 4–6

1 lb (450 g) ripe black cherries
3 eggs
4 oz (100 g) plain flour

2 oz (50 g) caster sugar
½ pint (300 ml) milk

Stone the cherries and arrange them on the base of a well-greased ovenware dish. Break the eggs into a basin and add the flour and sugar. Beat until well mixed and pour in the milk slowly, beating well to make a creamy batter. Pour over the fruit and bake at 375°F/190°C/Gas Mark 5 for 45 minutes. Sprinkle with some extra caster sugar and serve at once with cream or custard.

Tewkesbury Saucer Batters

Serves 3

12 oz (350 g) soft fruit
3 oz (75 g) caster sugar
1 egg

3 oz (75 g) self-raising flour
7 fl oz (200 ml) milk
Caster sugar for sprinkling

Tewkesbury is in the fruit-growing area of Gloucestershire, and the fruit-packing season was the time for local women to earn extra money in the days before farmers turned to pick-it-yourself systems. The women used to take home a little of the fruit and turn it into a simple pudding baked in saucers. Raspberries, black-berries, blackcurrants and gooseberries are all suitable for these puddings.

Mix the fruit and sugar together and put into a covered ovenware dish. Put on the lower shelf of the oven at 400°F/200°C/Gas Mark 6. Separate the egg. Whisk the egg yolk with the flour and milk to make a creamy thick batter. Whisk the egg white to soft peaks and fold into the batter. Grease 6 large old saucers and divide the batter between them. Bake at 400°F/200°C/Gas Mark 6 for 20 minutes. Slip three of the baked batters onto a warm serving dish. Quickly spoon on the hot fruit and cover with the remaining baked batters. Sprinkle with caster sugar and serve.

Yorkshire Pudding

Serves 4–6

4 oz (100 g) plain flour
Pinch of salt

1 egg
½ pint (300 ml) milk

This pudding originated as a 'dripping pudding', cooked in the pan that normally stood under the meat rotating on the spit to catch the meat juices and fat. When wheat flour came into common use at the beginning of the eighteenth century, northern cooks used this rich fat for cooking batters. A recipe of 1737 in The Whole Duty of a Woman specified a pancake batter put into a hot toss-pan (frying pan) with a bit of butter in the bottom. This pan was to be placed under the meat instead of a dripping-pan, and the pan was to be shaken frequently by the handle to make the pudding light and savoury. The pudding was eaten with all kinds of meat, and sometimes dried fruit was added to the batter, when the pudding was known as a Lincolnshire Pudding. The batter pudding could be eaten right through a meal: first with gravy to diminish the appetite, then with the meat as is customary today, and finally the leftovers were eaten with treacle or butter and sugar to finish a meal.

In 1747 Hannah Glasse recommended that the pudding should be dried out over a hot fire, as it must have been rather soggy when cooked under the meat, and it was then served with melted butter. A hundred years later Eliza Acton observed that a Yorkshire Pudding was thinner than the kind made in the south, and was cooked 'at an enormous fire' and was not turned. She said that the pudding would be double in size and much lighter if turned when firm and cooked on the other side as well.

Today the pudding has to be baked in the top of the oven over the meat. Fat from the meat is used to grease the pan and give flavour to the batter, and according to tradition the pudding should be cooked in a large tin and cut into slices. To make sure of a light pudding with well-risen crisp sides, the batter should be thin, the baking tin large, and the fat hot before pouring in the batter, which must be baked at a high temperature. A slightly thicker batter will give a heavier pudding.

Stir the salt and flour in a mixing bowl. Break the egg into the centre of the bowl and gradually work in half the milk, beating well to make a smooth batter. Beat in the remaining milk.

Set the oven at 425°F/220°C/Gas Mark 7. Put a tablespoon of fat from the roasting meat (or lard) into a 12 × 8 in (30 × 20 cm) baking tin. Put into the oven until smoking hot. Pour in the batter and put at the top of the oven. Bake for 40 minutes until well-risen, crisp and golden. If the meat is cooked on a rack in a roasting tin, the batter may be poured into the tin 40 minutes before serving time, and cooked in the old way under the meat.

Toad in the Hole

Serves 4–6

1 lb (450 g) pork sausages
1 oz (25 g) lard

Double recipe Yorkshire
Pudding (see p. 108)

While this can be a delicious dish, it has sometimes been an excuse to use up leftover scraps of inferior meat. Traditionally, it was made with lamb chops or pieces of tender steak, but today it makes an excellent way of extending sausages. Choose good sausages with plenty of chunky pork filling, well flavoured with herbs and spices.

Grill the sausages all over for 5 minutes under a hot grill. Set the oven at 425°F/220°C/Gas Mark 7 and put the lard into a large meat roasting tin. If preferred, the fat which runs from the sausages may be used instead of the lard. Heat in the oven to smoking point and pour in ½ in (1.25 cm) Yorkshire Pudding batter. Bake for 5 minutes. Arrange the sausages on top and pour in the remaining batter. Bake for 35 minutes and serve at once with gravy.

Yorkshire Cheese Pudding

Serves 4

4 oz (100 g) plain flour
Pinch of salt
1 egg
½ pint (300 ml) milk

1 oz (25 g) dripping
1 tablespoon chopped parsley
8 chopped sage leaves
3 oz (50 g) grated cheese

This recipe appears in a little book of 1940s' cookery ideas, designed to make the best of rationed food. It makes a good supper dish with vegetables, or can be used with meat instead of the more traditional plain Yorkshire Pudding. If possible, use bread flour, which contributes to an airy crispness.

Sift the flour and salt into a basin. Make a well in the centre and break in the egg. Add a little of the milk and whisk together, gradually adding the remaining milk, until the batter is creamy. Put the dripping into a roasting tin and heat at 425°F/220°C/Gas Mark 7 for 3 minutes until smoking hot. Quickly stir the herbs and cheese into the batter and pour into the hot fat. Bake for 40 minutes until puffed and golden. Serve at once.

12 Boiled and Steamed Puddings

Etonians will remember the chilly welcome given to those ungraceful rolls of suet pudding accompanied by inadequate treacle, and known to their hungry youth as 'Aunt's Leg', or, in its saucepan-shaped variety as 'Hayne's Hat', reminiscent of those furry concertinas worn as head coverings by their younger contemporaries.

Thus lamented Lady Jekyll in the 1920s. One of her contemporaries has told me that his friends called their school pudding 'Brother, Where Art Thou?' because the currants were so far apart and searching for each other. The long tradition of school nicknames for puddings continues with my son's references to 'Matron's Leg' and 'Boiled Baby', and certainly the filling length of a roly-poly pudding does not please everybody.

   The earliest boiled puddings seem to have been the medieval pottages, stews of meat, vegetables, and cereals, enlivened in richer circles by imported dried fruit and spices, which could disguise poor ingredients or enhance good ones. It was but a short step to cutting down on the meat content of some of them, increasing the thickening cereal and sweetening ingredients and making a more solid dish. The traditional Christmas pudding is a direct descendant of these early pottages, with its combination of suet (replacing meat), grated carrot (replacing the root vegetables), dried fruit and spice, and breadcrumbs and flour providing the cereal content.

Since all cooking was done in water in a single cauldron over an open fire, it became necessary to separate the pudding from surrounding meat and vegetables, and it was enclosed in a bag or cloth. It might be in a cannonball shape when based on the old pottage, but sometimes a basic pastry made from suet and flour was wrapped around ingredients in a long roll shape and was tied in a cloth, which in Suffolk was called a 'pudden-poke'. In that county a boy had to eat a 'yard of pudden' before he was considered a man. The cloth was traditionally wrung out in water, then floured before being tied around the pudding.

This type of cooking was obviously cumbersome, and flavours became very mixed. As industry developed and people were able to afford more cooking utensils, it became more acceptable to put puddings into basins before arranging them in the single cauldron. The basin was balanced on a piece of pierced wood, but still surrounded by other carefully packed loose ingredients, or other filled basins. This meant that pudding mixtures could be placed on toppings of fruit, jam or treacle, or could be arranged in layers. Suet crust could form a complete casing for sweet or savoury fillings, or could just form a topping. The old pudding cloth was now tied over the top of the pudding, but today is replaced by greased paper and foil.

While many of these puddings were complete savoury or sweet dishes, plain suet puddings were still prepared, boiled in a cannonball shape, to serve before meat and cut the appetite. Mrs Gaskell, an acute observer of the social scene, records the gradual dying-out of this custom in Cranford, and it would appear from this that in smart circles the custom had ended with the eighteenth century:

We had pudding before meat, and I thought Mr Holbrook was going to make some apology for his old-fashioned ways. 'When I was a young man, we used to keep strictly to my father's rule: "No broth, no ball; no ball, no beef" and always began dinner with broth. Then we had suet puddings, boiled in the broth with the beef, and then the meat itself. If we did not sup our broth, we had no ball, which we liked a great deal better; and the beef came last, and only those had it who had done justice to the hall and the broth.'

Sussex Drip Pudding was a variant of this, being boiled in a cloth, then sliced and dipped into the hot beef drippings from the meat, before being browned in front of the fire or in the oven while the gravy was being made.

Boiled or steamed puddings may be prepared in cloths, but it is difficult to form them into a cannonball shape. An old lady told me that this was most easily achieved if the cloth was arranged in a round mixing basin before filling and tying. Today, the cannonball is more easily prepared in a basin. The long pudding may be tied into a cloth or foil, and a clean old tea towel is the ideal shape for this. A little space must be allowed so that the pudding can expand, and the ends must be tied tightly. When covering a pudding in a basin, tie a loop of string over the top, as this makes it easier to lift the pudding from the saucepan.

Puddings may be made by rubbing in or creaming the fat, where butter or other fat is substituted for suet. Breadcrumbs will lighten a mixture and may take the place of some of the flour in a recipe. Eggs should be at room temperature to avoid curdling, and liquids should be added last to give the right consistency. A 'soft dropping consistency' which is needed for most puddings means that the mixture just drops from a spoon when shaken lightly. Basins should be well-greased and the mixture should come almost to the top.

Puddings may be steamed in a perforated pan over hot water, but not everybody has a steamer. The simplest method is half-steaming, which means placing the basin in a saucepan on an inverted saucer so that the pudding mixture is not too near the source of heat. Put in boiling water to come halfway up the basin, put on a close-fitting lid, and simmer for the required length of time. Always top up with boiling water so that the pudding retains its heat and the pan does not boil dry.

If a basin is covered with a cloth, or a long pudding is prepared in a cloth, it can be totally immersed in boiling water, covered and then simmered. Let all puddings stand for a few minutes after removing from the water so that they shrink slightly and are easy to turn out.

This little nineteenth-century rhyme shows the loving care with which a good boiled pudding should be prepared.

Mother Eve's Pudding

If you want a good pudding, to teach you I'm willing,
Take twopennyworth of eggs, when twelve for a shilling,
And of the same fruit that Eve had once chosen,
Well pared and well chopped at least half a dozen;
Six ounces of bread (let your maid eat the crust);
The crumbs must be grated as small as the dust;
Six ounces of currants from the stones you must sort,
Lest they break out your teeth and spoil all your sport;
Six ounces of sugar won't make it too sweet,
Some salt and some nutmeg will make it complete.
Three hours let it boil, without hurry or flutter,
And then serve it up – without sugar or butter.

Invitation to the opening of 163rd Pudding Season on 12 October 1930 at Ye Olde Cheshire Cheese, Fleet Street.

Be it known to all good citizens of thys ancient citye of London that ye famous pudding will be served for ye first time thys season on ye 12th day of October at 7 of ye clock. Many days hath ye hirelings scoured ye country side for ye Plover Bird and tasty mushrooms to mix with ye steak, kidney and succulent Oyster. Then with spieces from ye far West Indies Ye Pudding hath been built up to prodigious size, and plunged into ye boiling cauldron to be tended day and night be ye Chief Custodian. Perchance its fragrant aroma hath already been wafted from ye Upper Chamber.

The recipes of this famous old tavern have always been closely-guarded secrets, but it was always said that their famous pudding had to be cooked for 24 hours. The inclusion of plover and spices with the more traditional ingredients is interesting, but the plover would not be a practicable addition today.

Steak and Kidney Pudding
Serves 4–6

8 oz (225 g) self-raising flour
Pinch of salt
4 oz (100 g) shredded suet
1 lb (450 g) chuck steak

3 lambs' kidneys or 4 oz
  (100 g) ox kidney
Beef stock (optional)

This may well be everybody's favourite pudding and there is something very delicious about the melting steak and kidney that has simmered for hours in its suet crust. As usual with traditional dishes, there are endless variations. Purists despise onion in the pudding, but many people like a little finely chopped onion or grated shallot. Oysters were traditional and in the days when they were very cheap served to bulk out expensive beef and add savour. Tinned ones may be substituted now, and cockles or mussels are also sometimes used with similar results. Large, dark, meaty 'horse' mushrooms are very like oysters in texture and add dark richness to the gravy. The meat must be well-seasoned and some people include a pinch of herbs, and I have sometimes detected a trace of tomato flavouring in restaurant puddings.

Prepare the suet crust by mixing the flour, salt and suet and adding enough water to make a firm dough. Roll out and line a greased pudding basin with three-quarters of the dough. Cut the steak into thin pieces and chop the kidney into small pieces. Either wrap a piece of steak around each piece of kidney, or just mix the two meats. Add onions, oysters, or mushrooms according to taste. Put the meat into the bowl and add just enough water or beef stock to cover the meat. Cover with the remaining dough and seal the edges firmly. To cover, tie on a piece of greased greaseproof paper and kitchen foil and put into a pan with water to come halfway up the basin. Cover and boil for 4 hours. Do not turn out the pudding; wrap a large white napkin round the basin and serve in slices from the basin.

Game Pudding

A richly tempting pudding may be made with a single variety of game or a mixture. Use a brace of partridges or old grouse, venison or hare. The birds may be jointed or the flesh stripped and cut into pieces. As hare joints are very large, they are best stripped and cut into pieces. Mix the game with half its weight in chuck steak, and season well. Add some onions or mushrooms if liked, and a sprinkling of herbs. Use red wine or stout as half the liquid inside the pudding. Prepare the crust as for Steak and Kidney Pudding and boil for 3 hours.

Pigeon Pudding

Pastry
8 oz (225 g) self-raising flour
½ teaspoon salt
4 oz (100 g) shredded suet
¼ pint (150 ml) cold water

Filling
3 pigeons
8 oz (225 g) chuck steak, cubed
3 hard-boiled egg yolks
Salt and pepper
Pinch of ground mace
Beef stock

Pigeons have always been rather a nuisance in the countryside, particularly when they steal seed corn, peas and greenstuff in the garden. The countryman combines his rough shooting (pigeon are classed as vermin, not game, and are not protected) with a gift for the kitchen, and pigeon flesh is always welcome for its rich flavour and firm texture. Only the breasts of pigeon are worth eating, so there is no need to waste time plucking the birds. Instead, use a sharp knife to make an incision along the breastbone, and then peel off the skin and cut out the two breasts whole.

Mix the flour, salt, suet and water to make a soft dough. Roll out in a circle on a floured board. Cut out one-third segment of the suet pastry and reserve. Line a greased pudding basin with the large piece of pastry and bring the edges together so there is no gap in the pastry. Cut the breasts from the pigeons and arrange in the basin with the cubed steak, roughly chopped egg yolks and seasoning. Add just enough stock to cover the meat. Roll the remaining pastry to form a lid and put onto the filling, sealing the edges firmly with a little water. Tie on a piece of greaseproof paper and a piece of kitchen foil. Put into a pan with boiling water coming halfway up the basin. Cover and boil for 3 hours, adding more boiling water from time to time so that the pan does not boil dry. Remove foil and paper, and serve the pudding with potatoes, root vegetables and greens.

Rabbit or Chicken Pudding

Here is another variation of a meat-filled savoury pudding, which can be made in true country fashion according to what ingredients are available. For Rabbit Pudding, use rabbit joints flavoured with sage, onions, mushrooms and tomatoes. Chicken Pudding is nicest made with pieces of the flesh (no bones) mixed with half its weight in salt pork, some chopped onion and a liberal flavouring of parsley. Prepare the crust as for Steak and kidney Pudding, boil for 3 hours, and serve with parsley sauce.

Norfolk Plough Pudding

Pastry
8 oz (225 g) self-raising flour
½ teaspoon salt
4 oz (100 g) shredded suet
¼ pint (150 ml) cold water

Filling
1 lb (450 g) pork sausage meat
4 oz (100 g) streaky bacon
　rashers
1 large onion
2 teaspoons chopped fresh sage
½ oz (15 g) demerara sugar
Stock

Plough Monday is the first Monday after 6 January (Twelfth Night), and was the day on which spring ploughing began after the merry-making Twelve Days of Christmas. In fact, the day was often another feast, as a decorated plough was drawn through the streets by young men in fancy costumes known as Plough Witches. There was often sword-dancing or the performing of an ancient folk play known as the Plough Play. Money collected at this merry-making was used to maintain a Plough Light by the Ploughmen's Guild in some churches, but this disappeared after the Reformation and the money was given to help with parish expenses. Some Plough Puddings are suet rolls wrapped around bacon rashers with onions, sage, pepper and a little black treacle. As Norfolk is a great wheat-growing county, this version is a little more special, and more easily made in a basin.

Mix the flour, salt, suet and water to make a soft dough. Roll out in a circle on a floured board. Cut out a one-third segment of the suet pastry and reserve. Line a greased pudding basin with the larger piece of pastry and bring the edges together so that there is no gap in the pastry. Press the sausage meat into the pastry all round the basin. Chop the bacon and onion, and mix them together with the sage and sugar. Put into the centre of the pudding and add just enough stock to cover the filling. Roll the remaining pastry to form a lid and put onto the filling, sealing the edges firmly with a little water. Tie on a piece of greaseproof paper and a piece of kitchen foil. Put into a pan with boiling water coming halfway up the basin. Cover and boil for 3 hours, adding more boiling water from time to time so that the pan does not boil dry. Remove foil and paper and serve with gravy.

Bedfordshire Clanger

Savoury Filling
1 small onion
1 tablespoon lard
8 oz (225 g) lean pork
1 teaspoon sage
1 cooking apple
2 oz (50 g) cooked peas
Salt and pepper

Sweet Filling
2 eating apples
Grated rind and juice of
  1 orange
1 oz (25 g) caster sugar
2 oz (50 g) stoned dates
2 oz (50 g) sultanas

Pastry
12 oz (225 g) self-raising flour
Pinch of salt
6 oz (150 g) shredded suet

This pudding was a meal for workers, similar to the Cornish pasty and to the Lancashire Collier's Foot, which was another complete all-in-one package. It was reputedly devised by the hat-makers of Luton, who left the complete meal for their husbands, but it could also be taken into the fields. The long suet pudding contains meat and vegetables at one end and fruit at the other, so that a hungry person could eat right through from first to second course. A more convenient modern version can be made with shortcrust pastry and baked. This recipe makes two Clangers, and nowadays each will serve 2 people.

Make the savoury filling first. Chop the onion finely and cook in the lard until soft and golden. Mince the pork and sage and cook gently for 5 minutes, stirring often. Peel, core and chop the apple and add to the pork. Continue cooking for 5 minutes, then stir in the peas, season to taste, and cool.

Make the sweet filling by mixing peeled and chopped apples with the grated rind and juice of the orange, the sugar, chopped dates and sultanas.

Make up the suet dough by stirring together the flour, salt and suet and mixing with enough cold water to make a firm dough. Roll out the dough and cut two 10 in (25 cm) circles. Roll out the trimmings and cut two 10 in (25 cm) strips of pastry. Stand one on each circle and press lightly to form a wall. Put savoury filling close to one side of the wall and sweet filling on the other. Bring up the edges and pinch them together to form a pasty shape. Tie each

Clanger into a small floured pudding cloth, flattening the tops slightly. Put into a pan of boiling water and boil for 1 hour.

Norfolk Mussel Pudding
Serves 4–6

8 oz (225 g) plain flour
1 teaspoon baking powder
Pinch of salt

3 oz (75 g) shredded suet
50 prepared mussels
Salt and pepper

Those who enjoy mussels love this pudding, which is still very cheap to make. The mussels must be thoroughly scrubbed and the little stringy 'beards' removed. Any mussels that do not close when tapped should be discarded. It is best to soak the mussels in a bowl of cold water with a little oatmeal or porridge oats for 8 hours. They will open to feed and any dirt will be exuded. Put the mussels into a thick heavy pan in a single layer and cover with a lid. Heat very gently and the mussels will open in a few minutes, and can be lifted from their shells.

Prepare the dough by mixing the flour, baking powder and salt, and stirring in the suet. Add enough cold water to make a firm dough and roll into a rectangle. Spread the mussels on the dough and season well. Roll up like a Swiss roll, tie in a floured cloth and boil for 1½ hours. If liked, add a little finely chopped onion and bacon to the filling.

Suffolk Onion Pudding
Serves 4

4 oz (100 g) plain flour
2 oz (50 g) shredded suet

8 oz (225 g) onions
Salt and pepper

This simple pudding was often served with a piece of boiled bacon or beef, and could be boiled in the same pot.

Mix the flour and suet and add just enough cold water to make a firm dough. Roll out into a rectangle about ¼ in (6 mm) thick. Chop the onions finely and arrange on the dough. Season well with salt and pepper. Roll up like a Swiss roll and tie into a floured cloth. Boil for 1½ hours and serve cut in thick slices with a knob of butter on each.

Buckinghamshire Bacon Badger

Serves 4–6

8 oz (225 g) self-raising flour
4 oz (100 g) shredded suet
Pinch of salt
¼ pint (140 ml) cold water
1 large potato

1 lb (450 g) bacon
1 large onion
2 teaspoons chopped fresh sage
Pinch of pepper

It was a country tradition to extend a little meat with vegetables and herbs, wrap them in a suet crust, and then boil the pudding. The Buckinghamshire version is always known as a 'badger' and does indeed look like that rather well-rounded animal.

The bacon should be a good mixture of fat and lean, and cheap bacon pieces are ideal for this pudding.

Mix together the flour, suet, salt and water to make a firm dough. Roll out thinly on a floured board to a rectangle about 12 × 9 in (30 × 22 cm). Peel the potato and dice. Chop the bacon into 1 in (2.5 cm) cubes. Peel the onion and grate it coarsely. Mix the potato, bacon, onion, sage and pepper together and spread on the suet pastry, leaving 1 in (2.5 cm) all round the edge. Damp the edges lightly and roll up like a Swiss roll. Press the ends together to hold the filling in place. Tie in a floured cloth, or in a piece of grease-proof paper and then foil. Tie the ends tightly, but allow room for expansion. Put into a pan of boiling water and boil for 3 hours, adding a little more boiling water if necessary so that the pan does not boil dry. Remove the cloth or foil and put onto a hot serving dish. Cut in thick slices and serve with vegetables and gravy.

Bacon Puddings

The range of regional bacon and pork puddings similar to Buckinghamshire Bacon Badger is enormous, and they seem to come mainly from the Midlands and eastern counties, which even today are justly famous for their pork butchers and pork pies. It is obvious that a very filling meal could be made with a suet crust, a few scraps of pork or bacon and some flavouring, such as sage, onion or apple, but there were minor differences in each area.

In Northamptonshire suet crust was rolled round a mixture of chopped bacon and onion; Leicestershire Quorn Roll contained bacon and sage. Essex Pork Plugga (or Plugger for its filling qualities) was a suet roll made with streaky pork instead of bacon.

In Sussex the bacon, onion and herbs were actually mixed into the dough, which was made with milk and egg rather than water, then rolled into a ball in a cloth before boiling. In Suffolk the mixture of pork and onions was put into a basin lined and covered with suet crust, and was called a dumpling. In Buckinghamshire there was another pudding containing a mixture of liver, streaky bacon and onion, rolled up like a Swiss roll and boiled; in Staffordshire a pudding was made in a basin, and omitted the bacon completely, combining only liver and onions in a suet crust.

Pease Pudding   *Serves 4*

8 oz (225 g) dried whole   1 oz (25 g) butter
    or split peas   1 egg
Salt and pepper   Pinch of sugar

Pease pudding hot! Pease pudding cold!
Pease pudding in the pot nine days old.

So runs the old rhyme commemorating one of the old bag puddings, which may indeed be one of the very earliest native English dishes. Peas were a basic crop, which could be easily dried for winter, and which formed an important part of peasant diet. The dried peas were even ground to provide a type of flour that could be mixed with other grains for baking. Pease pudding is a traditional accompaniment to salt meat, another item in the staple diet. Any leftover pudding could be reheated for another day, so it is no wonder that the old rhyme sounded slightly despairing.

Wash the peas and soak them overnight in cold water. Drain well and tie them in a cloth, leaving room for them to swell. Put into a large saucepan and cover with boiling water. Boil for 2½ hours until the peas are soft. Take them out of the cloth and put through a sieve, or whirl in an electric blender. Mix with the salt, pepper, butter, beaten egg and sugar. Rinse the cloth and dust the inside with flour. Put in the pea mixture and tie into a ball. Put into fresh boiling water and boil for 45 minutes. If preferred, put the purée into a greased pudding basin, cover and steam for 1 hour.

Old-Fashioned Fruit Puddings

Serves 6–8

8 oz (225 g) self-raising flour
Pinch of salt
4 oz (100 g) shredded suet

1½ lb (675 g) prepared fruit
4–6 oz (100 g–150 g) sugar
4 tablespoons water

When people think of English puddings longingly, an old-fashioned suet pudding filled with fruit comes high on the list. The suet crust should be light and flaky and the pudding packed with lightly sweetened seasonal fruit. Apples, damsons, gooseberries and rhubarb are favourites, but fruits may be mixed, such as blackberries with apples. A good autumn mixture consists of apples, pears, plums and blackberries. One or two strongly flavoured summer fruits are also good – blackcurrants and cherries are excellent if carefully prepared. The blackcurrants must be stemmed, and the cherries are easier to eat if stoned – a mixture of sweet black cherries and sharp Morello cherries is best. The filling should not be watery, and the fruit will make its own rich juices. I like to add a little spice for subtle flavouring. Try ginger and orange rind with rhubarb, cloves with apples, cinnamon with blackcurrants.

Stir together the flour, salt and suet and add just enough cold water to make a soft but firm dough. Roll out the dough and use three-quarters of it to line a greased basin. Prepare the fruit in the appropriate way: e.g., peel, core and slice apples; chop rhubarb, or top and tail gooseberries. Mix the fruit and sugar and fill the basin. Sprinkle on the water and any preferred spice. Cover with a lid of the remaining dough and seal firmly. To cover, tie on greased greaseproof paper and kitchen foil, and put into a large pan with boiling water to come halfway up the pudding. Cover and boil for 3 hours. Turn out carefully onto a warm serving plate – it is a good idea to use a deep plate or bowl to serve the pudding, as the filling will spill out when cut. Serve with custard or cream.

Mrs Townley's Fulbourn Apple Pudding

Serves 6–8

8 eating apples
2 oz (50 g) butter
Grated rind of 1 lemon
6 oz (150 g) caster sugar
8 oz (225 g) apricot jam

8 oz (225 g) plain flour
1 teaspoon baking powder
Pinch of salt
4 oz (100 g) shredded suet

This recipe dates from 1847.

Peel and core the apples and cut them into thin slices. Put into a pan with the butter, lemon rind, sugar and jam. Heat gently, stirring well until the apples are soft, and leave to cool. Prepare a suet crust by mixing the flour, baking powder, salt and suet and mixing to a firm dough with cold water. Roll out the dough and line a greased pudding basin with three-quarters of it. Fill with the apple mixture and cover with a lid of dough, sealing the edges well. To cover tie on a piece of greased greaseproof paper and kitchen foil and put into a pan with boiling water coming halfway up the basin. Cover and boil for 2 hours. Turn out and serve with warm apricot jam and cream. The manuscript recipe suggests that the filling is also good for Apple Charlotte (see p. 53) or for serving with rice or whipped cream.

Rhubarb Basin Pudding

Serves 4-6

8 oz (225 g) self-raising flour
1 teaspoon salt
3 oz (75 g) shredded suet
8 tablespoons cold water
1½ lb (675 g) rhubarb

2 oz (50 g) stoned raisins
4 oz (100 g) caster sugar
½ teaspoon grated lemon rind
½ teaspoon ground ginger

Stir together the flour, salt and suet and mix with the water to make a soft dough. Turn out on a floured surface and knead lightly until smooth. Cut off one-third of the pastry for a lid, and roll out the rest to a 14 in (35 cm) circle. Grease a pudding basin with butter and sprinkle with a little of the sugar. Put in the circle of pastry, which will overhang the rim of the basin. Press the pastry lightly into place so that it fits the basin.

Cut the rhubarb into 1 in (2.5 cm) lengths and mix with the raisins, sugar, lemon rind and ginger. Put into the pastry-lined basin. Place the pastry circle on top and press firmly round the edge to seal. Cover with well-greased greaseproof paper and then a piece of kitchen foil and tie round the rim of the basin. Put into a large saucepan and pour in boiling water to come halfway up the sides of the basin. Put on the lid and boil for 2½ hours, adding more boiling water occasionally, so that the pan does not boil dry. Remove the basin from the saucepan and leave to stand for 5 minutes so that the pastry shrinks slightly from the sides of the basin and the pudding is easier to turn out. Turn onto a warm serving plate and sprinkle with a little caster sugar. Serve with cream or egg custard.

Sussex Ponds and Kentish Wells

Serves 6–8

8 oz (225 g) self-raising flour
4 oz (100 g) shredded suet
¼ pint (150 ml) mixed milk and water

4 oz (100 g) butter
4 oz (100 g) demerara sugar
1 large thin-skinned lemon

There are two versions of this pudding, known as Sussex Pond and Kentish Well. These two counties share a border, so it is easy to see why they may also have shared a pudding. The important part of the pudding is the rich filling of sugar and butter, which oozes out when the pudding is cut. The Kentish version often contains dried fruit in a suet crust. The Sussex version omits the dried fruit, but the filling contains a whole lemon in its skin. When the pudding has been boiled, the lemon has almost melted into the butter and sugar and it gives a wonderfully rich flavour to the sauce.

Another version, with a thin-skinned lemon that explodes, is called Lemon Bomb. Sussex is famous for scooped out pits dotted over the county which look rather like pudding basins. They are sometimes called dewponds, as they fill up with dew and rain, but are reputedly the remains of ancient iron-workings. Perhaps this feature of the landscape gave the pudding its descriptive name.

It is important to use a deep dish for turning out the pudding, as there is plenty of filling to spill out. When a lemon is included, each person should be given a small piece of the fruit.

Stir the flour and suet together in a bowl until well mixed. Add the liquid and mix to a soft dough. Roll the dough on a floured board into a large circle. Grease a pudding basin. With a sharp knife, cut out one quarter of the dough circle, and reserve this to use as a lid. Put the remaining dough into the basin and join the two cut ends so that the basin is completely lined. Cut half the butter into small flakes and put into the basin with half the sugar. Leave the skin on the lemon and do not cut the fruit. Prick the whole lemon all over with a thin skewer. Place it on top of the butter and sugar. Cover with small pieces of the remaining butter and the sugar.

Roll the reserved pastry into a circle to make a lid. Put on top of the filling and press the edges together to seal them firmly. To cover, tie on a piece of greased greaseproof paper and kitchen foil.

Put into a large pan of boiling water, so that the water comes halfway up the pudding. Put on a lid and boil for 3½ hours, adding more boiling water to the pan from time to time so that it is always halfway up the pudding. To serve, turn the pudding very carefully into a deep dish. The inside of the pudding is filled with a rich lemon-flavoured sauce, and each person should be served with a section of lemon.

Great Western Victory Roll *serves 4–6*

4 oz (100 g) carrots
4 oz (100 g) potatoes
4 oz (100 g) plain flour
2 oz (50 g) sugar or honey
2 oz (50 g) raisins
1 teaspoon bicarbonate of soda

½ teaspoon ground nutmeg
½ teaspoon ground mixed spice
½ teaspoon salt

Those who mourn the Great Western Railway also deplore the passing of individuality in railway catering. Once upon a time 'home cooking' was the basis of the splendid meals that were served, and food buyers for the railway visited the London markets daily to purchase meat, vegetables, etc. for the restaurant cars, station refreshment rooms and station hotels. Provincial restaurant car depots and stations bought fresh local produce. During the Second World War the railway caterers had to observe rationing regulations, but this recipe used by the GWR shows how they contrived to produce customers' favourite recipes. Another entry from the same source gives a good recipe for make-do Christmas Pudding, and it is hard to imagine a homemade celebratory pudding in today's dining cars. The Victory Roll may sound odd, but, in fact, carrots have been used for centuries to add sweetness to puddings, and potatoes have likewise been used to give lightness.

Peel the vegetables thinly, and grate them very finely. Stir together the remaining ingredients and work in the grated vegetables. Shape into a cylinder and tie into a floured pudding cloth, or wrap in greased greaseproof paper and kitchen foil. Immerse in a pan of boiling water and cook for 4 hours. Unwrap carefully and serve at once with custard.

Rotherfield Sweet-Tooth

Serves 6

12 oz (350 g) plain flour
1 teaspoon baking powder
3 oz (75 g) shredded suet
3 oz (75 g) currants
2 oz (50 g) sultanas
2 oz (50 g) chopped mixed
  candied peel

Pinch of salt
Milk
4 tablespoons honey
2 tablespoons soft butter

A delicious variation of the Kentish Well or Sussex Pond Pudding came from an old shepherd at Rotherfield in the 1930s.

Stir together the flour, baking powder, suet, currants, sultanas, peel and salt. Add a little milk gradually, working it in to make a firm dough and being sure the ingredients are evenly distributed. Form the dough into a ball. With the fingers, pull the dough apart in the centre and put in the honey and butter. Damp the torn edges of the dough and pinch them together over the honey filling. Put the ball of dough into a well-greased pudding basin. Cover with greased greaseproof paper and kitchen foil, and tie securely. Put into a pan with boiling water to come halfway up the sides of the basin. Cover and boil for 2½ hours, from time to time adding more boiling water to the pan so that it is always halfway up the pudding. Turn out carefully and cut into slices, being sure that each person has some of the runny filling.

Sussex Plum Duff

Serves 4–6

6 oz (150 g) self-raising flour
3 oz (75 g) shredded suet
4 oz (100 g) currants
4 oz (100 g) raisins

4 oz (100 g) demerara sugar
Pinch of ground mixed spice
About ¼ pint (150 ml) milk

'Plum' was a general name for dried fruit, and 'duff' is probably a corruption of dough. This filling pudding was quick to make and could be cooked in a pot over an open fire along with the rest of the meal. This is a Sussex version of a countrywide favourite. Puddings were still cooked in cloths in Sussex until well into the 1930s.

Mix together the flour, suet, currants, raisins, sugar and spice. Mix with the milk to make a stiff dough. Wring out a pudding cloth in boiling water and sprinkle one side with a little flour. Put the dough into the centre of the floured side and tie up like a football. Drop into a pan of boiling water, cover and boil for 1½ hours, adding more boiling water to the pan so that it does not boil dry. Unwrap carefully and serve with custard, or melted redcurrant jelly.

Simpson's Treacle Roll   *Serves 6*

1 lb (450 g) plain flour
12 oz (350 g) shredded suet
4 oz (100 g) caster sugar
2 teaspoons baking powder

1 egg
½ pint (300 ml) cold water
4 oz (100 g) golden syrup

This pudding is one that appears regularly at Simpson's in the Strand, and over which otherwise sane men have been known to turn lyrical. Serve it with plenty of extra golden syrup.

Put the flour, suet, sugar and baking powder into a bowl and stir together until well mixed. Add the egg and water and knead to a smooth dough. Roll out the dough on a floured board into a square ¼ in (6 mm) thick. Spread with golden syrup and roll up the dough, sealing the edges firmly. Wrap in a piece of greased greaseproof paper and tie into a cloth. Steam for 1½ hours and serve with plenty of warm golden syrup.

Victorian Chocolate Pudding   *Serves 4–6*

1 lb (450 g) day-old white bread
1 pint (600 ml) milk

2 oz (50 g) dark soft brown sugar
2 oz (50 g) plain chocolate

Break the bread into pieces and make into fine crumbs. Put into a bowl with the milk and sugar and leave to soak for 15 minutes. Grate the chocolate and stir into the mixture. Put into a greased pudding basin and cover with a piece of greased greaseproof paper and a piece of kitchen foil, tied on securely. Put into a saucepan with hot water to come halfway up the sides of the basin. Cover with a lid and boil for 2 hours, adding more boiling water from time to time so that the pan does not become dry. Leave until completely cold before turning out. Serve with custard, ice cream, or Chocolate Sauce (see p. 199).

Spotted Dog

8 oz (225 g) self-raising flour
Pinch of salt
4 oz (100 g) shredded suet

1 oz (25 g) sugar
8 oz (225 g) currants or raisins
¼ pint (150 ml) cold water

This is a long suet pudding spotted with currants like a Dalmatian dog. On the other hand, Spotted Dick consists of suet pastry rolled round a filling of raisins and sugar, and is also known as Plum Bolster (for its resemblance to a long pillow or bolster) or Raisin Roly Poly. The pudding may be served with custard or sweet white sauce, although it is best with brown sugar and butter, or with melted redcurrant jelly.

Stir together the flour, salt, suet, sugar and dried fruit. Mix to a firm dough with water. Form into a cylinder about 8 in (20 cm) long and put on a pudding cloth that has been wrung out in boiling water and sprinkled with flour. Roll the pudding in the cloth and tie the ends tightly but leave room for expansion. Put into a pan of boiling water, cover and boil for 2 hours, adding more boiling water if necessary to prevent boiling dry. Turn the pudding onto a hot dish and serve with custard.

Suffolk Raisin Roly Poly

8 oz (225 g) plain flour
½ teaspoon salt
1 teaspoon baking powder

4 oz (100 g) shredded suet
¼ pint (150 ml) cold water
12 oz (350 g) stoned raisins

Sweet suet puddings were very popular in the country, as they provided energy for farmworkers and filled up families when meat was scarce and too expensive for everyday use. These puddings were originally boiled in a cloth in a pan suspended over an open fire along with the rest of the meal. Suet for the puddings was chopped by hand, and the raisins would also have to be carefully stoned. The pudding needs boiling for 3 hours.

Sift the flour, salt and baking powder together. Stir in the suet and mix to a soft dough with the water. Roll out on a lightly floured board to form an oblong strip about 12 × 8 in (30 × 20 cm) and ¼ in (6 mm) thick. Spread the raisins on top, leaving 1 in (2.5 cm) margin at each side and at one end. Brush the edges with a little cold water, and roll up like a Swiss roll. Press the ends lightly together and dredge the pudding lightly with flour. Wring a pudding cloth out in boiling water and sprinkle one end with flour. Put the pudding on the floured end and roll up in the cloth, allowing room for expansion. Tie the ends of the cloth tightly and put into boiling water. Boil for 3 hours, adding more boiling water as necessary so the pan does not boil dry. Remove the cloth carefully and turn out onto a hot dish. Sprinkle with a little sugar and serve with custard.

Apple Suet Roll

Serves 1 0

8 oz (225 g) self-raising flour
Pinch of salt
Pinch of ground mixed spice
4 oz (100 g) shredded suet
2 large cooking apples

2 oz (50 g) currants
2 oz (50 g) light soft brown sugar
Grated rind of 1 lemon
2 tablespoons golden syrup

Sift the flour, salt and spice together and stir in the suet. Mix well and add just enough cold water to make a firm dough. Roll out ¼ in (6 mm) thick into an oblong. Peel and core the apples and chop them finely. Arrange on the dough, leaving 1 in (2.5 cm) uncovered at each side. Sprinkle with currants, sugar, lemon rind and syrup. Roll up the dough like a Swiss roll. Rinse a pudding cloth and dust with flour inside. Tie the suet roll into the cloth and put into a large pan of boiling water. Cook for 2 hours. Unwrap carefully and place on a warm serving plate. Serve with custard, melted golden syrup, or apricot Jam Sauce (see p. 203).

Individual Castle Puddings

Canary Pudding mixture (see p. 130) may be used to make individual puddings that look like little castles. Grease 6 individual castle pudding moulds (dariole moulds) and fill two-thirds full with pudding mixture. Cover with greased greaseproof paper and kitchen foil and tie securely. Put into a pan of boiling water coming halfway up the moulds and steam for 40 minutes. Add more boiling water to the pan if necessary to prevent it boiling dry. Flavourings may be varied as with Canary Pudding, but the little golden puddings look particularly tempting when crowned with caps of hot Jam Sauce (see p. 203).

129

Canary Pudding

4 oz (100 g) butter
4 oz (100 g) caster sugar
A few drops of vanilla essence

2 eggs
4 oz (100 g) self-raising flour
Pinch of salt

This is a good basic sponge pudding that can be varied infinitely with different flavourings or sauces. Perhaps its name derived from the fact that it was golden yellow like a canary, or perhaps it was at its best served with a sauce made from canary wine?

Cream the butter and sugar until light and fluffy. Add the essence and eggs and beat well. Sieve in the flour and salt and fold in gently. If necessary, a little milk may be added to give a soft dropping consistency. Put into a greased pudding basin. Cover with a piece of greased greaseproof paper and kitchen foil, and tie securely. Put into a pan with boiling water coming halfway up the basin, and cover. Steam for 1½ hours, adding more boiling water to the pan if necessary to prevent it boiling dry. Turn out onto a warm serving dish and serve with jam sauce, melted golden syrup, or custard.

Variations

The vanilla essence may be omitted and replaced by grated orange or lemon rind, ground ginger, or mixed spice. Sultanas, chopped mixed peel or glacé cherries may also be added.

Hampshire Six-Cup Pudding

4 oz (100 g) plain flour
3 oz (75 g) fresh white
  breadcrumbs
4 oz (100 g) shredded suet
5 oz (125 g) soft brown sugar

5 oz (125 g) mixed dried fruit
¼ pint (150 ml) milk
1 teaspoon bicarbonate of
  soda

The pudding derives its name from the fact that the ingredients were originally measured in large cups, in the days before every kitchen had a set of scales. Sometimes a pudding is described as a cup pudding because individual portions were steamed in cups – a development from the earlier method of boiling puddings tied in cloths. The cups in this recipe have been translated into standard measurements.

Stir together the flour, breadcrumbs, suet, sugar and fruit. Heat the milk to lukewarm. Remove from heat and stir in the soda. Mix the milk into the other ingredients to make a soft mixture. Put into a greased pudding basin. Cover with greased greaseproof paper and a piece of kitchen foil and tie with string. Put into a pan of boiling water, so that the water comes halfway up the basin. Put on a lid and boil for 4 hours. Add more boiling water to the pan as it becomes necessary. Turn the pudding out onto a hot plate and serve with custard.

Trinity College Pudding
Serves 8

8 oz (225 g) shredded suet
8 oz (225 g) fresh white
   breadcrumbs
2 oz (50 g) ratafia biscuits
4 oz (100 g) stoned raisins
4 oz (100 g) stoned prunes
4 oz (100 g) sugar

2 oz (50 g) chopped mixed
   candied peel
1 oz (25 g) plain flour
Pinch of salt
1 teaspoon ground mixed spice
2 eggs and 5 egg yolks
3 fl oz (75 ml) brandy

There seems to be a pudding named after every college in Oxford and Cambridge if one browses through old manuscript books and Victorian printed books. Doubtless each college had its speciality, but perhaps the housewife named her favourite steamed pudding according to family allegiances. There are Peterhouse, Magdalene, Trinity and dozens of other variations, but basically they seem to have the familiar foundation of bread, suet and dried fruit, which would be welcomed by undergraduates and would not overtax the cooks. This is rather a special version recorded by Wyvern (Colonel Kenny-Herbert) in his 1881 Sweet Dishes, and he suggested that it was a High Table favourite.

Mix the suet and the breadcrumbs. Crush the ratafia biscuits and add to the bread with the other dry ingredients. Work in the eggs, egg yolks and brandy and put into a greased pudding basin. Cover with greased greaseproof paper and kitchen foil and tie securely. Put into a pan with boiling water to come halfway up the basin. Cover and boil for 3 hours, adding more boiling water to the pan as necessary to prevent it boiling dry. Turn out onto a warm serving dish and serve with a rum sauce.

Aunt's Pudding

5 oz (125 g) fresh white
  breadcrumbs
2 oz (50 g) sugar
4 fl oz (100 ml) milk
3 eggs

2 oz (50 g) butter
Grated rind and juice of
  1 lemon
Pinch of ground nutmeg
4 oz (10 g) stoned raisins

Like the range of puddings named after Oxford and Cambridge colleges, there is a family range of homely puddings recorded in print and manuscript. Perhaps they were the favourite puddings of those from whom they borrowed their names, or perhaps they had been donated to the family by the person in question. Even Mrs Beeton recorded Aunt Martha, Aunt Nelly and Aunt Polly as pudding namesakes, possibly from those readers who contributed her recipes, while many manuscripts have recipes for Kate's, Mary Ann's or My Cousin's Pudding. These puddings were the usual steamed mixtures of suet, flour, breadcrumbs and dried fruit with variations, but this one is nice and light.

Put the breadcrumbs and sugar into a bowl and pour on boiling milk. Beat in the eggs and butter. Add the lemon rind and juice to the mixture with the nutmeg. Butter a pudding basin and stick the raisins all over the inside. Add the pudding mixture very carefully. Cover with a piece of greased greaseproof paper and kitchen foil and tie securely. Put into a pan with boiling water halfway up the basin. Cover and boil for 1¼ hours, adding more boiling water to the pan if necessary to prevent it boiling dry.

Syrup Layer Pudding

12 oz (350 g) self-raising
  flour
Pinch of salt
5 oz (125 g) shredded suet

12 oz (350 g) golden syrup
2 tablespoons lemon juice
4 oz (100 g) fresh white
  breadcrumbs

This is the ideal syrup pudding for those who do not want to mess about with pudding cloths. It is richly syrupy and lightened by breadcrumbs.

Sieve the flour and salt into a mixing bowl and stir in the suet. Add enough cold water to make a soft dough that can be rolled out.

Grease a pudding basin. Warm the syrup with the lemon juice and pour a little of the mixture into the basin. Roll out the dough and cut a piece the size of the bottom of the basin. Put this lightly in place. Sprinkle on one-third of the breadcrumbs and pour in some syrup mixture. Top with a slightly larger circle of pastry, one-third breadcrumbs and more syrup mixture. Cut out two more circles from the pastry, one the same size as the top of the basin, and the other slightly smaller. Continue arranging pastry, bread-crumb and syrup layers, ending with the large piece of pastry. Cover with greased greaseproof paper and a piece of kitchen foil, tied on securely. Put into a large pan with boiling water to come halfway up the basin. Cover and steam for 1¾ hours, adding more boiling water to the pan as necessary to prevent it boiling dry. Turn onto a warm serving plate and serve with custard.

Burbage Pudding

Serves 4–6

4 oz (100 g) white breadcrumbs
4 oz (100 g) shredded suet
4 oz (100 g) light soft brown sugar

½ teaspoon bicarbonate of soda
Pinch of salt
3 oz (75 g) strawberry jam
1 egg

Sometimes spelled 'Berbage', this pudding appears in a number of books, but I have not been able to trace its origin, or discover whether it was named after a person or a house. There were, of course, at least two actors of that name, and certainly this rather light steamed pudding is more showy and likely to appeal to an actor's temperament than the heavier varieties. It is traditionally made in a brick-shaped mould, and I find an oblong terrine very satisfactory. Serve the pudding with a pouring egg custard, or strawberry Jam Sauce (see p. 203).

Stir together the breadcrumbs, suet, sugar, soda and salt. Put the jam and egg into another bowl, and mix well together. Stir into the dry ingredients until thoroughly mixed. Put into a well-greased 1 lb (450 g) oblong terrine or pie dish. Cover with greased greaseproof paper and kitchen foil, tied on securely. Put into a shallow saucepan with boiling water halfway up the container, or into a steamer. Cover and steam for 3 hours, adding more boiling water to the pan so it does not boil dry. Leave the dish to stand for 5 minutes and then turn on to a warm serving dish.

Cabinet Pudding 1   *Serves 4–6*

8 oz (225 g) glacé cherries   3 oz (75 g) sugar
8 oz (225 g) spongecake   4 eggs
¾ pint (450 ml) single cream   3 tablespoons brandy

There are many variations on this recipe, which appears to derive from the French. Diplomate – a similar confection of sponge, brandy, candied or dried fruit or jam. The name of the English version (Mrs Beeton calls it Chancellor's Pudding) has an obvious derivation. Some recipes suggest serving the pudding hot with a wine or pineapple sauce; some puddings are steamed and others baked; one version is prepared and then frozen without cooking; and a twentieth-century version substitutes bread for spongecake and raisins for glacé fruit. The result is always a rich pudding for special occasions.

Butter a pudding basin or mould and arrange the halved cherries over the bottom. Cut the spongecake into 1 in (2.5 cm) cubes and put into the basin. Heat the cream and sugar gently until lukewarm. Beat the eggs enough to mix the yolks and whites thoroughly. Stir in the cream, mix well and leave until cold. Add the brandy and pour gently onto the cake cubes. Leave to stand for 30 minutes. Cover with a piece of greased greaseproof paper and kitchen foil, tied on securely. Steam in a pan of boiling water for 1 hour. Leave to stand for 5 minutes and turn out onto a serving plate. Serve hot or cold.

Cabinet Pudding 2   *Serves 6*

4 oz (100 g) currants   3 eggs
1½ oz (40 g) chopped mixed   Milk
  candied peel   1 oz (25 g) caster sugar
1 oz (25 g) sultanas   Grated rind of 1 lemon
10 oz (300 g) spongecake   Pinch of ground nutmeg
2 oz (50 g) butter

Grease a pudding basin very well with butter. Sprinkle the base with a few of the currants, and all the peel and sultanas, and try to make some of the fruit adhere to the sides of the basin. Cut the spongecake in thin slices and arrange in layers with the currants and a little butter between each layer.

Break the eggs into a measuring jug and make up to 1 pint (600 ml) with milk. Add the sugar, lemon rind and nutmeg and beat together until well mixed. Pour this liquid into the pudding basin very slowly so that it soaks into the spongecake. Cover with a piece of greased greaseproof paper and a piece of kitchen foil, and tie securely with string. Leave to stand for 2 hours, so that the spongecake softens. Put the basin into a large saucepan and add boiling water to come halfway up the basin. Cover and boil for $1\frac{1}{2}$ hours, keeping the water topped up by adding boiling water from time to time. Remove from the pan and leave to stand for 3 minutes, then turn out on a warm serving plate. Serve with custard.

Speech House Pudding

Serves 4–6

2 oz (50 g) butter
1 oz (25 g) caster sugar
2 eggs
2 oz (50 g) plain flour

1 large teaspoon raspberry jam
½ teaspoon bicarbonate of soda
1 tablespoon milk

The Speech House in the Forest of Dean in Gloucestershire is now a hotel, but was originally one of six lodges where the Ancient Forest Courts were held. The oath was not taken on the Bible but on a sprig of mistletoe, relic of far earlier ceremonies. The pudding, which is a light sponge, appears under many names in old cookery books; sometimes it is known just as Raspberry Pudding. My favourite version appears in an early Victorian manuscript book from Suffolk, where it is known as Kiss Me Quick Pudding. A later housewife has prudently crossed out the original title and renamed it Jam Pudding.

Cream the butter and sugar until light and fluffy. Separate the eggs and work the yolks into the butter. Fold in the flour and jam. Dissolve the soda in the milk and fold into the mixture. Whisk the egg whites to stiff peaks and fold into the pudding mixture. Put into a greased pudding basin, cover with a piece of greased greaseproof paper and kitchen foil, tie securely. Put in a pan with boiling water to come halfway up the basin and steam for 3 hours, adding more boiling water to the pan as necessary to prevent it boiling dry.

Sir Watkin Williams Wynne's Pudding

5 oz (125 g) fresh white
  breadcrumbs
4 oz (100 g) caster sugar
3 oz (75 g) shredded suet
Grated rind and juice of
  1 lemon
2 eggs

Sauce
2 eggs
1 oz (25 g) caster sugar
1 tablespoon brandy
2 tablespoons warm water

Successive generations of this Welsh Border family ran a pack of foxhounds, hunting mostly in Shropshire and Cheshire. Their version of bread pudding is light and was originally mixed with beef marrow instead of suet. It may be served with custard, but the correct accompaniment is a whipped brandy sauce. Wyvern (Colonel Kenny-Herbert) writing in 1881 gives a recipe for Sir Watkin's Pudding, which is more elaborate and contains apricot jam and Curaçao. It is served with apricot sauce. The following recipe, however, seems more likely to be suitable for a hunting squire.

Stir together the breadcrumbs, sugar and suet. Separate the eggs. Add the lemon rind and juice to the dry ingredients with the egg yolks. Whisk the egg whites to stiff peaks and fold into the mixture. Put into a greased pudding basin and cover with a piece of greased greaseproof paper and kitchen foil, tied on securely. Put into a pan with boiling water to come halfway up the basin. Cover and steam for 2 hours, adding more boiling water to the pan to prevent it boiling dry.

To make the sauce, put all the ingredients into a bowl over hot water and whisk over low heat until firm and creamy.

Figgy Pudding 1

Serves 6

2 cooking apples
1 lb (450 g) dried figs
1 medium carrot
8 oz (225 g) butter
4 oz (100 g) dark soft brown
  sugar

6 oz (150 g) wholemeal
  breadcrumbs
4 oz (100 g) wholemeal flour
Grated rind and juice of
  1 lemon
2 eggs
2 tablespoons black treacle

As Christmas carol time came around again, my carload of school fodder used to shriek their favourite 'Yes, we all love figgy pudding'

*taught to them by an inspired master. For some reason, it was a very
enthusiastic shouting song, and they made the most of it, although
their taste for dried figs was minimal. Possibly 'figgy' indicated just
a rich fruit seasonal pudding in the old days, since in Cornwall the
word is still used for raisins in cakes and puddings. The first recipe,
which comes from Yorkshire, is really the nearest to what dried
fruit puddings once tasted like; the second is a lighter modern
version.*

Peel and core the apples and cut them into pieces. Put the figs,
apples and carrot through the fine blade of a mincer. Cream the
butter and sugar until light and fluffy. Work in the breadcrumbs
and flour, and then the minced fruit. Put the lemon rind and juice
into a bowl with the eggs and treacle, and mix well together. Add to
the pudding and beat well. If necessary, add a little milk; the
mixture should be stiff. Put into a large greased pudding basin, or
two smaller ones. Cover with a piece of greased greaseproof paper
and kitchen foil, and tie securely. Put into a pan with boiling water
to come halfway up the basin. Cover and steam for 5 hours, adding
more boiling water to the pan from time to time to prevent it
boiling dry. This pudding may be kept like Christmas Pudding.

Figgy Pudding 2

Serves 4-6

8 oz (225 g) dried figs
Grated rind and juice of
    1 lemon
4 oz (100 g) fresh white
    breadcrumbs
4 oz (100 g) shredded suet
4 oz (100 g) plain flour

1 teaspoon ground mixed spice
1 teaspoon baking powder
3 oz (75 g) dark soft brown
    sugar
2 eggs
2 tablespoons milk

Cut the figs into small pieces with kitchen scissors and put the
pieces into a bowl. Add the lemon rind and juice to the figs. Put the
breadcrumbs and suet into another bowl. Sift in the flour, spice
and baking powder. Add the sugar and stir the dry ingredients
together until well mixed. Add the figs, lemon juice, rind, eggs and
milk and beat well. The mixture should be of a soft dropping
consistency. Put into a well-greased pudding basin and cover with
greased greaseproof paper and kitchen foil, and tie securely. Put
into a pan with boiling water coming halfway up the basin. Cover
and steam for 3 hours, adding more boiling water to the pan if
necessary to prevent it boiling dry. Turn onto a warm serving plate,
and serve with golden syrup and/or custard.

Half-Pay Pudding

4 oz (100 g) shredded suet
4 oz (100 g) fresh white breadcrumbs
4 oz (100 g) plain flour

4 oz (100 g) currants
4 oz (100 g) stoned raisins
2 tablespoons black treacle
½ pint (300 ml) milk

The name of this pudding has always fascinated me, conjuring up the straitened circumstances of the many officers and gentlemen who had to put their families on short rations, which included economical bread pudding. The system of 'half-pay' was first mentioned in print in Samuel Pepys' Diary (1664), and was originally calculated at half an officer's pay, but during the reign of William III half a servant's allowance was included. This was paid as a retaining fee rather than a pension, on the assumption that the officer would eventually return to duty when needed, or would receive some other Crown appointment. The pay was granted when officers were disbanded, but in the early days it often happened that young officers lived on half-pay for years, while old veterans past service received no pension.

E. S. Turner in Gallant Gentlemen *(1956) said that 'by going on half-pay at the right moment and exchanging into other regiments, a man could work his way up to field rank without ever being faced by the tiresome necessity of commanding troops.' Field-Marshal Sir Edmund Ironside described the system as a 'miserable dole designed to enable the War Office to keep up a cheap pool of senior officers', and the practice was ended by Hore-Belisha in the 1930s. The pudding must certainly have fulfilled its purpose, as when Mrs Beeton first wrote her cookery book it cost 8d to make.*

Stir together the suet, breadcrumbs, flour, currants and raisins. Add the treacle and milk and beat well. Put into a greased pudding basin. Cover with greased greaseproof paper and foil, tied on securely, and put into a pan with boiling water to come halfway up the basin. Cover and boil for 3½ hours, adding more boiling water from time to time to prevent the pan boiling dry. Serve with custard.

Snowdon Pudding with Snow on the Mountain

Serves 8

8 oz (225 g) shredded suet
8 oz (225 g) fresh white
  breadcrumbs
6 oz (150 g) light soft brown
  sugar
1½ oz (40 g) plain flour
6 oz (150 g) lemon marmalade
6 eggs
4 oz (100 g) stoned raisins
Grated rind of 2 lemons

Sauce
1½ oz (40 g) sugar
Grated rind of 1 lemon
¼ pint (150 ml) water
1 oz (25 g) butter
2 teaspoons cornflour
6 fl oz (150 ml) medium
  white wine

Although this is a book on English puddings, I cannot resist this delicious Welsh pudding given to me by Babs Honey, whom I worked with for many years on a farming magazine. It is a lovely, light, lemony steamed pudding and the sauce represents snow on the mountain.

Stir together the suet, breadcrumbs, sugar and flour. Work in the marmalade and eggs. Reserve 1 oz (25 g) raisins and stir in the rest into the pudding with the grated lemon rind. Grease a pudding basin and sprinkle the reserved raisins in the bottom. Spoon in the pudding mixture carefully so that the raisins are not disturbed. Cover with a piece of greased greaseproof paper and kitchen foil and tie on securely. Put into a pan with boiling water to come halfway up the basin. Cover and steam for 1¾ hours, adding more boiling water if necessary to prevent the pan boiling dry.

Prepare the sauce while the pudding is cooking. Put the sugar, lemon rind and water into a pan and simmer for 10 minutes. Strain to remove the lemon rind. Add the butter to the liquid and work in the cornflour. Return to low heat and stir in the wine. Simmer for 5 minutes. Turn the pudding onto a warm serving plate and pour on the hot sauce just before serving.

Prince Consort Pudding

Juice of 2 fresh limes
2 oz (50 g) sugar
6 oz (150 g) stale spongecake
½ pint (300 ml) single cream

7 egg yolks
2 oz (50 g) dried apricots
1 egg white
2 oz (50 g) candied lemon
peel

George I was known as Pudding George to celebrate his passion for the heavy puddings enjoyed by the House of Hanover. Until his reign, lighter dishes such as syllabubs and jellies were the acceptable dishes for the upper classes, although boiled puddings were enjoyed by poorer families and by country families who needed more solid food to sustain their hard work. Solid puddings began to grow in favour, but became really acceptable to all ranks of society only at the beginning of Victoria's reign. When she married Albert, there was a flurry of puddings rejoicing in German names such as Coburg, Kaiser and Albert. These puddings were a little more special than the usual family ones, and included spongecake and cream in place of the everyday bread and milk. This one is worth making if fresh limes are available.

Squeeze the lime juice over the sugar and stir well to dissolve the sugar. Grate the spongecake into fine crumbs. Bring the cream just to the boil and pour onto the crumbs. Add the lime sugar and leave to stand until cold. Beat in the egg yolks, and finely chopped apricots. Whisk the egg white to stiff peaks and fold into the mixture. Butter a mould and decorate with thin strips of candied lemon peel. Pour in the pudding very carefully. Cover with greased greaseproof paper and kitchen foil and tie securely. Put into a pan containing boiling water to come halfway up the basin. Cover and steam for 1 hour, adding more boiling water to the pan if necessary to prevent it boiling dry. Turn out carefully onto a warm serving dish. Accompany the pudding with a sauce of melted redcurrant jelly flavoured with curaçao.

Hunting Pudding

Serves 6–8

1 lb (450 g) stoned raisins
8 oz (225 g) plain flour
8 oz (225 g) shredded suet
4 eggs

½ nutmeg, grated
2 fl oz (50 ml) brandy
Milk

This recipe appears in many handwritten recipe books of the eighteenth century and I have sometimes seen it called Leicestershire Pudding. A similar pudding, called Hunter's Pudding, appears in Cassell's Dictionary of Cookery (late nineteenth century), and the entry notes that this and plum pudding are very similar. The Dictionary also states that finely-minced cooked meat could be substituted for the suet, and the pudding could then be eaten cold. It could also be stored for several months, and might be reboiled, or cut into slices and fried (like today's Christmas Pudding). The reference to the inclusion of minced meat makes me think that this is a very early version of a boiled pudding, being yet another way of preserving meat through the winter months.

A later version of the pudding includes breadcrumbs, sugar, currants, and candied lemon peel, and is cooked in a pudding basin for 6–7 hours, which seems a corruption of the original to come more closely in line with the popular Victorian fruited puddings. Either the plain sixteenth-century version or the lighter and fruitier one would make a very solid meal at the end of a hard day's hunting, but one wonders if the name derives from the fact that a slice of cold pudding would make a good sustaining snack tucked into a sportsman's pocket.

Mix together the raisins, flour and suet. Add the beaten eggs, grated nutmeg and brandy and enough milk to make a stiff mixture. Put into a floured pudding cloth and tie into a ball, leaving room for expansion. Put into boiling water and boil for 5 hours, adding more boiling water during cooking so that the pudding does not boil dry.

Welcome Guest

4 oz (100 g) fresh white
  breadcrumbs
½ pint (300 ml) creamy milk
  or single cream
4 oz (100 g) dry breadcrumbs
4 oz (100 g) shredded suet

Pinch of salt
3 oz (75 g) ratafia biscuits
3 oz (75 g) candied peel
Grated rind of 1 large lemon
4 eggs
4 oz (100 g) caster sugar

Eliza Acton called this The Welcome Guest's Own Pudding, and described it as her own recipe in 1855, but it was copied many times under a briefer name into many housewives' notebooks. Later versions became simplified with the use of ground almonds, and by substituting butter or margarine for suet, but I prefer the original version. This could be transformed into Sir Edwin Landseer's Pudding if made in a mould decorated 'tastefully with small leaves of thin citron peel and split muscatel raisins in a pattern, and strew the intermediate spaces with well cleaned and well dried currants mingled with plenty of candied orange or lemon-rind shred small'.

Make the fresh crumbs very fine. Bring the milk or cream just to the boil and pour over these crumbs. Cover and leave until cold. Stir in dry breadcrumbs, suet and salt. Crush the ratafia biscuits coarsely and add to the crumbs. Cut the peel in very thin slices and add with the grated lemon rind to the pudding mixture. Whisk the eggs with the sugar until light and fluffy and add the pudding mixture, beating until well mixed. Put into a greased pudding basin, and tie on a piece of greased greaseproof paper and a piece of kitchen foil. Put into a pan with hot water to come halfway up the basin. Cover and boil for 2 hours, add more boiling water from time to time to prevent the pan boiling dry. Remove from the water and leave the pudding to stand in the basin for 3 minutes. Turn out on a warmed serving dish and serve with Wine Sauce (see p. 200).

Carrot Pudding

Serves 6

12 oz (350 g) carrots
8 oz (225 g) white
  breadcrumbs
4 oz (100 g) shredded suet
4 oz (100 g) currants

4 oz (100 g) stoned raisins
3 oz (75 g) sugar
3 eggs
½ teaspoon ground nutmeg
Milk

Root vegetables were frequently used in old-fashioned puddings. Potatoes gave lightness, while carrots, beetroot and parsnips were used for sweetening. Carrot pudding was a particular favourite in the eighteenth century, but seems to have been neglected in England in later years, and the only relic remains in the carrots added to some Christmas Puddings. Oddly enough, carrot cakes and puddings are still very popular in the United States – a good example of the early dishes that travelled with the settlers and remained traditional favourites while they died out in the land of their birth. This is Mrs Beeton's 1888 version, and she boiled or baked the pudding, noting that carrots reputedly contained the same kind of sugar as the sugar-cane.

Peel the carrots and boil them until tender. Drain well and mash them to a pulp. Add all the remaining ingredients with enough milk to make a thick batter. Put into a greased pudding basin, cover with greased greaseproof paper and kitchen foil and tie on securely. Put into a pan with boiling water to come halfway up the basin. Cover and boil for 2½ hours, adding more boiling water to the pan if necessary to prevent it boiling dry. Turn out and sprinkle on a little sugar before serving. If the pudding is preferred baked, it will take an hour at 375°F/190°C/Gas Mark 5.

Christmas Pudding

8 oz (225 g) self-raising flour

8 oz (225 g) fresh white
breadcrumbs

8 oz (225 g) shredded suet

8 oz (225 g) currants

12 oz (350 g) sultanas

12 oz (350 g) stoned raisins

8 oz (225 g) dark soft brown
sugar

6 eggs

Grated rind and juice of
1 orange

Grated rind and juice of
1 lemon

1 teaspoon salt

1 teaspoon ground mixed spice

½ pint (300 ml) old ale or stout

4 oz (100 g) chopped mixed peel

4 oz (100 g) chopped glacé
cherries

1 small grated carrot

1 small grated apple

Cratchit left the room alone – too nervous to bear witness – to take the pudding up and bring it in.

Suppose it should not be done enough! Suppose it should break in turning out! Suppose somebody should have got over the wall of the back-yard and stolen it, while they were merry with the goose – a supposition at which the two young Cratchits became livid! All sorts of horrors were supposed.

Hullo! A great deal of steam! The pudding was out of the copper. A smell like a washing day! That was the cloth. A smell like an eating-house and a pastry-cook's next door to each other, with a laundress's next door to that! That was the pudding! In half a minute Mrs Cratchit entered – flushed, but smiling proudly – with the pudding like a speckled cannon-ball, so hard and firm, blazing in half of a quartern of ignited brandy, and bedight with Christmas holly stuck into the top.

Charles Dickens, *A Christmas Carol*

A traditional English pottage of stewed meat and dried fruit in broth was a popular dish in the early fifteenth century. Wine was added with minced onions and herbs, a thickening of bread, some spices, red colouring and currants, along with pieces of beef in a little water. There were Elizabethan variations using veal or chicken, and adding raisins, additional spices, salt, pepper, and newly-imported dried prunes or 'plums'. The herbs and broth were gradually abandoned, but the dish was a favourite festive dish on All Saints' Day, Christmas Day and New Year's Day. By 1673 it was recorded as a special Christmas food, and the original stewed broth became Christmas pottage, plum pottage or porridge. This developed into the later plum pudding, which was thick with fruit and spices and laced with claret or sack (white wine). Meaty plum porridge was recorded as a Scottish national dish as late as 1826.

Early plum puddings were boiled in a cloth and completely spherical, but today it is more convenient to prepare the puddings in a basin. They store well in a dry place or can be frozen, and are boiled for a second time before use. This recipe is light in texture but dark and delicious, and makes 4 medium-sized puddings.

Mix together flour, crumbs, suet, dried fruit and sugar. Gradually work in all the other ingredients to give a stiff but not dry mixture. Add a little more beer or milk if necessary. Put into 4 × 1½ pint (900 ml) greased basins, leaving a 2 in (6 cm) space above the surface of the puddings. Cover with greased greaseproof paper and kitchen foil and tie securely. Put into a pan of boiling water, cover and boil gently for 8 hours, adding more water to the pan if necessary to prevent it boiling dry. Cool completely and replace paper and foil with clean pieces for storage. Store in a cool, dry place. Boil for 3 hours before serving with hard sauce, cream or custard.

Cannon Ball Pudding

It is fun to make a traditional cannonball Christmas pudding like Mrs Cratchit's, but a little care is needed. The pudding may be boiled in a cloth, but Prue Leith, that great contemporary cook, has devised an easier way of handling the mixture. She puts it into a greased polythene freezer bag before putting it into a cloth, and then suspends the pudding on a wooden spoon across the top of a large pan so that it does not touch the base of the pan. She stores the finished pudding in an ungreased polythene bag ready for reboiling on the day.

The pudding must be unwrapped with great care so that it rolls gently on to the warm serving plate.

Lighting The Pudding

The traditional pudding needs to be finished in the correct manner. Before serving, tuck in some silver charms and stick a piece of holly in the top. Warm some brandy in a small pan until it is just lukewarm. Take it to the table with the pudding, light with a match and pour over the pudding at once. It is not as easy to light the alcohol once it is poured over the pudding, and if the operation is completed in the kitchen the flames will have died out when the pudding reaches the table.

13 Baked Puddings

Baked puddings have only become family dishes in the last two hundred years, gradually replacing the earlier boiled and steamed variety. Today it is considered practical and economical to slip a pudding into the oven on Sunday while the meat is roasting, and the paraphernalia of pudding basins, covering and boiling water is considered tiresome. Few of our ancestors, however, knew the convenience of an oven until the end of the eighteenth century, and the kitchen range complete with oven was not in popular use until the third quarter of the nineteenth century.

In palaces and great houses ovens had been available since early times to bake puddings for the upper classes. Lower down the social scale, however, a brick baking oven was part of the equipment of farmhouses, but cottagers had to cook all their food at an open hearth. Pies might be made for special occasions, but had to be taken to the village baker's oven for completion, and the more delicate baked pudding was not suitable for transportation before or after cooking. In towns, houses were equipped with fires, but many people lived in sets of rooms and the only type of cooking they could handle was simple toasting. Until well into the nineteenth century much of the people's food in towns was purchased from the cookshop or pieshop, or from itinerant vendors.

The ingenious Benjamin Thompson, known as Count Rumford, was a heating engineer, among other occupations. He is credited with the invention of the first cooking range at the end of the eighteenth century, and in 1802 George Bodley of Exeter patented a closed-top cooking range. Gradually, the kitchen range developed until by the middle of the nineteenth century many old fireplaces were bricked up to accommodate the new iron cooking device, which could boil and bake with convenience. By 1880 Smith & Welstood produced a small cottage range, but many people still suspended pans from the old fireplace iron cranes over the new cooker. The introduction of gas to towns during that period stimulated the development of cookers and increased the use of the oven.

The earliest baked puddings were heavy affairs and were simply adaptations of favourite boiled bread and suet mixtures. It is difficult now to realize the important part that bread played in so many people's lives. It was truly the staff of life in the days when most people subsisted on a diet of salt bacon, hard cheese, dark chewy bread and thin beer. The growing of wheat and the laws for the sale of this vital commodity played an important part in English history, and there were times when wages were calculated on the value of a loaf of bread.

Many people had to eat large quantities of bread to fill empty stomachs, and children in particular ate a great deal of it. Meat was rare and expensive, fish was not easily transported, and many local cheeses were very hard and difficult to digest. Children ate bread spread with lard (butter was too expensive for many people) as a treat, while bread-and-milk was standard food for the young and for invalids. The offering of a bowl of bread-and-milk as a soothing supper has only died out in the past twenty-five years as easily digested breakfast cereals have been developed and become children's favourites. Charles Spurgeon in the eighteenth century said 'you cannot put a quartern loaf into a child's hand; you must break it up and give him the crumb in warm milk'. My feeling about the somewhat fierce Thomas Carlyle softened when I read in

Sartor Resartus his early memory of supper:

On fine evenings I was wont to carry forth my supper (breadcrumb boiled in milk) and eat it out-of-doors. On the coping of the Orchard-Wall, which I could reach by climbing, or still more easily if Father Andreas would set-up the pruning ladder, my porringer was placed. There, many a sunset, have I, looking at the distant western mountains, consumed, not without relish, my evening meal.

Small wonder then that so many recipes are based on the traditional bread soaked in milk, sweetened and flavoured to taste. In the colleges of Oxford and Cambridge solid bread mixtures well-spiced and thick with dried fruit were boiled, baked or sometimes fried, and were special dishes designed to fill the poor scholars. The lighter bread-and-milk mixtures were more suitable for the ladies and children of middle-class homes where servants could control the shorter and more delicate baking operation in a domestic oven. The lighter sponge pudding, made with flour, was equally suitable for refined households and recipes became more delicious and in more common use as kitchen gadgets took over from the sturdy servants, who had taken up to 3 hours to beat up a light mixture. The following anonymous doggerel gives some idea of the pleasure that the early baked puddings could be expected to give.

18th Century Receipt for a Pudding

If the vicar you treat,
You must give him to eat,
A pudding to his affection,
And to make his repast,
By the canon of taste,
Be the present receipt your direction.

First take 2 lbs of bread
Be the crumb only weigh'd
For crust the good housewife refuses.
The proportions you'll guess
May be made more or less
To the size the family chuses.

Then its sweetness to make;
Some currants you take,
And sugar, of each half a pound.
Be not butter forgot.
And the quality sought
Must the same with your currants be found.

Cloves and mace you will want,
With rose water I grant,
And more savoury things if well chosen.
Then to bind each ingredient,
You'll find it expedient,
Of eggs to put in half a dozen.

Some milk, don't refuse it,
But boil as you use it,
A proper hint for its maker.
And the whole when compleat,
With care recommend the baker.

In praise of this pudding,
I vouch it a good one,
Or should you suspect a fond word,
To every guest,
Perhaps it is best
Two puddings should smoke on the board.

Two puddings! - yet - no,
For one will do
The other comes in out of season;
And these lines but obey,
Nor can anyone say,
That this pudding's without rhyme or reason.

Duck Puddings

3 oz (75 g) bread (without
  crusts)
3 fl oz (75 ml) milk
1 egg
2 oz (50 g) shredded suet

1 teaspoon plain flour
1 large onion
½ teaspoon chopped sage
Salt and pepper

These little savoury puddings do not contain any duck, but received their name from the fact that they were considered the perfect accompaniment to richly fat duck and pork. They also took the place of the stuffing we enjoy today, since a stuffed bird was difficult to cook on a spit, and the stuffing might not be cooked and could be dangerous. The herb-flavoured pudding could be prepared in the dripping pan under the spit, or when ovens came into general use, could be cooked in the meat pan with a rack for the bird or joint on top. Today it is easier to cook the puddings separately, and to put them round the roasting meat to finish cooking so that they absorb some of the rich juices in the old-fashioned way. These bulky puddings served to satisfy the appetite and cut down on the amount of meat eaten.

Break the bread into pieces and put into a bowl. Pour the milk over it, and leave to stand for 10 minutes. Beat well with a wooden spoon and work in the egg, suet and flour. Chop the onion finely and add to the mixture with the sage, salt and pepper. Grease 4 individual Yorkshire Pudding tins and put them in the oven with the accompanying meat until hot to the touch. Divide the mixture between the tins and bake at 425°F/220°C/Gas Mark 7 for 15 minutes. Lift out of the tins and put in the pan juices that surround the roasting poultry or meat. Continue cooking for 15 minutes.

Herb Pudding

Serves 4

6 oz (150 g) stale bread (without
  crusts)
½ pint (300 ml) milk
2 oz (50 g) shredded suet
2 oz (50 g) fine oatmeal

3 eggs
Salt and pepper
Pinch of cayenne pepper
Thyme, sage and marjoram

150

Here is another savoury baked pudding that is good with any meat. Yorkshire Savoury Pudding is a variation that is flavoured only with sage, but contains 4 large onions to the same quantity of dry ingredients.

In Cumberland a herb pudding is traditionally served in spring and contains onions, leeks, blackcurrant leaves and herbs with oatmeal and barley. The herbs include Easterledge, from which the pudding is often named. The pudding is considered to help the old country custom of 'clearing the blood' at the beginning of the year.

Break the bread into small pieces. Bring the milk to the boil and pour over the bread. Leave to get cold and then mix in the suet and oatmeal. Beat the eggs and mix into the bread with the seasonings and herbs. Beat well and pour into a hot roasting tin containing a little melted dripping. Bake at 400°F/200°C/Gas Mark 6 for 40 minutes. Serve with the meat and plenty of gravy.

Swanley Harvest Custard   Serves 4

8 oz (225 g) stale bread	1 egg
1 pint (600 ml) milk	Salt and pepper
4 oz (100 g) grated Cheddar Cheese	Pinch of ground nutmeg

The harvest field was a busy place before the coming of the great harvesters, when gangs of men worked all day far from home, and their wives brought packed meals and cooling drinks out in baskets. This dish was carried cold to the harvest, or else was hot and fresh to revive the men in the evenings. This recipe dates from the beginning of this century and was recorded in the late 1930s in Kent by Mrs Arthur Webb, who commented that mustard sauce was often served with the dish.

Remove crusts from the bread and break the bread into pieces. Boil the milk and pour it over the bread. Leave for 20 minutes then beat thoroughly together. Gradually beat in the cheese, egg and seasoning. Pour into a greased pie dish. Bake at 375°F/190°C/Gas Mark 5 for 30 minutes until the top is brown and crisp.

Fish Pudding

Serves 4

1 lb (450 g) white fish
1 teaspoon salt
Pinch of pepper
¾ oz (20 g) plain flour

1 egg
1 oz (25 g) butter, melted
¼ pint (150 ml) parsley sauce
4 oz (100 g) peeled shrimps

A boiled fish pudding used to be considered a suitable dish for an invalid, but this version is rich and very good for a family meal. Cod, haddock, halibut or whiting may be used for this dish.

Put the raw fish through the fine blade of a mincer 4 times, or else purée in an electric blender. Put into a bowl and mix with the salt, pepper, flour, beaten egg, butter, parsley sauce and shrimps. Beat with a wooden spoon until light and fluffy. Put into a greased pudding basin. Cover with a piece of kitchen foil. Stand the basin in a roasting tin containing 1 in (2.5 cm) hot water. Bake at 350°F/180°C/Gas Mark 4 for 40 minutes. Turn out and serve hot in slices with more parsley sauce, or with white sauce flavoured with capers.

Bread Pudding

Makes 12 slices

8 slices bread (medium toast thickness from a large loaf)
½ pint (300 ml) milk
12 oz (350 g) mixed dried fruit
2 oz (50 g) chopped mixed peel
1 eating apple
3 tablespoons soft dark brown sugar

2 tablespoons dark orange marmalade
1½ oz (40 g) self-raising flour
2 eggs
Squeeze of lemon juice
1 teaspoon ground cinnamon
4 oz (100 g) butter

This is one of the favourite country dishes, which can be eaten as a pudding with custard, or cut into squares to eat cold as a cake. It is still widely sold in the Midlands and East Anglia, and looks like a very heavy, damp fruit cake. It is extremely solid and nourishing, and is a wonderful way of using surplus bread, which is made palatable with dried fruit, sugar and plenty of spice. In Norfolk the pudding is sometimes called Nelson's Cake or Nelson Slices (the admiral was born and bred in the county), and it can also be found under that name in Plymouth, Devonshire, so perhaps it was a favourite of both cooks and seamen on the old ships. There are dozens of recipes, but this is the best I know, given to me by that great cookery writer, Helen Burke.

Break up the bread, including the crusts, and soak in the milk until soft. Beat well with a fork so that all the bread and crust become a soft cream mixture. Add the dried fruit and peel. Grate the apple with its peel and add to the mixture. Stir in the sugar, marmalade, flour, eggs, lemon juice and cinnamon. Melt the butter and pour half of it into the bread mixture. Beat well and put into a greased roasting tin 11 × 8 in (27.5 × 20 cm). Pour on the remaining butter in a thin stream to cover the surface. Bake at 300°F/150°C/Gas Mark 2 for 1½ hours, and then at 350°F/180°C/Gas Mark 4 for 30 minutes. Cut into squares and eat hot with egg custard. Some people prefer to leave it until cold, then sprinkle thickly with icing sugar and slice to eat as cake.

Bread and Butter Pudding
Serves 4–6

4 thin bread slices from large loaf

1 oz (25 g) butter

2 oz (50 g) currants

1 oz (25 g) chopped mixed peel

2 eggs

1 egg yolk

½ pint (300 ml) creamy milk

Grated rind of ½ lemon

Pinch of ground nutmeg

2 tablespoons brandy or rum

1 oz (25 g) granulated sugar

This dish has been popular for more than two hundred years and appears in many eighteenth-century cookery books. As with all old recipes, there are many variations. Some include glacé cherries (although these tend to colour the pudding too much), others spread the butter with marmalade or lemon curd as well as butter, while Prince Charles's favourite version includes bananas, black treacle and brandy.

Remove the crusts from the bread. Butter the bread slices and cut each in two triangles. Arrange layers of bread, currants and peel in a greased pie dish. Beat the eggs, egg yolk and milk together, and stir in the lemon rind, nutmeg and brandy or rum. Pour over the bread and leave to stand for 1 hour. This soaking is the secret of a good bread and butter pudding. Just before cooking, sprinkle the sugar on top of the pudding. Bake at 350°F/180°C/Gas Mark 4 for 30 minutes until the top is firm and crusty.

Epicure's Bread Pudding

Serves 4–6

6 oz (150 g) butter
6 oz (150 g) caster sugar
6 eggs
3 oz (75 g) sultanas
3 oz (75 g) raisins

3 oz (75 g) ground almonds
Grated rind of 1 lemon
Pinch of ground cinnamon
10 oz (300 g) fresh white
   breadcrumbs

Cream the butter and sugar until light and fluffy. Separate the eggs and add the yolks one by one, beating well. Add the dried fruit, almonds, lemon rind and cinnamon. Whisk the egg whites to soft peaks and fold into the mixture. Sprinkle in the breadcrumbs gradually and mix lightly together. Butter a straight-sided ovenware dish or soufflé dish and sprinkle it with caster sugar. Put in the pudding mixture. Bake at 400°F/200°C/Gas Mark 6 for 35 minutes. Serve at once with thin cream.

Cold Bread and Butter Pudding

Serves 4–6

6 thin bread slices from a large
   loaf
2 oz (50 g) butter
4 oz (100 g) sultanas
2 oz (50 g) currants

Pinch of ground mixed spice
1 pint (600 ml) creamy milk
2 oz (50 g) sugar
1 vanilla pod
1 egg and 4 egg yolks

This simple but delicious pudding was found by cookery writer Ambrose Heath when he dined with writer E. V. Lucas at a St James's club. He recommended that it should be eaten very cold.

Remove the crusts from the bread. Soften the butter slightly and spread it on the bread right to the edges. Put the sultanas and currants into a bowl and pour on boiling water to cover. Leave to stand for 15 minutes and drain thoroughly. Put a layer of bread slices into a well-greased pie dish. Sprinkle on half the fruit and spice. Cover with more bread and the remaining fruit and spice. Make the final layer of bread with the butter side upwards. Put the milk, sugar and vanilla pod into a saucepan and bring just to boiling point. Remove from heat and leave to stand for 20 minutes. Take out the vanilla pod. Whisk the egg and egg yolks together in a basin and gradually whisk in the milk. Strain over the bread in the pie dish and leave to stand for 1 hour. Put the pie dish into a baking tin and pour in hot water to come halfway up the sides of the dish.

Bake at 350°F/180°C/Gas Mark 4 for 50 minutes. Remove the pie dish from the water and leave until completely cold.

Bread and Butter Pudding with Marmalade

Serves 4–6

6 × ¼ in (5 cm) slices white bread (large loaf)
2 oz (50 g) butter
3 tablespoons dark orange marmalade
1½ oz (40 g) demerara sugar

2 oz (50 g) chopped mixed candied peel
Grated rind of 1 lemon
3 eggs
1 pint (600 ml) milk
1 oz (25 g) chopped mixed nuts
½ teaspoon ground ginger

Cut the crusts from the bread. Soften the butter slightly and spread it on the bread. Make three sandwiches with the marmalade and cut each sandwich into 4 triangles. Butter a pie dish and put in half the triangles. Sprinkle with one-third demerara sugar, the peel and lemon rind. Put the remaining triangles on top. Beat the eggs and milk together and strain over the bread. Mix together the remaining sugar with the nuts and ginger, and sprinkle on top of the pudding. Bake at 350°F/180°C/Gas Mark 4 for 40 minutes. Serve hot with cream.

Uncle Toby

Serves 4–6

6 oz (150 g) white breadcrumbs
3 oz (75 g) unsalted butter
4 oz (100 g) caster sugar
1 pint (600 ml) creamy milk

2 eggs
Grated rind of 1 lemon
3 fl oz (75 ml) medium sherry

Doubtless Uncle Toby liked his little tipple, but perhaps the family thought it advisable for him to have the sherry in the pudding. It is a light, delicious pudding that is quick to prepare.

Put the crumbs into a bowl with the butter cut into thin flakes and the sugar. Bring the milk to the boil and pour over the crumbs. Stir well and leave until just cold. Beat the eggs, lemon rind and sherry together until just mixed, and beat into the crumb mixture. Put into a greased pie dish and bake at 350°F/180°C/Gas Mark 4 for 40 minutes. Serve hot or cold, preferably with Sherry Sauce (see p. 200).

Jam Roly-Poly

Serves 4–6

6 oz (150 g) self-raising flour
Pinch of salt
3 oz (75 g) shredded suet

¼ pint (150 ml) cold water
8 oz (225 g) jam

This pudding, known as Suety Jack in the Potteries, is made with suet pastry and may be boiled or baked. Lady Jekyll, writing in 1922, recommended the use of stoneless damson or plum jam for baked suet roly-poly puddings, and certainly the bland pastry needs a dark sturdy jam as contrast. She also suggested putting the pudding on a baking tin greased on one side only, and tilting the tin inside the oven to keep the required 'roly' shape and prevent the spreading of the pudding.

The best jams to use are strawberry, raspberry, blackcurrant or plum, which contrast with the pale crust.

Stir together the flour, salt and suet and mix to a firm dough with water. Roll out to a rectangle 8 × 12 in (20 × 30 cms) and spread thickly with the jam. Roll up firmly and put onto a greased baking sheet. Bake at 425°F/220°C/Gas Mark 7 for 40 minutes until golden brown.

Baked Syrup Roll

Serves 4–6

10 oz (275 g) self-raising flour
5 oz (125 g) suet
2 oz (50 g) demerara sugar
1 egg

¼ pint (150 ml) milk
2 oz (50 g) fresh white
   breadcrumbs
8 oz (225 g) golden syrup

This sweet, sticky pudding is a great favourite with those who like golden syrup. It is a good idea to bake the pudding in a loaf tin or similarly-shaped dish, rather than on a baking sheet, as this will help to contain the filling and retain the roll shape.

Put the flour, suet and sugar into a bowl. Stir well and then work in the egg and milk until thoroughly mixed to make a firm dough. Roll out the dough on a floured board to an oblong 12 × 15 in (30 × 37.5 cm). Sprinkle on the crumbs to within 1 in (2.5 cm) of the edge. Spoon on the syrup. Fold the edges of the dough over the filling and then roll up from the narrow edge. Seal the edges firmly by pinching them lightly and put seam downwards in a greased 2 lb (900 g) loaf tin. Bake at 350°F/180°C/Gas Mark 4 for 1¼ hours. Cover the pudding with a piece of foil or greaseproof paper when it is well browned. Lift carefully onto a warm serving dish and serve with more golden syrup and thick cream or custard.

Peterhouse Pudding

Serves 4–6

8 oz (225 g) white breadcrumbs
½ pint (300 ml) milk
2 eggs
4 oz (100 g) sultanas

4 oz (100 g) shredded suet
2 oz (50 g) sugar
Pinch of ground allspice
8 oz (225 g) shortcrust pastry

As with boiled puddings, there are many baked dishes attributed to Oxford or Cambridge colleges. This and the next are among the best.

Put the breadcrumbs into a mixing bowl. Heat the milk to boiling point and pour onto the crumbs. Mix well and leave until cold. Beat the eggs and work into the crumb mixture. Stir in the sultanas, suet, sugar and spice. Line a pie dish with the pastry. Put in the mixture and bake at 375°F/190°C/Gas Mark 5 for 1 hour. Serve hot with custard.

Magdalene Pudding

Serves 4

4 oz (100 g) unsalted butter
4 oz (100 g) caster sugar
2 eggs
4 oz (100 g) plain flour

Pinch of ground nutmeg
Grated rind of ½ lemon
3 tablespoons (45 ml) brandy

Cream the butter and sugar until light and fluffy. Separate the eggs, and beat the yolks into the creamed mixture with a little of the flour. Fold in the remaining flour and nutmeg, and stir in the lemon rind and brandy. Whisk the egg whites to stiff peaks and fold into the mixture. Grease a pie dish and put in the mixture. Bake at 375°F/190°C/Gas Mark 5 for 40 minutes. Serve with Hard Sauce (see p. 201).

Toffee Apple Pudding

Serves 4-6

8 oz (225 g) self-raising flour
4 oz (100 g) shredded suet
1½ lb (675 g) eating apples
1 tablespoon lemon juice

4 oz (100 g) light soft brown
  sugar
2 oz (50 g) golden syrup
2 oz (50 g) demerara sugar

This is a pleasant variation on the traditional suet pudding filled with apples, and is more acceptable to those who do not like steamed puddings, and to children. Use crisp eating apples for the best results so that they keep their shape in the golden crust.

Sift the flour into a basin and stir in the shredded suet. Add just enough cold water to make a soft dough that can be rolled. Divide the dough in half and roll out one piece to fit a 7 in (17.5 cm) square tin. Grease the tin very well with butter and line it with the dough. Peel and quarter the apples and remove the cores. Cut the apples into thin slices and arrange in the tin. Sprinkle with the lemon juice and soft brown sugar. Roll out the second piece of dough and place on top of the apples. Seal the edges well by pinching them together. Bake at 400°F/200°C/Gas Mark 6 for 20 minutes. Spread the top with golden syrup and sprinkle with demerara sugar. Continue baking at 350°F/180°C/Gas Mark 4 for 20 minutes until the top is like golden toffee. Serve with custard or cream.

Eve's Pudding

Serves 4-6

1 lb (450 g) cooking apples
3 oz (75 g) light soft brown sugar
4 oz (100 g) butter
4 oz (100 g) caster sugar
2 eggs

4 oz (100 g) self-raising flour
Grated rind of 1 lemon
¼ teaspoon vanilla essence
Extra caster sugar for sprinkling

Peel and core the apples and chop coarsely. Put in to a greased ovenware dish and sprinkle on the brown sugar. Mix the fruit and sugar lightly together. Cream the butter and caster sugar. Work in the eggs, sifted flour, lemon rind and essence, and mix to a soft batter. Spread over the apples. Bake at 350°F/180°C/Gas Mark 4 for 40 minutes. Sprinkle the surface with caster sugar and serve at once with cream or custard.

Fruit Crumble

Filling
1 lb (450 g) ripe fresh fruit
½ oz (15 g) butter
3 oz (75 g) light soft brown sugar
Pinch of ground cinnamon
6 tablespoons water

Topping
2 oz (50 g) butter
1 oz (25 g) light soft brown sugar
3 oz (75 g) plain flour
Pinch of ground ginger

Although the crumble is now well-established in our kitchens, and is a lifesaver for the cook who loathes pastry-making, it does not appear in old book of English recipes, nor is it recorded in handwritten books until the twentieth century. The earliest reference I have found is in my 1930 edition of that American classic Fanny Farmer's Boston Cookbook, although it is not in the 1972 edition. It seems to be a typically makeshift concoction of a busy cook, and I suspect that the dish developed during the Second World War, when ingredients like sugar and fat were scarce and cooks did their best to dress up basic fruit. This seems to be confirmed by the fact that the English crumble usually consists of stewed fruit topped by a fat-and-flour pastry mixture without water. The result is dull and insipid compared with the American version containing butter, brown sugar and spice over fresh fruit, cooked to a golden crispness. On the basis of the transatlantic crumble, I have devised my own English version, which avoids the wateriness and paleness we normally see. If apples are used, choose eating apples with good flavour, which keep their shape when sliced. I prefer halved eating plums, blackcurrants, black cherries, apricots, or gooseberries with plenty of sweetening. If fresh cherries or apricots are not available, well-drained canned fruit may be used, but no additional sugar is necessary.

Prepare the fruit (e.g., peel, core and slice apples, halve plums or apricots, top and tail gooseberries). Put into a greased ovenware dish and dot with flakes of butter. Sprinkle with sugar and cinnamon, and stir the fruit lightly to mix. Add the water. If canned fruit is used, do not add sugar, but sprinkle with a little syrup from the can. Put the topping ingredients into a bowl and rub the butter in lightly until the mixture is like coarse breadcrumbs, being careful not to rub too hard or make the mixture too fine. Sprinkle on top of the fruit and press down *very lightly* with a fork. Bake at 350°F/180°C/Gas Mark 4 for 45 minutes until the top is crisp and golden. Serve hot with cream or custard.

Mrs Rowse's Figgy Obbin

Serves 4–6

8 oz (225 g) plain flour
Pinch of salt
4 oz (100 g) lard
4 tablespoons cold water

8 oz (225 g) stoned raisins
1 oz (25 g) butter
A little milk for glazing

'Figs' in Cornwall are raisins, but obbins often contain currants or dates instead. This sweet baked roll is good with custard or clotted cream, and any leftovers may be eaten like cake, or used for a packed meal.

Prepare pastry with the flour, salt, lard and water. Roll pastry into a rectangle 12 × 9 in (30 × 22.5 cm). Cover to within ½ in (1.25 cm) of edges with raisins. Dot with butter cut into small pieces. Moisten edges of pastry with water. Roll up evenly like a Swiss roll, starting from the short edge. Pinch edges together and seal the join securely. Lightly mark several times across the top of the roll with a knife and brush with milk to glaze. Put on a greased baking tray and bake at 400°F/200°C/Gas Mark 6 for about 30 minutes. Reduce heat to 325°F/170°C/Gas Mark 3 for 30 minutes.

Apple Bolster

Serves 4–6

8 oz (225 g) self-raising flour
½ teaspoon salt
4 oz (100 g) shredded suet
9 tablespoons milk
1 lb (450 g) cooking apples

2 oz (50 g) light soft brown sugar
2 oz (50 g) sultanas
¼ teaspoon ground mixed spice
¼ teaspoon ground cinnamon

This is another version of the filled suet roly-poly pudding (see p. 129), named for its resemblance to the old-fashioned long pillow, and baked rather than boiled.

Stir the flour, salt and suet together. Reserve 1 tablespoon milk and mix the rest into the flour. Mix to a soft dough and turn out onto a floured surface. Knead lightly and roll out to a 12 in (30 cm) square.

Peel and core the apples and cut the flesh into small pieces. Mix with the sugar, sultanas and spices, and arrange on the suet pastry to within 1 in (2.5 cm) of the edge. Dampen the edges of the pastry with a little water and roll up like a Swiss roll. Seal the ends and put onto a greased baking tray with the seam downwards. Brush the surface with the reserved milk. Bake at 200°F/400°C/Gas Mark 6 for 40 minutes. Serve hot with custard or cream.

Devonshire Apple Drugget   *Serves 4–6*

6 large cooking apples
4 tablespoons water
5 oz (125 g) fresh brown
   breadcrumbs
3 oz (75 g) butter
4 oz (100 g) light soft brown
   sugar

2 eggs
Grated rind of 1 lemon
2 oz (50 g) quince jam or orange
   marmalade
Pinch of ground cloves
Caster sugar for sprinkling

The dictionary defines drugget as a soft woollen carpet, and the word is nowadays applied to a rather cheap drab length of stuff put down to protect good flooring or valuable carpets. Hardly an attractive name for the pudding, but the recipe does produce a soft billowy, light brown square, so it may be appropriate.

Peel the apples and cut them in quarters. Remove the cores and cut the apples in slices. Put into a pan with the water and simmer to a pulp. This should not have any surplus liquid, so be sure that it is simmered until just dry. Put 3 oz (75 g) breadcrumbs in a bowl and pour on the hot apple. Add 2 oz (50 g) butter, sugar, eggs, lemon rind, quince jam or marmalade and cloves. Mix very thoroughly. Grease a 7 in (17.5 cm) square tin very well and sprinkle it with 1 oz (25 g) breadcrumbs. Pour in the apple mixture. Cover with the remaining breadcrumbs and dot with flakes of the remaining butter. Bake at 350°F/180°C/Gas Mark 4 for 1 hour. Turn out and sprinkle with caster sugar. Serve in squares with thick cream.

Derbyshire Bakewell Pudding

Most people know this dish today as a rather solid kind of tart filled with an almond flavoured cake. The dish should consist of a pastry case with a filling of rich custard made from butter and eggs, but is subject to endless variations. The story goes that the landlady of the Rutland Arms instructed her cook to add an egg and sugar to the pastry for a strawberry tart. The cook misunderstood Mrs Greaves' instructions and poured an egg mixture on top of the jam, and the result was so successful that the dish remained a favourite and became a local speciality.

Modern cookery writers have their own versions. Mrs Roundell (1898) spread pastry with 'candied preserve' and topped it with a mixture of lemon rind and juice, melted butter, sugar, breadcrumbs and egg yolks before baking. Lady Clark of Tillypronie (1909) made it with puff pastry, strawberry jam and strips of candied peel. On this went a mixture of eggs, butter, sugar, pounded blanched almonds, brandy and nutmeg. Ambrose Heath (1937) preferred to use fresh raspberries in a pastry case sprinkled with sugar and topped with a spongecake mixture, which was iced after baking.

The Queen's Own Staffordshire Yeomanry Pudding

Serves 4–6

8 oz (225 g) shortcrust pastry
3 oz (75 g) raspberry jam
4 oz (100 g) butter
4 oz (100 g) caster sugar
4 egg yolks
3 egg whites
2 oz (50 g) ground almonds
4 drops of almond essence

The mystery of Bakewell Pudding deepened when I found it in a Leicestershire notebook of the 1930s with a different title and containing raspberry jam and blanched almonds in the filling. This second title is supposedly given to a rich version of Queen of Puddings (see p. 164), but since Staffordshire and Derbyshire are neighbouring counties it could well be that the Staffordshire Yeomanry were particularly fond of the pudding from Bakewell.

However, I then discovered that the dish was a speciality of the

Swan Hotel, Lichfield, and a recipe dated 10 October 1838 gave the pudding a thin pastry base spread with raspberry jam and topped with a filling of 8 egg yolks, 2 egg whites, 8 oz (225 g) each of sugar and melted butter flavoured with almonds. Best of all, with this recipe was a poem written by Rowland Warburton, Esq. at that time to explain the triumph of the dish.

Line the dish with thinnest paste,
Raspberry jam upon it place,
Freshest eggs in beated state,
Whites of two and yolks of eight.
With lump of sugar pounded fine,
Butter melted must combine.
Half a pound of each apply
Flavour'd well with almonds dry.
Mix the whole, let it be,
Pour'd upon the Raspberry.
Oven slowly heat and in it
Bake the dish for 90 minutes.
Sound the trumpets, beat the drums,
Smoking hot the pudding comes.
Yeoman stout prepare to strike
Feasting, fighting, both alike,
Silver spoon instead of sword,
Brandish'd at the Lichfield board
Napkin for a standard spread,
Wav'd in triumph overhead,
Sugar far excels saltpetre,
Raspberries than bullets sweeter.
Puddings slash'd instead of foemen
Cut away, my Stafford Yeomen.

It seems a rather overblown tribute for a pleasant pudding, but I give here the Yeomanry version with raspberry jam, which seems to give a richer flavour than the Bakewell strawberry jam.

Roll out the pastry to line an 8 in (20 cm) pie plate or sandwich tin. Spread the jam on the base of the pastry. Melt the butter and when it is boiling hot, pour onto the sugar, egg yolks and whites, almonds and essence. Beat well and pour onto the jam. Bake at 400°F/200°C/Gas Mark 6 for 30 minutes. Eat while freshly baked.

163

Queen of Puddings

5 oz (125 g) fresh white
  breadcrumbs
1 oz (25 g) sugar
Grated rind of 1 lemon
1 pint (600 ml) milk

2 oz (50 g) butter
4 large eggs
4 tablespoons raspberry jam
4 oz (100 g) caster sugar

Basically this is a light baked pudding made with breadcrumbs and topped with crisp meringue, but there are variations. One recipe includes mixed peel and nutmeg in the breadcrumb base; another includes jam in the meringue topping. This version is the one most commonly used, with a soft bottom layer, thick jam on top, and a crown of golden meringue.

Put the breadcrumbs, sugar and lemon rind into a basin. Put the milk and butter into a pan and heat to lukewarm. Pour onto the crumbs and leave to stand for 10 minutes. Separate the eggs. Beat the egg yolks into the crumb mixture. Grease a pie dish and pour in the crumb mixture. Bake at 350°F/180°C/Gas Mark 4 for 30 minutes until just firm. Warm the jam so that it will spread easily, and very gently spread it on the pudding without breaking the surface. Whisk the egg whites to stiff peaks and fold in the caster sugar. Pile onto the pudding and continue baking for 10 minutes until the meringue is lightly browned and crisp. Serve hot with cream.

Monmouth Pudding

¾ pint (450 ml) milk
8 oz (225 g) fresh white
  breadcrumbs
3 oz (75 g) granulated sugar

¼ teaspoon vanilla essence
2 oz (50 g) butter
4 egg whites
8 oz (225 g) red jam

In Victorian seaside nursing homes and spas (hydros) pastry was considered too robust for the digestions of the inmates, and bread-based 'hydropathic puddings' were served instead. Summer Pudding (see p. 78) is the classic example. This pudding from the Welsh border reveals bold red and white stripes when cut in slices.

Bring the milk to the boil. Put the breadcrumbs into a large basin and pour the milk over them. Leave to soak for 10 minutes, then mix with a fork and add the sugar, vanilla essence and butter. Whisk the egg whites to stiff peaks and fold into the crumb mixture. Spoon half the jam into a greased ovenware dish and pour half the mixture on top. Spoon on the rest of the jam and finish with the breadcrumb mixture. Bake at 325°F/170°C/Gas Mark 3 for 45 minutes until set. Dust with a little caster sugar and serve hot.

14 Dumplings

'The county of hardy men whose housewives make the best dumplings in the world, and whose people speak the purest English', wrote George Borrow, born appropriately at Dumpling Green, near East Dereham, Norfolk in 1803. Norfolk and Suffolk are the traditional home of dumplings, as the heart of the English wheatlands. In the Fenlands, dumplings are traditionally called 'swimmers', but the true Norfolk yeast dumplings which take exactly twenty minutes to cook, should be called 'floaters'. The suet variety are derided by Norfolk men as 'sinkers'.

Although today we think of a dumpling as a suet and flour mixture boiled with salt meat, the true dumpling did not contain suet. It was made in three varieties: from yeast dough, from flour and water only, or from thick egg and milk batter. C. Anne Wilson in her *Food and Drink in Britain* (1973) says that dumplings originated in Norfolk, and that from Elizabethan times Norfolk dumplings were a byword far beyond that county. Bread dough was the basis of these dumplings, or pot-balls, boiled in the stewpot just like other puddings. They were meant to cut the appetite before meat, or even to replace the meat itself. The use of bread dough for small puddings is not confined to England, for it was quite natural for the housewife to pinch off small pieces of the dough to prepare in a variety of ways, often as a treat for children. Scandinavia, Holland, Germany and Austria all have their national boiled or fried dumplings, versatile tummy-fillers and cake substitutes.

The Norfolk rules for preparing dumplings should be adhered to strictly for success. Farmers' wives used to make them to weigh exactly 4 oz (100 g) each. They are still made from proved bread dough rolled into balls and left to prove again for 10 minutes to the size of a tennis ball. They are then put onto a plate and slipped into a large saucepan containing fast-boiling water. With the lid put on immediately, they are kept boiling for exactly 20 minutes, then put into hot soup plates. Traditionally, the dumplings had to be of exactly the same size, and the pan had to be large enough to accommodate the swelling puddings. The lid must never be lifted until cooking time is completed, and the dumplings must be served at once with gravy. Dumplings should never be cut with a knife, but torn apart with two forks at once so that they do not become heavy. Leftover dumplings were sometimes sliced and toasted like bread.

A dressing of butter and sugar dates back to Tudor times, when Gervase Markham reported on the new fashion for eating homely cereals such as oats, wheat, barley and rice with butter. Treacle was, of course, popular with children. This type of dressing was often used on the small batter dumplings (see Chapter 11), which were also attributed to Norfolk and Suffolk and were very popular in the eighteenth century. At the same time, a kind of butter shortcrust was more attractive than plain bread dough that was used to enclose jam or fruit. Small pies of shortcrust were sometimes fried, or could be moulded into balls and boiled. In 1855 Eliza Acton recommended that suet instead of butter in the crust gave a lighter result, and thus the large boiled filled pudding was reproduced in individual sizes. The larger filled puddings were also known in Suffolk and Buckinghamshire as dumplings.

With the greater use of ovens, it became more convenient to bake than boil for hours, and apples covered in shortcrust pastry evolved as baked dumplings, which remain a favourite. Mrs Beeton shows delightful pictures of the pastry formed into a long sausage and wrapped around apples and pears before being glazed and baked. The result is most attractive, showing the shape of the whole fruit. Charles Lamb reported that Coleridge declared that 'a man cannot have a good conscience who refuses apple dumpling, and I confess that I am of the same opinion'. Many people would still agree with him.

Norfolk Dumplings

Serves 4–6

½ oz (15 g) yeast
1 teaspoon caster sugar
¼ pint (150 ml) hot water

2 tablespoons milk
1 lb (450 g) plain flour

It is generally considered that yeast dumplings are the true Norfolk dumplings. Hannah Glasse called them just Yeast Dumplings in the mid-eighteenth century, and wisely said 'as good a way as any to save trouble is to send to the baker's for half a quartern of dough (which will make a great many) and then you have only the trouble of boiling it'. Obviously, when a farmer's wife was making her own bread, it was easy to take pieces from the risen dough and toss them into the pot with boiling meat or vegetables. Eliza Acton said that they should be served with wine sauce or raspberry vinegar, but that in some counties the sauce was made from sweetened melted butter, mixed with a little vinegar.

Cream the yeast and the sugar. Pour the water and milk over the yeast and pour the liquid onto the flour. Mix well and leave to rise in a warm place for 2 hours. Knead well and form into 8 dumplings. Leave them to stand for 10 minutes. Put into a large pan of boiling water, cover and boil for exactly 20 minutes. Serve at once with gravy, eating the dumplings with two forks. If liked, they may be eaten with melted butter and sugar, although this is not traditional in Norfolk.

Hard or Suffolk Dumplings

8 oz (225 g) plain flour   Pinch of salt
½ pint (300 ml) cold water

Hannah Glasse gave an eighteenth-century recipe for Hard Dumplings with the same plain ingredients as this recipe. She recommended that they should be prepared 'as big as a turkey's egg' and boiled for 30 minutes, preferably with a good piece of butter. She also recommended the addition of a few currants, and a final dressing of melted butter. In a second recipe she suggested the addition of butter to the dough.

These dumplings have become traditionally associated with Suffolk, and a correspondent, Dorothy Hall, has told me how they used to be made and eaten:

My mother used to make for my father what he called his Suffolk dumplings, he coming from Suffolk. She used to mix flour with some cold water and shape it into a ball, then put into a steamer and leave it to stand for a while. Then the steamer plus dumpling was put over a pan of boiling water and allowed to cook – to steam. When ready, it had blown up ever so much and my father used to pull it apart with two forks and put syrup upon it. When my mother and I had it, we put gravy from the meat on it. That was between 50 and 70 years ago. Some years ago I saw a very interesting comment on this recipe, but it was called a Sussex dumpling, made from 1 lb [450 g] of plain flour and ½ pint [300 ml] cold water, divided into 4 or 8 dumplings. The maker said it was 'light as love' and the secret was to leave the dumplings for several hours in a warm place, then throw them into a pan of fast boiling water and boil rapidly for 20–45 minutes according to size. They will be as light as a feather because flour and water mixed and left in heat will ferment.

Mix the flour and water together with the salt to make a firm dough. Roll with the hands to make 6 balls. Roll lightly in a little flour and put into a pan of fast-boiling water, cover and boil hard for 20 minutes. Serve hot with butter, gravy or syrup, tearing the dumplings slightly apart with two forks to let the steam out as soon as they are taken from the pan, so that they do not become heavy in the middle.

Savoury Herb Dumplings

Serves 4 or more

4 oz (100 g) self-raising flour
2 oz (50 g) shredded suet
Pinch of salt

2 teaspoons chopped mixed
  herbs or parsley

Suet dumplings are easy and quick to make. They are a perfect accompaniment to boiled salt beef, and go equally well in beef stews, or with boiled bacon. Small ones make a generous garnish for soup.

In Scotland these used to be known as Green Dumplings, and were made in spring with green hawthorn buds, nettle tips, grass, dandelion leaves, daisy stems, young corn shoots and turnip tops, indeed anything that tasted sweet and was not poisonous. The greenstuff was washed and chopped finely and worked into the dough until it was completely green.

Stir together the flour, suet and salt and add the herbs. Mix with just enough cold water to make a soft dough. Divide into 8 pieces and form into small balls. Add to the cooking liquid 20 minutes before serving time.

Derbyshire Oatmeal Dumplings

Serves 4–6

3 oz (75 g) medium oatmeal
3 oz (75 g) plain flour
Salt and pepper

1 small onion
1 oz (25 g) beef dripping

These dumplings have a pleasantly nutty flavour that goes well with a rich beef stew.

Stir together the oatmeal, flour and plenty of seasoning. Grate the onion finely. Melt the dripping and cook the onion in it for 3 minutes, until just golden. Stir the onion and dripping into the dry ingredients and add just a little cold water to bind the mixture. Form into 8 balls. Add to the stew 30 minutes before serving.

Lowestoft Buttons

4 oz (100 g) plain flour
6 fl oz (175 ml) milk
Salt and pepper

2 oz (50 g) butter
1 oz (25 g) fine white
  breadcrumbs

These little dumplings make a light supper or luncheon dish; they must be served very hot and freshly cooked. A similar recipe from the neighbouring county of Norfolk, recorded in 1765, was made with the addition of eggs, and eaten hot with 'a lump of fresh butter'. The writer remarked that they were called Drop Dumplings or Spoon Dumplings.

Sift the flour into a bowl and gradually add the milk to make a thick batter, which should just drop from a spoon when shaken. Season with salt and pepper and beat well. Have a large pan of boiling water ready and quickly drop in teaspoonfuls of batter. Cover and boil for 5 minutes. Drain in a colander and pile onto a hot dish.
  While the dumplings are cooking, prepare the crumb topping. Melt the butter in a small frying pan and stir in the breadcrumbs. Fry until golden and sprinkle over the hot dumplings.

Mrs Crowfort's Dumplings

Serves 4

2 eggs
4 oz (100 g) plain flour

8 tablespoons milk

These dumplings from Suffolk, 1863, are smaller versions of the boiled batter so popular in Victorian times. They were to be served with thick gravy made from the pan juices of roast meat.

Break the eggs into a bowl and work in the flour and milk to make a firm batter. Put into two pieces of cloth, tie firmly and put into a pan of boiling water. Boil for 45 minutes and serve hot with gravy.

Fashionable Apple Dumplings

1 lb (450 g) plain flour
2 teaspoons baking powder
3 oz (75 g) butter or lard

½ pint (300 ml) milk
4 large eating apples
Orange or lemon marmalade

In the middle of the nineteenth century these were still boiled in the old way in small knitted or closely-netted cloths. Eliza Acton recommended the former for 'the prettiest effect, which gives quite an ornamental appearance to an otherwise homely dish'. May Byron, writing in 1923, recommended covering the apples with a kind of scone dough, which gives very satisfactory results.

Sift the flour and baking powder together and rub in the butter or lard. Mix to a firm dough with the milk and roll out thinly. Cut into 4 large squares, that will enclose the apples. Core the apples without peeling them and place one on the centre of each piece of pastry. Fill the cavities with marmalade and then enclose each apple completely in the pastry, sealing all joins firmly. Tie into four floured cloths and put into a pan of boiling water. Boil for 1 hour and unroll carefully onto warm plates. Serve with hot apricot jam or custard.

Baked Apple Dumplings

4 medium-sized cooking apples
12 oz (350 g) shortcrust pastry
2 oz (50 g) caster or soft brown
   sugar

1 oz (25 g) butter
Pinch of ground mixed spice
2 oz (50 g) raisins or sultanas

When ovens came into popular use, baked fruit dumplings became popular, retaining the shape of the older, boiled dumpling, but enclosed in a shortcrust pastry. The apples are cored and the cavity filled with dried fruit, or mincemeat, sugar or honey, butter and spice. They used to be popular for shooting luncheons on farms. In Cornwall, clotted cream was spooned into each dumpling just before serving.

Peel and core the apples. Roll out the pastry and cut into 4 squares, each large enough to enclose an apple. Put an apple on the centre of each piece of pastry. Fill the cavities with sugar, butter, spice and raisins or sultanas. Draw up the edges of the pastry round each apple and press them together. Turn the apples over so that the joins come underneath. Put onto a floured baking sheet. Brush with a little beaten egg or milk. Bake at 400°F/200°C/Gas Mark 6 for 30 minutes. Sprinkle a little caster or icing sugar on them and serve with cream or Hard Sauce (see p. 201).

Hereford Apple and Orange Dumplings   *Serves 4*

12 oz (350 g) shortcrust pastry
1 teaspoon sugar
4 cooking apples
2 oz (50 g) sultanas
Grated rind of 1 orange
Milk for glazing
Caster sugar

Sauce
Juice of 1 orange
½ oz (15 g) cornflour
2 tablespoons orange
  marmalade
1 oz (25 g) light soft brown
  sugar

Mix pastry with the sugar and divide into four pieces. Roll out circles that will enclose the apples. Peel and core the apples and place one in the centre of each piece of pastry. Fill the apples with sultanas and orange rind. Bring the pastry up over the apples and seal firmly. Turn upside down on a baking sheet and decorate the tops with pastry leaves made from the trimmings. Brush with milk and sprinkle lightly with caster sugar. Bake at 400°F/200°C/Gas Mark 6 for 10 minutes, then at 350°F/180°C/Gas Mark 4 for 30 minutes.

Make the sauce by mixing the orange juice with enough water to make up ½ pint (300 ml). Mix a little of the liquid with the cornflour. Heat the orange juice with the marmalade and sugar until the sugar has dissolved. Stir in the cornflour and bring to the boil, stirring well. Simmer for 2 minutes and serve hot with the dumplings.

Shropshire Apple Cobs

Yet another variation on the baked dumplings is this tempting dish, which consists of peeled and cored apples filled with honey. These are placed on circles of shortcrust pastry and sprinkled with mixed spice. The apples are then covered with a lid of shortcrust pastry and baked until crisp. They are sent to table with a crown of 3 or 5 cloves stuck in the centre of each top.

Lady Savill's College Dumplings
Serves 4–6

2 tablespoons sugar
2 tablespoons fresh
  breadcrumbs
2 tablespoons shredded suet
2 tablespoons currants
Pinch of ground nutmeg

Grated rind and juice of
  ½ lemon
1 egg
Deep fat for frying
Caster sugar for sprinkling

These are also known as New College Puddings, and they are like the traditional suet-and-breadcrumb mixture made into filling puddings for the 'poor scholars' of Oxford and Cambridge colleges on special occasions (see Chapter 11). The New College Pudding is always fried in dumpling form. I have retained Lady Savill's method of measuring her early twentieth-century version, as it is so quick to use. The spoons should be heaped up.

Stir together the dry ingredients and mix with the lemon rind and juice. Mix with beaten egg and press together into 4–6 small balls. Fry in a wire basket in hot deep fat for about 6 minutes until golden, and serve sprinkled with sugar.

Light and Good Lemon Dumplings
Serves 4

10 oz (250 g) fine breadcrumbs
8 oz (225 g) shredded suet
1 oz (25 g) plain flour

Grated rind and juice of 1 large
  lemon
4 oz (100 g) caster sugar
3 eggs

This recipe received its glowing title from Eliza Acton who said in 1855 that 'they will be extremely light and delicate: if wished very sweet, more sugar must be added to them. The syrup of preserved ginger would be both a wholesome and appropriate sauce for them.'

Mix together the breadcrumbs, suet and flour. Mix the lemon rind and strained juice with the flour mixture and stir in the sugar and beaten eggs. Mix thoroughly and divide into 4 portions. Tie in well-floured cloths and boil for 1 hour. Serve with syrup from a jar of ginger.

Sir Robert Walpole's Dumplings with Wine Sauce

4 oz (100 g) shredded suet
3 oz (75 g) dry white
  breadcrumbs
4 oz (100 g) currants
1 oz (25 g) chopped mixed
  candied peel
Pinch of ground cinnamon
1 oz (25 g) sugar
1 egg and 1 egg yolk

Sauce
¼ pint (150 ml) sweet white
  wine
2 oz (50 g) unsalted butter
1 oz (25 g) sugar

These dumplings were recorded by Mrs Maciver of Edinburgh in Cookery and Pastry (1773). They bear a strong resemblance to a contemporary recipe for French Dumplings, and are a small, rich version of the Scots Clootie (cloth) Dumpling, so perhaps they have their origins in France, which contributed so much to Scots cookery. They certainly were popular in Walpole's Norfolk, and I recently talked to a young Norfolk woman who remembers her grandfather calling this dish Poor Man's Christmas Pudding. Despite the name, he enjoyed the spiced fruit dumplings with juices from the roast beef – a direct link with the savoury-and-sweet pottages of medieval times. The little dumplings were originally made in 'small nets, wrought of pack-thread', but today they are more easily enclosed in small pieces of cloth before boiling.

Put the suet, breadcrumbs, currants, peel, cinnamon and sugar into a bowl and mix well together. Add the egg and egg yolk and mix to a very stiff dough. Divide the mixture into four portions and form into balls. Cut four 8 in (20 cm) squares of clean white cloth and grease them lightly. Put a ball of dough into the centre of each piece and tie tightly, but allow room for expansion. Drop into a pan of boiling water and boil for 1 hour.

Prepare the sauce just before serving. Heat together the wine, butter and sugar over low heat until the sugar has dissolved. Untie the dumpling cloths and put the dumplings onto a warm serving plate. Pour over the hot sauce and serve at once.

Sweet Boiled Patties

Serves 6

8 oz (225 g) plain flour
3 oz (75 g) shredded suet

Pinch of salt
6 tablespoons jam

*Eliza Acton gave this recipe in 1855 for little jam dumplings, which
could be made with buttercrust, but she felt that suet made them
lighter. Use a strongly flavoured jam such as damson or raspberry
for the best contrast with the pastry.*

Stir together the flour, suet and salt and mix to a soft dough with a
little cold water. Divide into 12 pieces and roll out into circles. Put
some jam in the centre of each circle and mould the dough round
the filling so that it cannot escape. Put into a pan of boiling water,
cover and boil for 12 minutes. Drain and serve at once.

15 Pies and Tarts

But the pie, the pie of all pies, the quintessence of pie-ity is the apple pie. Firstly the crust. Let us settle down to this grave matter, the confection of crust.... There must be a serious touch in pie crust, solid but not cludgy, crisp but not powdery. To this day, floured hands and a wide apron seem to mark the summit of female powers. Their poetry, I admit, is interesting, their pictures admirable, but their apple pies show the master hand. Well might our cooks say: 'I care not who may make a nation's laws so long as I may make its pies'.

Edward Bunyard, that great fruit nurseryman, writing in the 1940s, might be surprised to see today's cooks making their pies with the aid of frozen pastry or packet mixes (often commercial fillings too) instead of rejoicing in the 'floured hands and wide apron', but still the pie and flan are popular dishes, showing that some effort has been made in the kitchen.

Pies have been great English favourites for centuries, and indeed the *Oxford English Dictionary* states that the pie 'is not known outside England'. This is somewhat misleading, for as early as the ninth century, the abbey of Fontenelle in France received dues of goose pies and chicken pies. Nevertheless, although the open flan is popular in some European countries, the pie with a top crust only seems to be peculiarly English. The plate pie, with crust top and bottom, does occur in some areas of France, probably sharing a common medieval ancestry.

The early popularity of English pies has been recorded in nursery circles: Simple Simon met a pieman, Little Jack Horner ate a Christmas pie (his 'plum' was in fact the deeds of valuable lands), and the king was delighted by his blackbird pie. Such pies were considered a great diversion at banquets, when a crust was baked and then placed over a dish of live birds. When the birds flew out, the men loosed their falcons to bring them down. Sometimes the pie would contain a dwarf to entertain the company with his tricks, including falling into a bowl of custard.

The earliest pies seem to have been made with a kind of hot water crust, ancestor of the one used today for pork, veal and game pies. The flour was mixed with hot butter and water or ale boiled together, and sometimes coloured with saffron or egg yolks. Some pastes were mixed with stock or cream, but basically a solid pastry was made that would stand without support in an oven, and formed a 'coffin' or 'coffer' for savoury contents. These pies would travel long distances, and the pastry formed a container for the meat like a pâté dish. Often the pastry was not eaten with the contents, but was discarded to be eaten by servants. Fine white flour was used, since barley meal crust was likely to crack, and rye crust was very dark. Gradualy, a finer wheat crust evolved, mixed cold with butter, water and eggs, which must have been similar to good flan pastry.

The Elizabethans were very fond of open dish tarts made with short, rich pastry. The Florentine, a particular favourite, was made with pastry so thin 'that ye may blow it up from the table'. It was filled with a mixture of chopped veal, kidney, dried fruits, spices and sugar, with the occasional addition of spinach. The bottom pastry was almost flat and the filling mounded in the centre. It was covered with another piece of pastry and baked, and then iced with rosewater and sugar. This finish, rather like our royal icing, continued until Victorian times on top-crust pies.

Rich shortcrust made with butter was prepared with eggs and flavoured with spices, and rolled out, like today's puff pastry, around layers of butter. It was then baked in sections, then sugared and served like a biscuit. Sir Hugh Platt gave this pastry the name of puff paste in 1603, and it was used for florentines and fruit tarts and, later, jam tarts. Its use continued in the eighteenth century for little sweet and savoury pies, which were sometimes fried.

The earlier pies had consisted of mixtures of meat sweetened with dried fruit or honey and spices, but by the beginning of the Georgian period meat savoury pies were not sweetened, and the sweet pie had a stronger identity of its own, although we have a relic of the sweetened savoury pie in mince pies. Early sweet pies contained artichoke hearts and potatoes with beef marrow, candied and dried fruits and spices, and were moistened with white wine and rosewater under the iced lid. The early standing (hot water crust) fruit pies gave way to open fruit tarts made with puff pastry that needed less time in the oven. Sometimes they were filled with whole fruit, but more often with a well-cooked, thick, heavily spiced and sweetened fruit purée, to which dried or candied fruit might be added. Flans were commonly made with a cream and egg filling, the name deriving from the medieval 'flawn' or 'flathon'.

The recipes in this chapter clearly show these early origins, although they may be made with today's prepared pastry. If a good sweet shortcrust is preferred, substitute 1 oz (25 g) fine semolina for the equivalent flour in a standard shortcrust pastry recipe. Add a little sugar and mix with an egg yolk and a little cold water for a crisp, sweet short pastry. The use of butter, lard or white fat is a matter of preference when making pastry. A mixture of butter and lard makes a well-flavoured short pastry, but professional cooks nowadays like to use hard block margarine, which resists the high temperature needed for baking (particularly puff pastry) and gives a lighter texture.

The crusts of fruit pies are not usually decorated before baking, probably because they used to be glazed with icing afterwards. The easiest way to finish a top-crust pie is by brushing with water and caster sugar before or during baking. The old type of icing can be prepared by mixing 4 oz (100 g) icing sugar to a stiff paste with a stiffly whisked egg white. Ten minutes before a pie is completely cooked, take it from the oven and leave to cool for 5 minutes. Spread the icing roughly on top and return to the oven for 10 minutes. Do not oversweeten the pie-filling if this finish is used.

Apple Pie

1 lb (450 g) cooking apples
8 oz (225 g) crisp eating apples
4 oz (100 g) sugar
1 teaspoon grated lemon rind

2 cloves or pinch of ground
   cinnamon
½ pint (300 ml) water
8 oz (225 g) shortcrust pastry
Caster sugar for sprinkling

The Romans developed several apple varieties in Britain from the native wild crabapple. The fruit was small, but sweeter than the wild fruit, and some varieties were kept for a winter use spread out in rows in lofts. Some of the earliest kitchen implements to be found are bone knives and corers that were used for apples (metal stained the fruit). One of the earliest named apples was the pearmain, recorded in the early thirteenth century, and by the fifteenth century there were pippins, bittersweets, blanderelles and pome- waters. The costard, a very large apple, was popular from the thirteenth to the seventeenth centuries, and was sold in London by coster (costard) mongers.

Fresh fruit in excess caused diarrhoea, and the skins often carried germs, so it was considered wise to cook the fruit. Apples were made into a purée for many dishes, including tarts, which were a great favourite with Elizabethan cooks. They made the apples into a purée with red wine, sugar, cinnamon and ginger. Apple pies can be made into two-crust plate pies, but the English favourite is a deep pie with a single crust. A mixture of cooking and eating apples gives the best result, with a mixture of textures and flavours, and a little grated lemon rind gives a subtle flavour. Some people like to put a couple of cloves in the pie, but a pinch of ground cinnamon may be more acceptable. In the early autumn a handful of blackberries goes well in apple pie.

Peel, core and slice the apples. Arrange in a 2-pint (1 l) pie dish, sprinkling with the sugar, lemon rind and spice. Add the water. Roll out the pastry to cover the apples. Make a small slit in the centre to allow steam to escape. Brush the lid with water and sprinkle with a little caster sugar to give an even coating. Bake at 400°F/200°C/Gas Mark 6 for 20 minutes. Reduce heat to 375°F/190°C/Gas Mark 5 and continue baking for 20 minutes. Serve warm with cream or custard.

Warden Pie
Serves 4–6

8 oz (225 g) sweet shortcrust
   pastry
5 large pears
2 oz (50 g) sugar

Grated rind and juice of
   1 lemon
Blade of mace
Milk for glazing
1 tablespoon caster sugar

Wardens were the old English winter pears, invaluable for their keeping qualities. Because they were larger and much harder than other English pears and the imported French varieties, they were often described as a different fruit, and the phrase 'wardens and pears' often appears in old books. Hard fruit, such as wardens and quinces, was often baked for long hours in sweetened wine or cider to make it palatable, and it had to be pre-cooked before being included in pies. Today, we rarely include pears in pies, perhaps because modern commercial fruit is rather soft and sweet, and lacks the necessary body and fragrance, although in France one sometimes sees a spectacular tart containing whole pears complete with stalk. For this modern version of an old favourite, look for a firm well-flavoured pear.

Line an 8 in (20 cm) greased pie plate with half the pastry. Peel the pears and cut them into quarters. Take out the cores and arrange the pears in the pastry case. Sprinkle with half the sugar. Sprinkle the lemon rind and juice over the pears. Put the pear peelings and cores into a pan with just enough water to cover. Add the mace. Simmer until the pear peelings are tender. Strain the liquid and stir in the remaining sugar. Simmer again until the liquid forms a thin syrup. Cool and pour over the pears. Cover with the remaining pastry and seal the edges well by pinching with finger and thumb. Brush with a little milk and bake at 375°F/190°C/Gas Mark 5 for 25 minutes. Sprinkle with caster sugar and continue baking for 5 minutes. Serve with thick cream.

Kentish Apple Pie

1½ lb (675 g) cooking apples
4 oz (100 g) sugar
4 cloves
6 tablespoons water
4 oz (100 g) Cheddar cheese

Pinch of ground nutmeg
Sprinkle of white pepper
1 teaspoon caster sugar
8 oz (225 g) shortcrust pastry

There is a saying 'An apple pie without some cheese is like a kiss without a squeeze', and it is an old tradition to eat a piece of mature cheese with a wedge of apple plate pie. This recipe, however, combines the two most successfully.

Peel the apples and cut them into quarters. Remove the cores and cut the apples into thick slices. Put a layer of apples into a 2 pint (1 l) pie dish and sprinkle with sugar. Continue adding apples and sugar in layers, tucking in the cloves halfway down the layers. Pour in the water. Cut the cheese in very thin slices and place over the apples. Sprinkle with nutmeg, pepper and caster sugar. Cover with the pastry and bake at 375°F/190°C/Gas Mark 5 for 45 minutes.

Cherry Pie

Serves 6

12 oz (350 g) shortcrust pastry
1½ lb (675 g) ripe black cherries

4 oz (100 g) sugar
2 tablespoons tapioca flakes

Nobody seems to know why, but a cherry pie is always supposed to be round. Perhaps this dates from the days when pies were taken to be baked in communal ovens, and the shapes would help to identify the different types (pies were often decorated with initials, leaves or other patterns for the same reason). To help thicken the filling, I like to add some tapioca flakes, which do not flavour the pie but give a jelly-like finish to the fruit juices.

Line an 8 in (20 cm) greased pie plate with half the pastry. Stone the cherries and mix them with the sugar and tapioca flakes. Put into the pastry case and top with the remaining pastry. Seal the edges firmly and cut a slit in the top. Bake at 400°F/200°C/Gas Mark 6 for 20 minutes, and then at 350°F/180°C/Gas Mark 4 for 20 minutes. Serve with sweetened whipped cream flavoured with brandy.

Fried Apple Pies

1 lb (450 g) eating apples
4 tablespoons water
3 oz (75 g) sugar
½ cinnamon stick
Grated rind of 1 orange

½ teaspoon ground dill seed
1 tablespoon rosewater
8 oz (225 g) puff pastry
Deep oil for frying

This eighteenth-century recipe for little apple turnovers is unusual in both ingredients and preparation. The apples were pippins, flavoured with cinnamon, orange rind, rosewater and dill, perhaps considered to be a digestive that would offset the richness of fried pastry.

Peel and core the apples and slice them thinly. Put into a pan with the water, sugar, cinnamon, orange rind and dill. Simmer for about 20 minutes until the fruit is soft. Leave to cool and then remove the cinnamon stick. Stir in the rosewater and mash the apples lightly to break up the slices. Roll out the pastry and cut into twelve 3 in (7.5 cm) squares. Put a little apple in the middle of each square and fold over the corners to form triangular pies. Seal the edges firmly with a fork. Fry in hot oil until crisp and golden on both sides, frying only three or four pies at a time. Drain well before serving hot.

Westmorland Three Deckers

1 lb (450 g) shortcrust pastry
1 lb (450 g) apples, plums or
  blackberries

4 oz (100 g) demerara sugar
Caster sugar for sprinkling

The inner layer of pastry in this dish is surrounded by syrupy fruit, and it is particularly good with strongly flavoured autumn fruit.

Roll out the pastry and cut out three 8 in (20 cm) circles. Line a greased 7 in (17.5 cm) pie plate with one pastry circle. Peel, core, and slice the apples (if plums are used, cut them in half and remove the stones). Arrange half the fruit in the pastry case and sprinkle with half the demerara sugar. Cover with another layer of pastry. Add the remaining fruit, and sprinkle with the rest of the demerara sugar. Cover with the third pastry circle and seal the edges firmly. Bake at 375°F/190°C/Gas Mark 5 for 1 hour. Sprinkle with caster sugar and serve hot.

Million Pie   *Serves 4–6*

8 oz (225 g) shortcrust pastry
2 oz (50 g) jam
1 lb (450 g) prepared vegetable
  marrow

1 egg
Pinch of ground nutmeg
1½ tablespoons sugar
Currants or raisins (optional)

*A 'million' was a type of vegetable marrow, which used to be treated
as a fruit rather than a vegetable. Because of its size, a marrow was a
useful bulk ingredient for hungry families, and its rather bland
flavour was improved with spices and dried fruit. One version of
this dish is simply made with marrow slices cooked with sugar,
raisins and water in a pie dish until tender, then covered with a
pastry crust. The marrow is very similar to the pumpkin, and it
could be that this recipe, which only appears in Norfolk, is a relic of
an earlier favourite.*

*To prepare the marrow, peel away the skin and remove the pith
and seeds. Cut the marrow in pieces and weigh out 1 lb (450 g)
before cooking.*

Line an 8 in (20 cm) greased sandwich tin or pie plate with the
pastry. Keep the pastry trimmings to decorate the top of the tart.
Spread the pastry with a thin layer of jam. Boil the marrow in just
enough water to prevent burning until it is soft. Drain off all liquid
and leave the marrow until cold. Add the egg and nutmeg to the
marrow and beat together with a fork until smooth. A few currants
or raisins may be added to the marrow filling if liked. Put into the
pastry case and sprinkle with a little more nutmeg. Cover with a
lattice of pastry strips. Bake at 400°F/200°C/Gas Mark 6 for 10–15
minutes, then at 350°F/180°C/Gas Mark 4 for 15 minutes until the
pastry is golden. Serve hot or cold.

Pumpkin Pie

The pumpkin was introduced from France in Tudor times,
although various kinds of gourds had been used in stews in
medieval times. The pumpkin was hollowed out and stuffed with
apples before baking, and this dish was enjoyed by poor people.
Richer folk sliced the pumpkin and fried it with herbs and spices,
then beat it with sugar and eggs. This mixture was put into a pastry
case with layers of apples and currants. The dish was reproduced
in America by the early colonists and became a national favourite.

Poor people began to imitate the pie with simple mixtures of apples and pumpkins, which provided useful bulk, but the pumpkin was never really popular and was replaced in British gardens by the marrow.

Buckinghamshire Cherry Bumpers

Serves 6

8 oz (225 g) shortcrust pastry
1 lb (450 g) black cherries

2 oz (50 g) granulated sugar
Caster sugar for sprinkling

The black cherry orchards of Buckinghamshire were once famous, and Cherry Pie Sunday at the end of August celebrated the end of cherry picking. These turnovers are delicious hot or cold, and an inn at Cadsden, near Princes Risborough, used to sell thousands of them with ale.

Roll out the pastry about ¼ in (6 mm) thick and cut into 4 in (10 cm) circles. Stone the cherries and sprinkle them with the granulated sugar. Heap the centre of the pastry circles with cherries and fold them over into turnovers, pinching the edges firmly together. Bake at 400°F/200°C/Gas Mark 6 for 30 minutes and sprinkle with caster sugar.

Norfolk Lent Pies

Serves 6

3 hard-boiled eggs
3 oz (75 g) currants
3 oz (75 g) stoned raisins
1 large eating apple
1 oz (25 g) dark soft brown sugar
1 oz (25 g) chopped mixed
  candied peel

½ teaspoon ground ginger
½ teaspoon ground cinnamon
4 tablespoons melted unsalted
  butter
12 oz (350 g) shortcrust pastry
Caster sugar for sprinkling

This seems to be very rich for Lenten fare, but the spicy filling is delicious.

Chop the egg whites finely and sieve the yolks. Mix with the currants. Chop the raisins and the peeled, cored apple. Mix with the currants, sugar, peel, spices and butter. Line a greased 7 in (17.5 cm) pie plate with half the pastry. Spread the filling on top and cover with the remaining pastry. Pinch the edges together firmly. Bake at 400°F/200°C/Gas Mark 6 for 25 minutes. Brush with water and sprinkle thickly with caster sugar. Continue baking for 10 minutes.

Kentish Pudding Pie

1 lb (450 g) shortcrust pastry
1½ pints (900 ml) milk
4 oz (100 g) unsalted butter

2 oz (50 g) sugar
2 eggs
Pinch of ground nutmeg
2 oz (50 g) currants

Sometimes known as Folkestone Pudding Pie, it evolved as a Lenten dish, since meat pies could not be eaten during that period, and people became tired of fish. The filling forms a kind of rice custard dotted with currants, and the pie is made in a pie dish, not a shallow tin.

Line a greased pie dish with the pastry. Bring the milk to the boil and sprinkle with the rice. Simmer for 15 minutes, stirring well. Cream three-quarters of the butter and work in the sugar and the eggs. Cool the milk and rice to lukewarm and beat into the butter mixture. Flavour with nutmeg. Leave until cool and then put into the pastry case. Sprinkle with currants and dot with flakes of the remaining butter. Bake at 350°F/180°C/Gas Mark 4 for 45 minutes. Serve hot or cold.

Blackcurrant Saucer Pies

Serves 4

Pastry
10 oz (300 g) plain flour
Pinch of salt
5 oz (125 g) margarine and lard
  mixed
1 oz (25 g) caster sugar

Filling
12 oz (350 g) blackcurrants
3 oz (75 g) caster sugar
Pinch of cinnamon
Caster sugar for sprinkling

Saucers, which were originally shallow dishes for serving sauces, and not accompaniments to teacups, were also convenient receptacles for baking individual portions of food. Large, thick saucers were used for batters and for small pies, but today these may be made in large individual Yorkshire Pudding tins. Cherries, raspberries and blackberries make equally good fillings.

Sift together the flour and salt. Rub in the fat until the mixture is like fine breadcrumbs. Stir in the sugar and add just enough cold water to make a firm dough. Roll out pastry and cut into 8 circles to fit 4 old, thick saucers. Grease saucers. Put a circle of pastry on each saucer. Mix the fruit, sugar and spice, and divide between the pieces of pastry. Cover with pastry lids and seal edges, pressing with a fork. Bake at 375°F/190°C/Gas Mark 5 for 30 minutes. Sprinkle with caster sugar and serve with cream.

Mince Pies

Makes 18 pies

1 lb (450 g) shortcrust pastry
1 lb (450 g) fruit mincemeat

White of egg
1 oz (25 g) caster sugar

Fruit mincemeat was originally made with finely chopped meat, dried fruit and spices. The combination of savoury and sweet was typical of medieval pottages, and spices served to disguise less-than-perfect meat. Even up to the beginning of the twentieth century, fruit mincemeat recipes included meat, usually boiled beef or ox tongue, but this has now been replaced by suet. Spiced dishes with dried fruit were widely enjoyed on feast days, particularly at Christmas time when they symbolized the Eastern offerings of the Three Kings. The original mince pies were shaped in an oval like a crib, and were often iced with a kind of royal icing made from egg whites and fine sugar baked in a low oven. It is traditional to eat a mince pie for each of the twelve days of Christmas to ensure happy months all through the year. They are particularly delicious hot with brandy butter or rum butter slipped under the lid just before serving.

Puff pastry may be used for mince pies, but this tends to be rather fatty and is only suitable if the pies are to be eaten when freshly baked.

Line 18 greased tart tins with the pastry. Put a good spoonful of mincemeat into each one. Cover each tart with a pastry circle and press the edges together firmly. Brush over with white of egg and sprinkle with sugar. Bake at 425°F/220°C/Gas Mark 7 for 15 minutes. Serve with cream, brandy butter or rum butter.

Cumberland Nickies

12 oz (350 g) shortcrust pastry   3 oz (75 g) dark soft brown sugar
8 oz (225 g) currants   1 tablespoon dark rum

The name of these currant pies comes from the traditional decoration of light cuts or 'nicks' made across the top lid of pastry. The edges of the pies should be absolutely plain, not pinched or given a fancy trim. Sometimes the Nickies were made with dough, but pastry was preferred by many farmers. The currants have to be very lightly moistened. This can be done with water, but Cumberland people love rum, traditionally imported to their ports from the West Indies, and these are often known as Rum Nickies.

Line a 7 in (17.5 cm) greased pie plate with half the pastry. Mix the currants and sugar and moisten with the rum. Spread on the pastry and cover with the second piece of pastry. Press the edges together firmly, but do not pinch or decorate. With a sharp knife, make light cuts to and fro across the top. Bake at 400°F/200°C/Gas Mark 6 for 30 minutes. Serve hot or cold.

Fruit Bakestone Cake

12 oz (350 g) fresh fruit   ¼ teaspoon ground nutmeg
½ oz (15 g) butter   8 oz (225 g) shortcrust pastry
2 oz (50 g) light soft brown sugar

The bakestone is one of the most ancient of all cooking utensils – simply a flat stone heated in the fire, on which bannocks, flapjacks, drop scones and other primitive breads could be baked. Today a heavy iron griddle or frying pan may be used instead. This cake, made with fresh fruit, is eaten hot with cream. Use juicy apples for the filling or mix them with blackberries or halved plums.

Peel, core and finely slice apples, or halve plums if used. Put the butter into a saucepan and add the fruit, sugar and nutmeg. Cover and stew gently, stirring frequently to prevent sticking, for about 10 minutes. The fruit should still be fairly firm and not pulpy, as it cooks a little more on the griddle. Divide the pastry in two and roll each piece into a 7 in (18 cm) circle. Moisten the edges of one circle and spread the fruit on top to within about ½ in (1.25 cm) from the edge. Place the other circle on top and press the edges lightly together. Brush a griddle or heavy frying pan with a little lard before heating. To test the heat sprinkle a little flour on the surface. If it turns golden brown in a minute, the heat is sufficient. Lift the cake onto the griddle, using a large fish slice and cook each side for about 10 minutes until golden brown. Dredge with sugar and serve in wedges with cream or custard.

Goggs' Lemon Pudding

Serves 4–6

3 oz (75 g) unsalted butter
4 oz (100 g) sugar
4 eggs
Grated rind and juice of
    1 lemon

3 oz (75 g) candied peel
8 oz (225 g) puff pastry

This recipe came from the 1865 notebook of Mrs Julia Spurrell of (appropriately named) Pudding Norton Hall, in Norfolk, to which 'Goggs' contributed a number of recipes. If whole peel is not available, use ready-chopped mixed candied peel, although the texture is rather soft and the flavour is not as well-defined as the old-fashioned variety.

Put the butter and sugar into a saucepan and stir over low heat until the butter has melted and the sugar has dissolved. Remove from the heat. Beat the eggs lightly with a fork and whisk into the sugar mixture. Add the lemon rind and juice to the sugar mixture and stir until well blended. Cut the candied peel into matchstick-thin strips. Line an 8 in (20 cm) greased flan tin with the pastry and bake blind at 425°F/220°C/Gas Mark 7 for 15 minutes. Arrange the strips of candied peel in the bottom of the pastry case and pour in the lemon mixture. Reduce heat to 375°F/190°C/Gas Mark 5 and continue baking for 25 minutes.

Cheesecake

4 oz (100 g) plain flour	2 eggs
Pinch of salt	1 teaspoon grated lemon rind
2½ oz (65 g) unsalted butter	2 teaspoons cornflour
Juice of 1½ lemons	2 tablespoons double cream
8 oz (225 g) soft curd cheese	1 tablespoon melted butter
2 oz (50 g) caster sugar	2 oz (50 g) raisins

Cheese tarts were recorded in 1265 when the Countess of Leicester spent money on 'cheese for tarts'. This was a rich, soft cheese, which was pounded in a mortar before being mixed with egg yolks, ginger, cinnamon and sugar to make a tart filling. In the fifteenth century the cheese was sometimes mixed with milk to a creamy consistency, or tarts were made with green cheese, which was soft. Occasionally, meat and dried fruit were added. The spiced cheese tarts of medieval times gradually gave way to curd tarts, which became known as cheesecakes in the seventeenth century. Fresh curds were mixed with eggs, spices and sometimes currants. By the middle of the seventeenth century, some recipes contained no cheese or curds, but were a custard mixture of sweetened eggs, butter, flour, cream and spices. A later lemon cheesecake was in fact filled with a mixture of lemon peel, egg yolks, sugar and butter, now known as lemon curd, although some people still call this confection lemon cheese. Some small cakes became known as cheesecakes, but these were little tarts filled with a lemon-flavoured spongecake mixture dotted with currants, which imitated the appearance of the curd tarts of former years. Today's popular cheesecake is a creamy unbaked affair on a biscuit crust base, but this is a modern American invention. The best American cheesecakes are, however, closely allied to those that remain in some European countries and are rich baked curd cheese mixtures. This recipe comes from Yorkshire and has a sharp creamy filling.

If curd cheese is not available, cottage cheese may be used, but the result is not so rich; the cottage cheese must be sieved.

Sift the flour and salt, and rub in the butter. Add the juice of ½ lemon and just enough cold water to make a firm dough. Roll out to line a 9 in (22.5 cm) greased tin. Bake blind at 425°F/220°C/Gas Mark 7 for 10 minutes. Sieve the cheese and mix with sugar, beaten eggs, lemon rind and the remaining lemon juice. Beat until smooth and then add the cornflour mixed with cream. Fold in the melted butter. Pour into pastry case and sprinkle on the raisins. Bake at 350°F/180°C/Gas Mark 4 for 30 minutes. Serve cold.

Lemon Cheesecake
Serves 4–6

Grated rind and juice of 1 large
   lemon
4 oz (100 g) caster sugar
4 eggs and 2 egg yolks

4 oz (100 g) unsalted butter
3 tablespoons double cream
6 oz (150 g) shortcrust pastry

There are many recipes for lemon cheescake in manuscript books, which are in fact versions of today's lemon curd (popularly called lemon cheese until about 1950). The use of the words 'curd' and 'cheese' point to the resemblance in texture of this pie filling to the earlier one made from cheese curds. The recipes indicate that the lemon cheese was not stored for use as a spread or cake filling as is now the practice, but was baked immediately in a pastry case. This Norfolk recipe of 1829 is a little unusual in including cream among the ingredients, and there is only a light flavouring of lemon. The original recipe recommended that the lemon mixture could be cooked over a 'slow fire' or baked in a crust.

Put the lemon rind and juice into a bowl with the sugar, eggs and egg yolks, and beat well together. Heat the butter gently until melted. Remove from the heat and stir in the cream. Stir into the lemon mixture and mix thoroughly. Line a 7 in (17.5 cm) greased sandwich tin with the pastry and pour in the lemon mixture. Bake at 375°F/190°C/Gas Mark 5 for 30 minutes. Serve hot or cold.

Old English Cheesecake
Serves 4–6

8 oz (225 g) shortcrust pastry
2 oz (50 g) butter
12 oz (350 g) soft curd cheese
3 oz (75 g) caster sugar
2 eggs

1 tablespoon brandy
2 tablespoons single cream
Pinch of ground mixed spice
2 oz (50 g) seedless raisins

Line an 8 in (20 cm) greased flan tin with the pastry. Prick with a fork and bake at 350°F/180°C/Gas Mark 4 for 30 minutes. Leave to cool. Cut the butter into pieces and cream with the cheese and sugar. Work in the eggs, brandy, cream and spice. Mix until smooth. Stir in the raisins. Put into the pastry case. Bake at 325°F/170°C/Gas Mark 3 for 40 minutes. Serve cold.

Jam Tart

8 oz (225 g) shortcrust pastry   6 oz (150 g) jam

The jam tart has always been a country favourite, being particularly useful for making the best of the oddments of pastry at the end of baking day. A simple jam tart has one type of jam filling, but housewives took great pride in fitting in as many differently coloured jams as possible. Four kinds of jam were normal, eight made a good show, and twelve jams made a triumphant tart. The different kinds of jam were separated by strips of pastry, and in the north of England, where women take particular pride in their baking skills, there were many decorative patterns with special names. The Red Cross was made with redcurrant jelly surrounded by lemon curd; the twelve-jam tart arranged in a star-shape of pastry was an Epiphany. The Well was useful for using up a small quantity of jam in the centre, surrounded by circles of one or more jams in constrasting colours.

Line an 8 in (20 cm) greased pie dish with pastry, and spread the jam in the base. Roll out the pastry trimmings and arrange in a pattern on the jam. Bake at 400°F/200°C/Gas Mark 6 for 30 minutes. Serve hot or cold.

Thame Tart

A sophisticated version of the jam tart was invented by John Fothergill, a famous inn proprietor who entertained Oxford undergraduates in the 1930s. This consists of a crisp pre-baked pastry case containing a thick layer of raspberry jam, topped by a layer of lemon curd and finished with a layer of thick cream. The combination of the three flavours and textures is superb.

Sussex Bailiff's Bliss

Serves 6

12 oz (350 g) sweet shortcrust
    pastry
4 oz (100 g) ground almonds
2 oz (50 g) caster sugar
2 oz (50 g) icing sugar

2 oz (50 g) stoned raisins
2 oz (50 g) glacé cherries
2 oz (50 g) walnut halves
3 eggs

The duller name for this Hastings pudding is Celebration Tart. There is a story that the tart was first served at the celebration banquet that followed the granting of the charter to the town of Hastings by Elizabeth I in 1588, when the bailiff became the first mayor of the town.

Line a greased 7 in (17.5 cm) flan tin or sponge sandwich tin with half the pastry. Mix together the almonds, caster sugar and icing sugar. Chop the raisins, cherries and walnuts and stir into the almonds. Mix well with the beaten eggs. Put into the pastry case and cover with the second piece of pastry. Bake at 425°F/220°C/Gas Mark 7 for 25 minutes. Serve with warm double cream.

Crit Tarts

Makes 18 tarts

8 oz (225 g) crit
4 oz (100 g) currants
4 oz (100 g) finely chopped
  apples
4 oz (100 g) cooked rice

2 oz (50 g) dark soft brown sugar
1 teaspoon ground nutmeg
1 teaspoon ground ginger
1 lb (450 g) puff pastry

Crit is also known as scratchings, cracklings or fritters, and consists of the crisp brown pieces of fat left when fat has been rendered down. These little crunchy morsels have traditionally been a tasty snack when sprinkled with salt. In the days when a housewife rendered down the fat from her cottage pig to make fine lard, these little pieces were always left in the pan, and were often worked into fruitcake mixtures or made into these little tarts, which are a cousin of mince pies.

Now that many households buy large pieces of meat for the freezer, it is easy to make crit again from the surplus fat. Cut the fat (pork and beef are nicest) into small pieces and put into a roasting tin. Either heat on top of the stove or in a low oven until fat runs. Keep pouring off this fat into a bowl until no more runs into the pan (this fat is excellent for pastry and fruit cakes). The little brown pieces of crisp fat that are left are the ones to use for tart filling.

Mix together the crit, currants, apples, rice, sugar and spices. Line 18 greased tart tins with the pastry (or make one large tart if preferred). Fill with currant mixture and cover with pastry. Bake at 400°F/200°C/Gas Mark 6 for 20 minutes until the pastry is risen and golden. Serve hot or cold.

Treacle Tart

8 oz (225 g) shortcrust pastry
8 tablespoons golden syrup
2 teaspoons lemon juice

2 oz (50 g) fresh white
 breadcrumbs
Pinch of ground ginger

Although this tart is a great favourite, and seems to be part of a long kitchen heritage, it is in fact a comparatively recent addition to English tables, as golden syrup was not made until the 1880s. Perhaps a clue to its origin lies in the old way of making gingerbread by mixing breadcrumbs with honey and spice. Many people flavour the crumbs-and-syrup tart filling with a pinch of ground ginger and lemon juice, and some nineteenth century tarts were made with dried fruit, peel and thick treacle, so perhaps festive gingerbread was a delicious memory and somebody decided that the mixture would taste just as good in a pastry case. Cornish Treacle Tart is made with the filling enclosed by two layers of pastry.

Line an 8 in (20 cm) greased pie plate with pastry. Mix the syrup and lemon juice and put into the pastry case. Mix the breadcrumbs and ginger and put onto the syrup. Bake at 375°F/190°C/Gas Mark 5 for 25 minutes. Serve hot or cold with cream.

Norfolk Treacle Tart

8 oz (225 g) shortcrust pastry
6 tablespoons golden syrup
Grated rind of 1 lemon

½ oz (15 g) butter
3 tablespoons single cream
2 eggs

I have always preferred this version of a treacle tart, which is less sweet and cloying than the kind made with breadcrumbs. The filling sets into a kind of lemon custard that is delicious. The neighbouring county of Suffolk favours a similar dish without the cream and this is known as a Treacle Custard (in East Anglia, custard tarts are usually known as custards). Both are equally good made with the earlier black treacle instead of golden syrup. Lady Freyberg, in her additions to her mother's (Lady Jekyll's) cookery book, Kitchen

Essays, gives a variation of this recipe. She says it is about 100 years old and has the designation Walpole House Treacle Tart – an interesting name in view of the very long association of the Walpole family with Norfolk.

Line a 7 in (17.5 cm) greased flan ring or sponge sandwich tin with the pastry. Warm the syrup until thin but not hot. Remove from the heat and gently stir in the lemon rind, butter, cream and beaten eggs. Pour into the pastry case and bake at 350°F/180°C/Gas Mark 4 for 40 minutes until the filling is set and lightly browned.

Custard Tart

Serves 4–6

8 oz (225 g) shortcrust pastry
½ pint (300 ml) creamy milk
2 eggs and 1 egg yolk

1 oz (25 g) caster sugar
Ground nutmeg

Custard tarts have been favourites for centuries, but today they mainly appear in country shops. When they are made at home, it is important to prepare the custard with creamy milk or, preferably, single cream to give a smooth richness that contrasts with crisp pastry. I like the simple nutmeg flavouring, but in earlier times the custard filling was often flavoured with cinnamon and orange-flower or rosewater in addition to the sprinkling of nutmeg.

Line an 8 in (20 cm) greased flan ring or sponge sandwich tin with the pastry, and bake blind at 400°F/200°C/Gas Mark 6 for 15 minutes. Put the milk into a saucepan and bring to the boil. Beat the eggs, egg yolk and sugar together and whisk in the milk gradually. Strain into the pastry case and sprinkle with nutmeg. Bake at 325°F/170°C/Gas Mark 3 for 35 minutes until the custard is set. It will become firmer as it becomes cold, but is nicest to eat while still slightly warm. Accompany with cream and/or fresh soft fruit such as raspberries.

Duke of Cambridge Tart

8 oz (225 g) shortcrust pastry
2 oz (50 g) chopped mixed
  candied peel
2 oz (50 g) glacé cherries

1 oz (25 g) angelica
3 oz (75 g) unsalted butter
3 oz (75 g) caster sugar
2 egg yolks

This tart was named after the seventh son of George III, uncle of Queen Victoria. The filling is just as good in small tartlets.

Line a 7 in (17.5 cm) greased flan ring or sponge sandwich tin with the pastry. Sprinkle the base with chopped peel. Cut the cherries and angelica in small pieces and sprinkle on the base. Put the butter, sugar and egg yolks into a small pan and bring gently to the boil, beating with a wooden spoon. When boiling, pour over the fruit in the pastry case. Bake at 375°F/190°C/Gas Mark 5 for 40 minutes. Serve warm with cream.

16 Sauces

The English have suffered for a long time from the jibe of Signor Francesco Caraccioli that we have 'sixty different religious sects, but only one sauce'. Certainly, we do not have the wide range of sauces offered by our continental neighbours, but, in fact, most of theirs are variations on classic themes, and many lack the sheer inspiration of those few English sauces of which we can be proud. Who does not enjoy the tingling bite of horseradish sauce with rare roast beef, the smoothness of redcurrant jelly with mutton, and the unexpectedness of green gooseberry sauce with mackerel?

In the sweet pudding department, the sauce range is similarly limited but good. Sadly, a blanket of packet custard seems to have become the obligatory accompaniment to English sweet courses. Many puddings do indeed welcome the sweet creaminess of custard, but it must be made with fresh eggs and milk, and this takes little time or trouble. Pouring cream, whipped cream and clotted cream are perfect and easy to serve with hot and cold puddings, but I find the habit of serving ice cream with hot puddings and pies unattractive, particularly if the ice-cream is of the over-sweet commercial variety which has never made contact with eggs or milk, let alone cream.

Wine sauces and jam sauces are particularly good partners for steamed and baked puddings, although melted jam or golden syrup may substitute occasionally if time is short. The great English pudding sauce, however, is almost certainly Hard Sauce. Usually made only once a year to accompany Christmas pudding and mince pies, it is equally delicious with many other puddings and pies. Through the last three centuries housewives have endlessly experimented with this sauce, choosing brandy, rum or sherry to partner rich butter and sugar. Sometimes the sugar is rich, dark and brown, and sometimes the best double-refined, finely ground to resemble today's caster and icing sugars. Some women added ground almonds, favourite spices, grated citrus fruit rind and juice; others whisked the ingredients with egg whites or cream, but all of them put an individual mark on this favourite sauce.

Custard Sauce

1 pint (600 ml) creamy milk	2 eggs
1 vanilla pod	1 oz (25 g) caster sugar

This takes no longer than packet custard to make but is far more delicious. If the vanilla pod is split, it will shed tiny black flecks into the milk, but the flavour will be much stronger.

Put the milk into a pan with the vanilla pod and bring just to boiling point. Leave to stand for 5 minutes and then remove the vanilla pod. Beat the eggs with the sugar and pour on the milk. Mix well and put through a strainer. Put into a bowl over hot water or into the top of a double saucepan and stir over low heat until the mixture will coat the back of a spoon. Take off the heat and stir occasionally for 2–3 minutes. Serve hot or cold.

Rich Vanilla Sauce

7 fl oz (200 ml) single cream
½ vanilla pod
2 oz (50 g) caster sugar

3 eggs and 3 egg yolks
2 teaspoons white rum

This sauce is very rich, and is excellent hot or cold with light sponge puddings, mousses and ices.

Put the cream, split vanilla pod and sugar into a bowl over hot water and heat gently for 15 minutes. Separate the eggs and put all the yolks into a basin. Remove the vanilla pod from the cream and pour the cream onto the eggs, beating enough to blend well. Return to the bowl over hot water and stir over heat until the mixture is like thick cream. Whisk the egg whites to stiff peaks. Pour the cream onto the whites, folding in the mixture until it is completely incorporated. Stir in the rum.

Chocolate Sauce

¼ pint (150 ml) water
4 oz (100 g) caster sugar

2 oz (50 g) cocoa

The best kind of chocolate sauce is dark and syrupy, and those that contain milk or cereal thickening never seem quite right to the true chocolate lover. This recipe is very easy, and very rich, and makes the perfect accompaniment to ice creams, mousses and sponge puddings. It is worth making a double quantity, as the sauce stores well in the refrigerator or freezer.

Put the water and sugar into a pan and stir over low heat until the sugar has dissolved. Bring to the boil and simmer for 1 minute. Tip in the cocoa and bring back to the boil, whisking all the time, until the sauce is smooth (a wire whisk is the best implement to use). Serve warm or cold. Stir the sauce occasionally as it cools, for it will thicken.

Wine Sauce

¼ pint (150 ml) sherry or
  madeira
½ oz (15 g) unsalted butter

½ (15 g) arrowroot
½ oz (15 g) caster sugar

Eighteenth-century wine sauces were a mixture of butter, sugar and wine warmed together. By 1855 Eliza Acton suggested a mixture of lemon-flavoured syrup with butter, a little flour for thickening, and sherry, madeira or 'good white wine', which gave a better flavour and was less rich. Florence White in Good Things in England *(1932) suggested the substitute of port wine and the addition of lemon juice, grated nutmeg and additional sweetening. She also gave an alternative, substituting orange rind and juice for the lemon. In other words, Wine Sauce was subject to the whim of the cook and the availability of ingredients. This simple version is excellent with steamed puddings and dumplings.*

Put the sherry or madeira into a small saucepan. Mix the butter and arrowroot together. Warm the liquid very gently and when lukewarm, add the butter and arrowroot. Heat and stir gently until the mixture thickens and clears. Stir in the sugar and serve hot.

Sherry Sauce

¼ pint (150 ml) water
1 oz (25 g) caster sugar
3 fl oz (75 ml) sweet sherry

1 tablespoon bramble jelly
½ teaspoon lemon juice

This sauce is very good with baked custard or custard-based dishes such as Bread and Butter Pudding (see p. 153).

Put the water and sugar into a pan and simmer for 10 minutes. Add the remaining ingredients and bring to the boil. Strain and serve hot.

Goodwood Sauce

2 oz (50 g) unsalted butter
3 oz (75 g) icing sugar,
  sieved

3 fl oz (75 ml) sweet white
  wine
3 fl oz (75 ml) brandy

This late-Victorian sauce is a very special version of Hard Sauce and it is perfect for Christmas pudding. The sauce should be made two or three hours before serving and be well-chilled before it is needed.

Cream the butter and sugar very thoroughly until light and fluffy. Add the wine and brandy little by little, whipping gently, until completely mixed. Put into the refrigerator or a cold place for 2–3 hours until well chilled.

Hard Sauce

4 oz (100 g) unsalted butter
4 oz (100 g) caster sugar

1 oz (25 g) ground almonds
1 tablespoon brandy

Sometimes known as Brandy Butter, this sauce was certainly in use in the early eighteenth century. It is the usual accompaniment to Christmas pudding, or others made with plenty of dried fruit and spice. The almonds are sometimes omitted, but they give a pleasant texture.

Cream the butter until soft. Add the sugar, and cream and mix together until very light and fluffy. Stir in the almonds and brandy. Put into a serving dish and chill, or form into small balls like butter balls.

Burnt Brandy

This simple finishing touch can make a boiled or baked pudding. Put 4 sugar cubes into a small pan with ¼ pint (150 ml) brandy. Heat gently until lukewarm. Light with a match and pour over the hot pudding.

Spiced Sugar

It is worth making up a jar of spiced sugar if you like fritters or fried bread dishes. The mixture may also be sprinkled on dumplings or custards just before serving. Just mix 1 part ground mixed spice with 3 parts caster or icing sugar, stir well and keep in a covered jar. If liked, the sugar may be prepared with cinnamon and sugar instead.

Mrs Wightman's Delicious Sauce

4 oz (100 g) unsalted butter
4 oz (100 g) caster sugar

3 tablespoons Jersey cream
6 tablespoons dark rum

This recipe dates from 1930.

Put the butter into a bowl and beat hard with a wooden spoon to a light cream. Add the sugar and continue beating until light and fluffy. Stir in the cream and then add the rum gradually, stirring well. Make the sauce an hour before serving. Serve with hot steamed puddings or Christmas pudding.

Cumberland Rum Butter

4 oz (100 g) unsalted butter
8 oz (225 g) dark soft brown
  sugar

¼ teaspoon ground nutmeg
3 tablespoons dark rum

While not strictly a pudding sauce, this is a delicious accompaniment to steamed pudding, Christmas pudding and mince pies. Rum is a great favourite in Cumberland, as the county ports were used for the importation of Jamaican sugar and its by-products. This sweet butter was traditionally placed in a silver dish or fine china bowl when a new baby arrived. Visitors who came in to congratulate the parents or attend the christening spooned out the rum butter to spread on biscuits, and in return filled the container with money for the baby. The woman who first cut into the bowl would be the next one to prepare such a dish, and butter made for a boy was said to be more 'infectious' than that for a girl.

Cream the butter until light and fluffy. Work in the sugar and nutmeg, adding the rum drop by drop until the mixture is smooth and creamy.

Raspberry Vinegar

2 lb (900 g) raspberries   Sugar
1 pint (600 ml) white vinegar

This curious fruit syrup was traditionally made in the country each summer. It was diluted with water to drink as a cordial, or used to soothe children's sore throats, but it was also extremely popular poured over plain batter puddings. The summery flavour must have been very welcome in the dark winter months.

Put the raspberries into a bowl and mash them well with a wooden spoon. Pour on the vinegar and cover with a cloth. Leave for 6 days, stirring well each day. Strain through a jelly bag without pressing, and measure the liquid. Allow 1 lb (450 g) sugar to each pint (600 ml) juice. Put sugar and juice into a pan and stir gently over low heat until the sugar has dissolved. Boil gently for 10 minutes, removing scum with a slotted spoon. Leave until cold and pour into bottles. Store in the refrigerator.

Jam Sauce

8 oz (225 g) jam   1 tablespoon brandy or
2 tablespoons water   rum (optional)
2 teaspoons lemon juice

A jam sauce may be used with steamed puddings or milk puddings. If the jam is rich and fruity, leave the fruit in, but if the jam is of poor quality the sauce is better sieved. Apricot, blackberry, raspberry and strawberry jams make particularly good sauces.

Put the jam, water and lemon juice into a small pan and heat gently until the jam has melted. Stir well and add brandy or rum just before heating. If the sauce has to be sieved, reheat it afterwards and then stir in the alcohol.

Guards' Sauce

½ pint (300 ml) double cream
1 oz (25 g) caster sugar
Finely grated rind of 1 lemon

½ teaspoon lemon juice
1 tablespoon brandy

The Hertfordshire Constitutional Magazine *of 1888 gave this recipe for a Christmas sauce to go with the pudding. It should be firm and resemble clotted cream.*

Put the cream into a bowl with the sugar and lemon rind, and whisk to stiff peaks. Stir in the lemon juice and brandy. Whisk until they are just incorporated. Pile into a serving dish and chill before serving.

British/American Conversion Tables

American measures

3 teaspoons	1 tablespoon
2 tablespoons	1 fl oz
1 American cup (16 tablespoons)	8 fl oz
1 American pint	16 fl oz

Equivalents

British	*American*
1 teaspoon	1 heaped teaspoon
1 tablespoon	$1\frac{1}{2}$ tablespoons
$\frac{1}{4}$ pint	$\frac{5}{8}$ cup
$\frac{1}{2}$ pint	$1\frac{1}{4}$ cups
$\frac{3}{4}$ pint	$1\frac{7}{8}$ cups
1 pint	$2\frac{1}{2}$ cups

Equivalent weights and measures

British	*American*
Almonds	
$2\frac{1}{2}$ oz ground	$\frac{1}{2}$ cup
4 oz whole, blanched	$\frac{3}{4}$ cup
Apples	
1 lb eating	4 medium-sized
1 lb cooking	3 medium-sized
1 lb sliced	$2\frac{2}{3}$ cups
Breadcrumbs	
2 oz fresh	1 cup
2 oz dried	$\frac{3}{4}$ cup
Cereals	
2 oz cracker crumbs	1 cup
3 oz oatmeal	1 cup
4 oz pearl barley/tapioca	$\frac{1}{2}$ cup
6 oz cornmeal, cracked wheat or semolina/ground rice	1 cup

205

Cottage cheese
2 oz	$\frac{1}{3}$ cup
6 oz	1 cup

Cornflour/cornstarch
1 oz	3 tablespoons
4 oz	$\frac{3}{4}$ cup

Cream
2 fl oz	4 tablespoons or $\frac{1}{4}$ cup
$\frac{1}{4}$ pint (5 fl oz)	$\frac{5}{8}$ cup
$\frac{1}{2}$ pint	$1\frac{1}{4}$ cups

Dried fruit
2 oz candied peel	$\frac{1}{2}$ cup
4 oz glacé cherries	under $\frac{1}{2}$ cup

Currants, raisins, sultanas
1 oz	2 tablespoons
6 oz	1 cup

Prunes or apricots
2 oz	$\frac{3}{8}$ cup
6 oz	1 heaped cup

Flour, plain/all purpose (sifted first)
1 oz	4 tablespoons
2 oz	over $\frac{1}{2}$ cup
3 oz	over $\frac{3}{4}$ cup
$3\frac{1}{2}$ oz	1 cup
4 oz	1 cup + 2 tablespoons
8 oz	$2\frac{1}{4}$ cups
1 lb	$4\frac{1}{2}$ cups

Gelatine
$\frac{1}{2}$ oz	2 tablespoons

Honey, jam, syrup, preserves
4 oz	$\frac{3}{8}$ cup
6 oz	$\frac{1}{2}$ cup

Nuts, large (i.e. walnuts)
2 oz shelled or ground   over ½ cup

Rice (uncooked)
4 oz   ½ cup

Soft fruits
In the USA these are sold in pints or quarts (4 cups = 1 quart)

Redcurrants, blackcurrants, blueberries/bilberries
4 oz   1 cup

Raspberries
5 oz   1 cup

Strawberries
6 oz   1 cup

Cherries
1 lb   2 cups

Solid fats
1 oz   2 tablespoons
8 oz   1 cup

Sugar
Caster/granulated or soft brown/dark brown
1 oz   2 tablespoons
8 oz   1 cup

Icing/Confectioners' (sifted first)
1 oz   ¼ cup
2 oz   under ½ cup
3 oz   ⅔ cup
4 oz   ¾ cup
6 oz   1 cup
8 oz   1⅔ cups
12 oz   2½ cups
1 lb   3⅓ cups

Yeast
¼ oz dried   1 packet active dried

SELECTED TERMINOLOGY

British	American
Apples, cooking	Green apples
Bicarbonate of soda	Baking soda
Cherries, cooking	Tart or sour cherries
Coconut, desiccated	Flaked or grated coconut
Cornflour	Cornstarch
Cream, double	Whipping or heavy cream
Cream, single	Light cream
Crystallized fruits	Candied fruits
Custard powder	Not available; use cornstarch, vanilla essence and yellow colouring (or packet vanilla pudding)
Glacé cherries	Candied cherries
Golden syrup	Not available; use light corn syrup
Hazelnuts	Cob nuts or filberts
Jam	Preserves
Jelly	Jello
Marrow	Large zucchini
Rice, round grain	Short grain rice
Semolina	Semolina flour (not readily available, use farina)
Sugar	
Caster or granulated	Granulated
Soft brown	Light brown
Demerara	Light brown
Icing	Confectioners'
Sultanas	Seedless white raisins
Syrup, golden	Not available; use light corn syrup
Treacle	Molasses
Wholemeal	Whole wheat

Index

A SELECTION OF BESTSELLERS FROM SPHERE

FICTION

CHANGES	Danielle Steel	£1.95 ☐
FEVRE DREAM	George R. R. Martin	£2.25 ☐
LADY OF FORTUNE	Graham Masterton	£2.75 ☐
FIREFOX DOWN	Craig Thomas	£2.25 ☐
MAN OF WAR	John Masters	£2.50 ☐

FILM & TV TIE-INS

THE DUNE STORYBOOK	Joan Vinge	£2.50 ☐
INDIANA JONES AND THE TEMPLE OF DOOM	James Kahn	£1.75 ☐
ONCE UPON A TIME IN AMERICA	Lee Hays	£1.75 ☐
SUPERGIRL	Norma Fox Mazer	£1.75 ☐
MINDER – BACK AGAIN	Anthony Masters	£1.50 ☐

NON-FICTION

THE YOUNG ONES' BOOK	Rik Mayall, Ben Elton & Lise Mayer	£2.95 ☐
WORST MOVIE POSTERS OF ALL TIME	Greg Edwards	£4.95 ☐
THE AGE OF DINOSAURS – A PHOTOGRAPHIC RECORD	Jane Burton & Dougal Dixon	£5.95 ☐
THE FINEST SWORDSMAN IN ALL FRANCE	Keith Miles	£1.95 ☐
POLITICAL QUOTES	Michael Rogers	£1.50 ☐

All Sphere books are available at your local bookshop or newsagent, or can be ordered direct from the publisher. Just tick the titles you want and fill in the form below.

Name_____

Address_____

_____

Write to Sphere Books, Cash Sales Department, P.O. Box 11, Falmouth, Cornwall TR10 9EN

Please enclose a cheque or postal order to the value of the cover price plus:

UK: 55p for the first book, 22p for the second book and 14p per copy for each additional book ordered to a maximum charge of £1.75.

OVERSEAS: £1.00 for the first book plus 25p per copy for each additional book.

BFPO & EIRE: 55p for the first book, 22p for the second book plus 14p per copy for the next 7 books, thereafter 8p per book.

Sphere Books reserve the right to show new retail prices on covers which may differ from those previously advertised in the text or elsewhere, and to increase postal rates in accordance with the PO